Professor Helen McGrath has worked psychologist in both a hospital setting and in private practice. She has also lectured for many years on a range of topics in psychology and educational psychology at Deakin University and run hundreds of workshops for professionals on aspects of psychology. She is currently an adjunct professor at Deakin University. Helen has also been involved in the development of a number of national and state frameworks in Australia that are related to the promotion of mental health and the safety and wellbeing of children and young people. She is the author/ co-author of twenty-two books for psychologists, other professionals and the general community, including *Bounce Back!*, *Difficult Personalities* and *Friends*.

Cheryl Critchley is a respected Melbourne investigative journalist with thirty years experience on a range of publications, including the Melbourne *Herald Sun* newspaper and *The Weekly Review* magazine. She has written about state and federal politics, psychology, education, general news and features, and had a long-standing parenting column. She is the author of six books on topics as diverse as AFL football, parenting and Melbourne Zoo's first baby elephant. Cheryl has a particular interest in psychology and is currently working on a book about her investigation into the controversial facilitated communication technique used with people with autism and severe physical and intellectual disabilities.

Cheryl Critchley and Dr Helen McGrath

WHY DID THEY DO IT?

MACMILLAN
Pan Macmillan Australia

Some of the people in this book have had their names changed to protect their identities.

First published 2015 in Macmillan by Pan Macmillan Australia Pty Ltd
1 Market Street, Sydney, New South Wales, Australia 2000

Copyright © Helen McGrath and Cheryl Critchley 2015

The moral rights of the authors have been asserted.

Cataloguing-in-Publication entry is available
from the National Library of Australia
http://catalogue.nla.gov.au

Typeset in 12.5/15.5 Granjon LT by Midland Typesetters, Australia
Printed by McPherson's Printing Group

Material reprinted with permission from the *Diagnostic and Statistical Manual of
Mental Disorders* (Fifth Edition, American Psychiatric Association, 2013).
All Rights Reserved.

The author and the publisher have made every effort to contact copyright holders for
material used in this book. Any person or organisation that may have been overlooked
should contact the publisher.

This book is dedicated to those who lost their lives and the family members and friends who loved and supported them, as well as the dedicated police who worked tirelessly to seek justice for all of those affected by the crimes covered in this book.

CONTENTS

FOREWORD

This is an interesting and unusual book in which the authors have combined their analytic and writing skills to produce a readable and informative account of the thought processes that appear to have motivated some of the worst murders in recent Australian history.

Most, if not all of them, have shocked the Australian public and the motivation for most appears inexplicable. A common reaction is to say 'They must have been mad', but in no case did they satisfy the criteria of legal insanity. To satisfy that criteria it would have needed to have been shown that they either did not know the nature and quality of their act or, if they did, did not know that it was wrong.

None of them did so, although one, Katherine Knight, made a bizarre attempt to do so after killing her partner, by mutilating and cooking parts of him with vegetables and setting up a tableau for his adult children to find when they visited.

The significance of this book is that it analyses their conduct in light of the personality disorders from which they suffered, not amounting to legal insanity, which largely explain their conduct.

As the authors point out, personality disorders are essentially extremes of the normal spectrum of personality. Three aspects of such disorders are sometimes dangerous to others, the first being a lack of resilience under stress that turns a problem into a crisis and the second an inability to adapt to changing circumstances, such as a partner wishing to leave a relationship.

When these are coupled with a third, namely a low level of empathy and concern for others, a situation of real danger may arise. I believe that these factors do much to explain the sort of conduct described in this book. A lack of empathy in particular is a real danger sign.

From my experience as a former chair of the Adult Parole Board and as a former judge of the Supreme Court of Victoria, I am aware that most psychiatrists agree that the prediction of dangerousness is extremely difficult.

This is the real problem that faces judges when sentencing offenders for offences falling short of murder, coupled as it is with the requirement that the punishment must fit the crime. A similar problem faces parole authorities when ordering their release.

Certainly not all people with personality disorders are necessarily dangerous and many are subject to them in a mild form and still function as ordinary members of the community.

However this book signals possible danger signs in a powerful way, by giving detailed accounts of the motivation of people with serious personality disorders and the possible consequences of failure to recognise them.

It contains an important discussion of personality disorders and their origins, which the authors point out are usually the result of a complex interplay of genetic and environmental factors; good parenting can work wonders with any child, but bad parenting can have the opposite effect.

Foreword

The detailed examples contained in the book may help readers to understand the motivation and behaviour of the people it profiles.

Hopefully it will give some assistance to decisions made by those dealing with persons suffering from severe personality disorders, whether they be partners or prospective partners of such persons, or professionals, including police, judges and lawyers and others involved in law enforcement and the helping professions. At the very least, such knowledge may sound a warning and a timely call for help and assistance from a prospective victim and a more knowledgeable response by courts, police and other professionals involved.

In my time at the Parole Board I interviewed many murderers and other violent criminals and I have no doubt that such a work would also have given great assistance to me and others in making decisions as to their future.

However the problem remains that courts and parole boards cannot punish people for what they might do as distinct from what they have done. Further, there is almost no prospect of curing personality disorders as there is of curing mental illness.

Some, but far from all of the cases discussed in this book, involved people with prior convictions for offences less than murder, which means that in the usual course they must be released.

For example it may be that Adrian Bayley should have received longer sentences for his offences, should not have been granted bail and should have had his parole revoked, which would have saved Jill Meagher. But it would not have saved a similar victim when the time came for his eventual release.

In relation to those who have not committed relevant prior offences like Robert Farquharson, there was little that would have enabled a court to have anticipated what he did. This is a problem often faced by Family Court judges and by magistrates, as my later experience in that court taught me. Normally it is routine to order unsupervised contact between parents. However there have been cases where such an order may place the children in danger and these are often difficult to identify. The information to be extracted from this book might at least sound a warning in such circumstances and dictate caution in making orders for contact with a parent with a personality disorder in circumstances where children may be endangered.

This book deserves a wide audience and should be read by all who are interested in criminal justice and will also appeal to a wider audience.

The Honourable Alastair Nicholson AO, RFD, QC
Justice of the Supreme Court of Victoria (1982–1988)
Deputy Chair and Chair of the Victorian Adult Parole Board (1982–1988)
Chief Justice of the Family Court of Australia (1988–2004)
Chair of the National Centre Against Bullying
Honorary Professorial Fellow, Melbourne Law School, University of Melbourne
Chair of Children's Rights International

HOW TO USE THIS BOOK

This book attempts to explain the motives behind some of Australia's most puzzling murders, in order to understand *why* they happened. As well as outlining the circumstances of each crime, the book explains how, in each case, a specific type of personality disorder, in combination with other factors, led to the murder. An outline of the relevant personality disorder is provided as an introduction to the applicable murders. Each chapter concludes with a short summary outlining what lessons can be learned from each case as well as a diagnostic chart for each perpetrator. At the back of the book you will find a glossary of technical terms, some useful contact details for those seeking assistance, references and further/recommended reading.

INTRODUCTION

Some crimes appear inexplicable. They are so awful, their details so shocking, that we struggle to comprehend how or why they could have happened. Some particularly gruesome murders leave us feeling horrified and even physically ill.

Why would a father deliberately drive his three sons into a dam and leave them to drown in his car?

Why would an apparently loving partner throw his fiancée to her death from the balcony of their fifteenth-floor apartment?

And why would a man kill his pregnant wife with a spear gun then wait several days before inflicting the same horror on his toddler daughter?

To most people, these crimes seem unspeakably evil. We can understand the distress felt when a relationship fails, or the anger that can occur during a custody dispute following a bitter family breakup, but when someone is prepared to kill a loved one to solve their problems or express their feelings, we are left shaking our heads.

Peter Caruso bludgeoned to death his wife Rosa because she finally defied him after of almost fifty years of acquiescing to keep

1

the peace. Gerard Baden-Clay killed his wife Allison when she challenged his repeated dishonesty and infidelities, and threatened to expose his carefully crafted public image. John Myles Sharpe killed his pregnant wife Anna and their young daughter Gracie because he didn't want another child. And Katherine Knight stabbed and skinned her partner John 'Pricey' Price when he announced he was leaving her.

Most people were shocked when they read about these murders. On the surface they looked like they could not possibly be the work of a rational person. But these killers knew exactly what they were doing. None were mentally ill (see page 356) and most were confident that they wouldn't be caught. Some felt that the murder was justified. Robert Farquharson believed that killing his three young sons and making it look like an accident would not only exact revenge on his ex-wife Cindy, but would see people in his small township pity him as the poor, wronged ex-husband rather than an inadequate man rejected by his wife.

For others, murder was a means to an end. Keli Lane killed her newborn girl, Tegan, because she did not fit into the aspiring Olympic water polo player's life plan. Angelika Gavare dismembered pensioner Vonne McGlynn simply because she wanted Vonne's home and possessions. Adrian Bayley wanted to silence Jill Meagher, whom he had sexually assaulted, after she told him off. Simon Gittany threw his fiancée, Lisa Harnum, from a fifteenth-floor balcony when he discovered that she was planning to leave him. And Roger Dean let fourteen nursing home residents die in a fire he had lit in order to cover up his theft of prescription medication.

Why?

Why are some people prepared to commit murder to solve a perceived problem, rather than address it rationally and within the law as most of us do? Why don't they feel guilt or remorse? And why do they think they will get away with it?

Just as perplexing are the actions of those who support a killer in the face of overwhelming evidence of their guilt. Why do they accept claims of innocence by someone who is clearly lying? And why do they continue to believe those lies after a thorough trial has found them guilty?

This book provides answers to questions such as these by using psychological analysis, combined with scientific evidence from research studies, to identify the reasoning and motives of murderers whose actions seem inexplicable. In doing so, we hope to reassure readers that neither they nor anyone they know is likely to experience the kind of harm inflicted by these murderers. Callous killers are, fortunately, very rare.

But the analysis of these cases can also help alert us to warning signs in partners, friends, family members and social acquaintances who may, despite appearances to the contrary, be capable of serious, harmful and criminal acts. While rare, these people do exist and they can be dangerous. They are often such good actors that their criminal behaviour comes as a complete surprise to those who know them. But when you dig a little more deeply, the signs may have been there: a pattern of selfishness, lack of compassion, controlling behaviour or callous indifference to suffering may indicate a seriously flawed personality.

We have analysed court documents and media coverage, visited some of the crime scenes and spoken to a number of people close to some of the murderers profiled in this book. This has enabled us to gain an insight into their behaviour and motives and the context in which the murders occurred. Professor Helen McGrath has also spent many years researching the available scientific information about personality disorders as well as counselling patients who have relatives, colleagues or partners whose lives have been affected by the behaviour of people with these disorders.

Our analysis aims to provide an understanding of these crimes, but it in no way excuses them. Nor do we wish to imply that all people with personality disorders such as avoidant, narcissistic, antisocial and borderline are dangerous. Most are neither dangerous nor violent. What we hope to convey is an understanding of why some people with certain personality disorders can cross the line and seriously hurt someone. Being alert to the potential signs can help all of us to feel a bit safer.

Mental disorders

The main resource used in this book for diagnostic purposes is the most recent version of the *Diagnostic and Statistical Manual of Mental Disorders* 5 (DSM 5, American Psychiatric Association, 2013, see glossary).

It defines a mental disorder as:

> ... a syndrome characterized by clinically significant disturbance in an individual's cognition, emotion regulation, or behavior that reflects a dysfunction in the psychological, biological, or developmental processes underlying mental functioning. Mental disorders are usually associated with significant distress in social, occupational, or other important activities. An expectable or culturally approved response to a common stressor or loss, such as the death of a loved one, is not a mental disorder. Socially deviant behavior (e.g. political, religious, or sexual) and conflicts that are primarily between the individual and society are not mental disorders unless the deviance or conflict results from a dysfunction in the individual, as described above.

The World Health Organization's International Classification of Diseases (ICD-10, 2010) describes a mental disorder as follows: '"Disorder" is not an exact term, but it is used here to imply the existence of a clinically recognizable set of symptoms or behavior associated in most cases with distress and with interference with personal functions.'

4

Introduction

A personality disorder is an example of a mental disorder, as defined above, but it is *not* a 'mental illness'. The killers featured all have one or more personality disorders. It is important to distinguish these from mental illness as they differ in several ways. An individual's *personality* is their relatively consistent, pervasive and permanent pattern of thinking, feeling and behaving. If this pattern becomes inflexible and maladaptive (dysfunctional and non-productive), is displayed in many areas of their life and causes personal or general distress to others, then it can become a 'personality disorder'. A UK study found that 4.4 per cent of the population – almost one in twenty-five people – is living with a personality disorder (Coid et al., 2006).

The DSM 5 defines a personality disorder as: 'An enduring pattern of inner experience and behavior that deviates markedly from the expectations of the individual's culture, is pervasive and inflexible, has an onset in adolescence or early adulthood, is stable over time, and leads to distress or impairment' (APA, 2013). More details of the specific DSM 5 criteria are provided in the glossary (see page 350). This pattern is manifested in two (or more) of the following areas:

1. Cognition (i.e. ways of perceiving and interpreting self, other people, and events).
2. Affectivity (i.e. the range, intensity, lability, and appropriateness of emotional response).
3. Interpersonal functioning.
4. Impulse control.

The DSM 5 adds that,

> The enduring pattern is inflexible and pervasive across a broad range of personal and social situations. The enduring pattern leads to clinically significant distress or impairment in social, occupational, or other important areas of

functioning. The pattern is stable and of long duration, and its onset can be traced back to at least adolescence or early adulthood. The enduring pattern is not better explained as a manifestation or consequence of another mental disorder. The enduring pattern is not attributable to the physiological effects of a substance (e.g. a drug of abuse, a medication) or another medical condition (e.g. a head trauma).

The ICD-10 describes personality disorders as: '... long-term patterns of thoughts and behaviors that cause serious problems with relationships and work. People with personality disorders have difficulty dealing with everyday stresses and problems. They often have stormy relationships with other people.'

Such disorders are distinguished from mental illness by several features. Personality disorders are enduring, relatively stable and potentially lifelong. They are deeply ingrained and maladaptive patterns of behaviours for which there are no reliably effective treatments. Conversely, mental illnesses – at least in part – are more commonly influenced by a 'disease' that adversely affects one or more organs, including the brain, in a way that significantly impairs normal functioning and for which medical treatments are more likely to be effective. Such illnesses usually have a recognisable onset and time span, and most result in severely impaired thinking and impaired perceptions of reality. The behaviours that are part of a mental illness often cause distress and harm to the sufferer more than to others.

Mental illness is a term used more in a legal context than in a medical context. Most legal definitions describe it as a clinically significant medical condition that significantly impairs (temporarily or permanently) the person's mental functioning and judgment, and strongly indicates that they need care, treatment and/or control. It is characterised by serious disturbance in one of more of the following: thought processes, emotions, orientation, mood, perceptions, memory and/or decision-making. It usually results in one or more of the following symptoms: delusions, hallucinations, serious disorder of thought, a severe disorder of mood and/or sustained or repeated irrational behaviour that indicates the presence of one of the above symptoms.

These indicators are mostly associated with the more severe mental disorders that often include a temporary or longer-term psychosis, such as schizophrenia, bipolar disorder, and some severe mood disorders, such as post-partum depression. When somebody is in a psychotic state, their thoughts and emotions are seriously impaired to the point where they are unable to distinguish what is real and what is not. Typical symptoms displayed by someone who is in a psychotic state include delusions, hallucinations (hearing voices, receiving 'commands' from people who aren't there, or 'seeing' things that are not there), seriously impaired memory, confused and irrational thinking, and a severe inability to effectively reason, solve everyday problems and make plans.

In law, a person who has been charged with a crime can claim 'mental impairment' and, if successful, they may be declared unfit for trial. They must be assessed as unable to assist in their own defence and unable to understand the court process. 'Mental impairment', which usually means mental illness, intellectual disability, brain damage and/or senility, can also be used as a defence during a trial. Some Australian states have laws that specifically exclude substance abuse from the definition of mental illness. It is possible for some people with a personality disorder to have a separate mental illness too, such as schizophrenia, but this isn't the situation in the ten cases explored in this book.

Are depression and anxiety mental illnesses? Mild to moderate depression is often a normal part of life and is not a mental illness. Most people have times when they feel sad or de-energised and their mood is low. This often occurs in response to a sad event or when we must quickly adjust to a new life situation, such as separation from a partner, being widowed, losing a job or the birth of a child.

Some people experience a more severe and prolonged period of depression that *is* considered a mental illness. An example outlined in the DSM 5 is major depressive disorder. Sufferers are likely to have a depressed mood most of the day, nearly every day. They feel chronically sad, empty, hopeless and teary, may lose weight or overeat, have problems with insomnia or oversleeping nearly every day, feel de-energised, lack the desire to engage in formerly pleasurable activities, have a diminished capacity to think clearly, concentrate and solve problems, and sometimes think about suicide. These symptoms are severe enough to cause clinically significant distress or impairment in their social life, work and other parts of their lives. In these cases, antidepressant medication can help.

Rather than behaviours that are controlled by an illness or disease, personality disorders are essentially extremes of the normal spectrum of personality. They reflect an individual's identity, characteristic lifestyle, style of relating to and communicating with others and, ultimately, their identity. The key features of any personality disorder are distorted and inflexible patterns of thinking and behaving, problematic emotional reactions and responses, problems with impulse control (sometimes too much, sometimes too little) and difficulties with interpersonal communication, empathy and relationships. A personality disorder can range from mild to severe, and two people with the same disorder may behave differently in some ways, depending on which combination of that personality disorder's criteria they meet.

Two aspects of all personality disorders are especially maladaptive, self-defeating and sometimes dangerous to others

(Millon et al., 2004). The first is a lack of resilience under stress. Someone with a personality disorder lacks the capacity to respond to problems and difficulties in their life with flexible and varied strategies. Unlike most other people, if their first strategy doesn't work, they won't try a different approach. Instead, they keep using the same strategy, often turning a problem into a crisis with even higher levels of stress and anger that adversely affect those around them.

The second aspect is stubbornness and an inability to adapt to changing circumstances. In situations that make new demands of them, such as a partner wanting to change something in their relationship, someone with a personality disorder will continue to try to control the outcome to suit themselves rather than rethink things in terms of their partner's needs. Again, this often leads to an interpersonal crisis.

These maladaptive ways of dealing with life's challenges and hurdles often lead to a series of repeated, ineffective and self-defeating behaviours that blight both their own lives and those of the people with whom they live, work or interact. In extreme cases, they can result in violence and even murder. In Gerard Baden-Clay's case, he continued to have extramarital affairs knowing the damage this could do to his family and his personal image. Keli Lane continued to fall pregnant despite the complications it caused in her life.

A third aspect of most personality disorders is a relatively low level of empathy and concern for others. Most of us can put ourselves in the shoes of someone else experiencing distressing emotions such as grief, sadness, worry or discouragement. We share some of a contestant's feelings of nervousness when we watch them answer a million-dollar game show question and feel sad when we watch a TV news item about cruelty to animals and see the pain and terror on the animals' faces. However, most people with serious personality disorders have a diminished capacity to empathise. That is why some are able to commit serious crimes without feeling guilt or remorse, cover them up and then calmly lie when they are caught.

Empathy has three main components: emotional recognition, emotional resonance and empathic concern. *Emotional recognition* (also referred to by some as 'cognitive empathy') is the ability to perceive how someone else is feeling and predict their intentions and needs by identifying their internal psychological state after seeing their expressions and actions and listening to their words. This type of empathy may require some perspective (i.e. imagining how you might feel in that situation). Taking it a step further, *emotional resonance* (also referred to by some as 'emotional empathy') is when you actually feel some of the same emotion that you recognise another person is feeling. If someone is crying after the death of a pet, you might find yourself feeling sad and maybe even notice tears in your own eyes. It often requires separation and management of your feelings at the time, so you can focus on the other person's feelings. *Empathic concern* occurs when, having recognised and understood that another person is worried or distressed, you say or do something to help them. This can range from speaking in a caring voice and using kind or reassuring words to offering physical assistance or protection.

Some aspects of empathy appear to be developmental. Mirror neurons in our brain are specialised brain cells that enable us to recognise, share and imitate the feelings and actions of others. As children develop, their experiences with other people help their brain to create efficient neural pathways and they become more and more capable of empathy. Children start to develop empathy from about the age of two and may cry when an adult or another child cries. The skills that underpin emotional recognition, emotional resonance and empathic concern are largely learned from childhood experiences of empathy, kindness, support and nurturance at home and at school. We also learn it from our own opportunities to show empathy, kindness, support and nurturance to family members, friends, classmates, neighbours and pets.

The degree to which those with personality disorders lack empathy will vary according to the type and severity of the disorder, but most will display a pattern of putting their needs ahead of the needs of others. They also lack insight into their own thinking and behaviour, and this can lead to problems.

Nature or nurture?

Personality disorders are usually the result of a complex interplay of genetic and environmental factors. Genetics don't directly cause a personality disorder but they often play a role in predisposing a person to develop one or more components of a disorder. Genes can predispose someone to behave in a certain way, or make them more susceptible to the negative effects of certain situations. In a health-related example, someone with the gene predisposing them to type 2 diabetes is more susceptible to the negative effects of becoming overweight than an overweight person without that gene. Other genes can minimise the effects of one specific gene, as can environmental factors. Similarly, other genes or negative environmental factors can exaggerate the effects of a specific gene.

The Australian Temperament Project (Vassallo et al., 2014) is a longitudinal research study that has collected data on a number of key behaviours in more than two thousand children. They started collecting data when the children were four to eight months old and collected it at fifteen time points until they were thirty years old. The researchers were able to identify different 'temperaments' in children that have tended to be relatively stable over time. Many children have shown small changes, but few have changed radically, suggesting that genetic factors play a significant role in the development of these traits.

The temperaments include:

Level of activity: The frequency and intensity level of a child's movement.

Reactivity: Emotional intensity level in situations of frustration, anxiety, annoyance etc.

Mood: Type and intensity, ranging from predominantly negative to predominantly positive.

Sociability: The level of interest in social interaction and the degree of shyness.

Persistence: The degree to which a child can pay attention to tasks/activities and see them through.

The level of 'heritability' is the degree to which genetic differences explain the differences between large groups of people in terms of specific behaviours and characteristics such as shyness or impulsivity. The influence of genetics is larger in some personality disorders than in others. But biology isn't destiny and many environmental factors also play a significant role.

Parenting significantly impacts on the development of a person's temperament and overall personality. Warm, caring parents who are calm and resilient under stress can help a child to self-calm and feel safe. Such parents also model resilience and show their children how to manage uncomfortable feelings and cope with difficult situations. Parents who directly teach their children to consider the rights, needs and feelings of others make it more likely that they will behave that way. Parents can also minimise a child's predisposition to be shy by teaching them specific social skills and encouraging them to connect with other people.

A child's attachment style, or how they establish emotional bonds, is developed through their early childhood experiences and becomes their working model for adult relationships. A child is more likely to develop a positive and trusting working model of how relationships should be when they are raised in a loving, secure, responsive and predictable family situation in which their physical and emotional needs are reliably met, boundaries about acceptable behaviour are clearly communicated and adults can be trusted to care for them and keep them safe. This helps the child develop a 'secure attachment' style that leads to confident and independent adult behaviour, the ability to trust others in relationships, positive social interactions and an ability to meet both their own and another person's needs.

However, when a child is raised in a family situation that is non-responsive to their needs, unpredictable, chaotic or unsafe, they are likely to develop a negative and non-trusting working model of relationships and an 'insecure attachment' style. As adults, they are less able to trust those close to them, more likely to fear isolation, have difficulties in managing feelings such as anger, and become over-controlling and/or over-reliant in relationships. These children are more likely to develop a personality disorder, especially if they already have a genetic predisposition to some of its components, such as emotionality, irritability, a lack of empathy, impulsivity, anxiety or shyness.

Often 'shared genes' also result in a 'shared environment'. This can increase the likelihood that the child will develop a personality disorder. A parent who has passed on a specific gene to their child may be more likely to parent in a way that reflects that same genetic predisposition in themselves. For example, a parent with a genetic predisposition for anxiety may pass it on to their child while also modelling anxious behaviour by over-focusing on potential danger in the child's world.

A child's early temperament can also influence the way in which their parents respond to them. Parents of babies with an easygoing and sociable temperament often find it relatively easy to be calm, warm and nurturing towards them. Parents of babies who are irritable, socially withdrawn or overly emotional may respond to them in a more impatient or avoidant way. Parents of babies who are fearful and inhibited may respond to them in a more protective way that calms them down but also reduces their confidence and independence. Robert Farquharson, a youngest child who was smaller than average for his age, appears to have been overprotected by his mother and his siblings to some degree. It is not uncommon for well-meaning relatives to behave in this way, but it may have reinforced his shy and inhibited personality to the point where he later found it hard to cope with adult life. Rather than look inwards, he blamed others when things went wrong.

Some environmental factors that influence how a child's personality develops are the result of random good fortune or misfortune. An example of good fortune is having regular contact with another adult who displays care and affection, such as a family friend, teacher, sports coach or grandparent. Conversely, the death of a parent when a child is young is an example of misfortune. Other factors that can affect a child's personality development include the quantity and quality of their friendships, whether they are bullied or included at school, the quality of their educational experiences and their involvement in positive or negative activities outside school, such as music, art, drama, sport and Scouts.

The cases outlined in this book illustrate how complex personality disorders can be and how several factors can combine with a personality disorder to produce tragic results. Violent behaviour is extreme aggression intended to cause serious harm to another person. Both personal and situational factors converge to enable a violent act to occur. Therefore, as we shall see, the answer to the question 'Why did someone commit this murder?' is nearly always an equation rather than simple cause and effect. Each additional personal or situational factor increases the likelihood of the outcome.

* In the References and Further Reading section, you will find a list of books you can read to find out more about domestic violence and the various personality disorders.

PART I

AVOIDANT PERSONALITY DISORDER

INTRODUCTION

Avoidant personality disorder (AvPD): When the mask comes off

You've probably never heard of avoidant personality disorder (AvPD). This isn't surprising given that only about one in fifty people have it and, unlike some of the more obvious personality disorders discussed in this book, it is less likely to be mentioned in the media. People with an AvPD are typically socially inept, anxious and awkward, preoccupied with their own shortcomings and inadequacies, and have deep-seated and painful feelings of self-consciousness. While some also lack knowledge of appropriate skills for social situations, many are aware of them but have difficulty enacting them.

AvPD begins by early adulthood and manifests in a variety of situations. Some may have a mild socially anxious and avoidant personality style and seem shy. Others have a more severe behaviour pattern that is consistent with an AvPD diagnosis. You may recognise somebody like this in your family, social or working life.

But they don't stand out from the crowd and that's how most of them like it. Like all of us, they want to be accepted, liked and respected but don't believe that they are the kind of person whom others *will* automatically accept, like or respect.

Some people with AvPD learn with professional help to adapt and cope by developing stronger social skills, managing and accepting situations, or gravitating towards workplace situations that they find less socially challenging. They may rely on the support of a longstanding but small group of family and friends. They may also do well if they have what has been termed 'a therapeutic relationship' with a partner who can provide acceptance, social and emotional support and build their confidence. In return, they can show their partner appreciation and offer other kinds of support. This kind of relationship can minimise the impact of an AvPD on the quality of life.

Others, like Robert Farquharson and John Myles Sharpe, don't cope. In their cases, the results were catastrophic. Farquharson reacted to his wife leaving him by deliberately drowning his three sons to take his revenge on her, while Sharpe killed his pregnant wife and young daughter because he resented his wife's decision to have a second child and wasn't willing to lose any of his assets through divorce. Farquharson and Sharpe both had strong, competent and socially confident partners but, unfairly, they increasingly resented the control their wives exercised over their lives, despite the fact that they had chosen to relinquish control. Their feelings of inadequacy developed into a festering rage against those incorrectly perceived by them to be at fault – their wives and, to a lesser extent, their own young children.

Recognising someone with an AvPD
Diagnosing a personality disorder is difficult and requires some professional knowledge, but you can get some idea by looking

at the criteria. The DSM 5 (APA, 2013) describes an AvPD as 'a pervasive pattern of social inhibition, feelings of inadequacy and hypersensitivity to negative evaluation, beginning by early adulthood and present in a variety of contexts', as indicated by four (or more) of the following:

1. Avoids occupational activities that involve significant inter-personal contact because of fears of criticism, disapproval or rejection.
2. Is unwilling to get involved with people unless certain of being liked.
3. Shows restraint within intimate relationships because of fear of being shamed or ridiculed.
4. Is preoccupied with being criticised or rejected in social situations.
5. Is inhibited in new interpersonal situations because of feelings of inadequacy.
6. Views self as socially inept, personally unappealing or inferior to others.
7. Is unusually reluctant to take personal risks or to engage in any new activities because they may prove embarrassing.

Prevalence
An estimated 2.4 per cent of the population has an AvPD during their lifetimes and slightly more women than men have the disorder (Grant et al., 2004).

Comorbidity (other disorders that often co-occur with AvPD)
Social Anxiety Disorder (SAD) has some similarities with AvPD and researchers have concluded that they are related but separate diagnoses. One study (Cox et al., 2009) found that almost 46 per cent of people with an AvPD also had many symptoms of SAD.

It is also important to remember that, like other personality disorders, the acuteness of an AvPD can range from mild to severe and two people with the same disorder may meet different criteria and thus will not necessarily behave in the same way.

Typical behaviours of someone with an AvPD

AvPD is far more severe than simple shyness. Those who have it see themselves as unlikable, inferior and inadequate compared to other people. They are also apprehensive that others will confirm this picture of them. Therefore they are always on the alert for, and hypersensitive to, any behaviour by others that appears to be critical, contemptuous or rejecting of them. Someone with an AvPD is deeply afraid of making a fool of themselves or being humiliated, so tries to avoid or minimise social and workplace situations in which they think they might perform poorly, embarrass themselves or be criticised. They frequently experience feelings of anger and shame out of proportion to the situation at hand because of their interpretation of how other people are seeing them.

No-one likes to be criticised, mocked or ridiculed. We all feel uncomfortable if we act foolishly or don't handle a social situation as well as we would have liked. But we get over it. We reflect for a while on what has happened and how we handled it and then try to think of better ways to deal with similar situations next time. But someone with an AvPD doesn't easily work it through and move on. Instead, they tend to keep thinking and brooding about what has happened, often blaming other people for making them feel inept or foolish. They link incidents, however small, with their memory of every other humiliation, slight or situation when others have 'made' them look inferior, incompetent or foolish.

As they obsess, they can become increasingly angry and resentful. This constant self-focus, coupled with their social difficulties, means they are less likely to develop skills for understanding and being empathic towards other people. Unsurprisingly, research confirms that they tend to start dating and marry (if at all) later than others.

Four subtypes of AvPD have been identified and they help to explain some of the small variations in the behaviour of those who have it (Millon et al., 2004). A person may fall entirely into one subtype, or have a combination of traits from several.

Robert Farquharson and John Myles Sharpe both fit into the 'conflicted' AvPD subtype. Those in this category fear being independent due to their feelings of inadequacy and seek others to assume the responsibility for many of the major areas in their life. But at the same time, they resent being dependent on another person. They feel misunderstood, unappreciated and demeaned and often become embittered, hostile and vengeful. They are masters at shifting blame. Others describe them as negative, moody, surly, resentful, withdrawn, complaining, irritable, uncooperative, cranky, sulky and prone to temper tantrums when something simple goes wrong (e.g. when they can't get something to work properly).

Men in this subtype are, more often than not, especially angry with women. They misinterpret relationships as struggles in which they are powerless and other people are dictators. They avoid conflict due to a lack of courage, a lack of confidence in their ability to respond assertively and a fear of retaliation. Instead, many people in the 'conflicted' subtype use passive-aggressive tactics to express their feelings, 'pay back' the person on whom they are dependent and try to gain a sense of control.

Their passive-aggressive behaviours can be many and varied, such as constant negative talk, nasty teasing or hostile humour and practical jokes ('I was only joking' or 'Can't you take a joke?'), refusal to cooperate, intentionally behaving in ways that they have been asked not to (such as leaving dirty clothes on the bathroom floor), failing to do their share of the work or take on their share of responsibility, intentionally doing unwanted jobs badly or procrastinating for so long that the other person gets fed up and does them. They may also complain about reasonable demands being placed on them, avoid obligations or claim to have forgotten them and give the 'silent treatment'. They often respond to complaints or suggestions that they have fallen short of the other person's expectations by walking away or making disrespectful comments ('whatever'; 'you're paranoid'; 'do it yourself then').

The other AvPD subtypes are:

Hypersensitive: Characterised by hypersensitivity plus distrust and fear of others. Those in this subtype assume that others are intentionally trying to undermine them and make them look bad.

Phobic: Characterised by excessive dependence on a relationship with one particular person. People who fit into this subtype tend to invest too much of their trust and their sense of self into this relationship and are always worried about the possibility of losing it. This ongoing sense of dread may be converted to phobias such as a fear of flying or a fear of heights.

Self-deserting: Characterised by the creation of a fantasy life to avoid the discomfort of having to interact with and relate to others. This minimises feelings of depression that can develop from obsessively thinking about what they perceive to be their own real inadequacies.

Like Farquharson and Sharpe, many people with an AvPD struggle with the emotional demands associated with a parenting role. Most don't physically harm others, but a surprisingly large number do. In a sample of fifty convicted murderers in a Brazilian jail, 22 per cent had a diagnosis of AvPD (Rigonatti et al., 2006). On the other hand, a study conducted in Finland found that only 2.6 per cent of convicted murderers had an AvPD (Laajasalo et al., 2013). However in a study of 562 convicted sexual offenders, including child molesters, AvPD was the most frequently identified personality disorder (Francia et al., 2010).

Some people with an AvPD – often those with higher intelligence/education levels and people in their life who can offer feedback – will attempt to influence how they are perceived, sometimes with a degree of success. For others, their lack of social competence and empathy means that often they don't get this right. They may, for example, show off, act as 'know-it-alls' or put others down in public to try to impress people. Some get it wrong by making the same joke, telling the same amusing story or making the same funny comments over and over. Disagreements are also tricky. Most people see them as an exchange of ideas, but someone with an AvPD will often incorrectly interpret disagreement as hostility towards them, 'having a go' or putting them down.

Many use alcohol as a social relaxant, but some develop a dependency, incorrectly believing that they are more interesting to people when they've had a few drinks. Many also smoke, which offers several potential benefits despite the fact that they find it difficult to break the habit (Pineiro et al., 2013). Smoking gives them something to do with their hands and calms them in social situations. 'Going outside for a smoke' allows them to take a break from the social demands of a situation, or leave if they sense they are not doing well or that someone might be mocking or disagreeing with them. Often the other smokers outside initiate conversation with them, so it seems like a 'comfortable' place to be.

What causes an AvPD?

Being shy, a little fearful around strangers and feeling anxious about challenges are not uncommon in childhood. Most children become less shy and more confident as they interact with others and develop new skills, especially social skills. Shyness, a reluctance to deal with new or unfamiliar people and situations, and social apprehension appear to increase in children who go on to develop an AvPD. These characteristics may become more obvious as children go to school, and become adolescents and young adults. Some of these traits may be genetic, such as social anxiety, negative affectivity (negative mood and reactions) and behavioural inhibition (a tendency to react more than most children with fear, restraint, withdrawal or all three to unfamiliar persons, situations or experiences).

The heritability of AvPD – the degree to which genetics plays a role in developing a disorder – is estimated to be .64 (Gjerde et al., 2012). This means that 64 per cent of the differences between those people in research studies who had an AvPD and those who didn't were due to genetic differences between them. There is some evidence that a gene called RGS2 may contribute to an AvPD by predisposing an individual to be more socially anxious and behaviourally inhibited. Other genes appear to contribute to an AvPD by predisposing an individual to experience high levels of negative emotions such as worry, nervousness, anger, guilt, feelings of rejection and sadness.

Research has found that adults with AvPD are more likely to have had a particular combination of 'life' factors in their childhood and adolescent years, some of which may interact with a genetic predisposition. These factors include poor athletic performance, lower levels of social involvement compared to other children, lower levels of peer popularity, fewer out-of-school activities and fewer school leadership opportunities.

They are also likely to have had fewer positive relationships with non-caretaking adults such as sports coaches, teachers and family friends when they are of primary school age (Rettew et al., 2003).

Parenting style also has some impact. The style most often related to the development of AvPD is overprotective, quite critical, focuses excessively on 'what people will think', incorporates shame and guilt-based discipline and offers low levels of parental warmth and affection (Johnson et al., 2006; Stravynski et al., 1989). AvPD is also related to being raised in a family where the parents are not separated but have significant ongoing conflict (Meyer and Carver, 2000). Most children who grow up to have an AvPD also report, as adults, that at least one of their parents had impaired social competence (Rettew et al., 2003). A parent's genetic predisposition inevitably affects how they parent as well, so a mother or father with a similar genetic predisposition as their child to an AvPD is more likely to parent this way.

Filicide

The term filicide is used when a parent kills one or more of their biological children under the age of eighteen, as Robert Farquharson did. One study identified five filicide categories, including: *altruistic*, where the parent believes death is in the child's best interests, which may be secondary to either psychotic or non-psychotic reasoning; *acutely psychotic*, where the parent is mentally ill, has no rational motive and is unable to differentiate fantasy from reality (relatively rare); *unwanted child*, where the child is regarded as a hindrance; *accidental*, where the child dies through abuse or neglect; and *spousal revenge*, where the parent kills the child to exact revenge on the other parent (West et al., 2009). Farquharson falls clearly into the spousal revenge category.

In Victoria, Brown et al. (2014) analysed forty local filicides committed between 2000 and 2009 and concluded that 71 per cent of male perpetrators had some prior contact with a health professional, such as a GP or psychologist, mostly about feelings of depression. Most had displayed a variety of direct or indirect warning signs of their intentions to those professionals, or to a friend or family member.

Familicide

John Myles Sharpe committed familicide, meaning he killed both his partner and biological child/children. Those who kill their partner and all their children, as Sharpe did, have also been described as 'family annihilators'.

Four categories of male family annihilators have been identified (Yardley et al., 2014). The men in all four were assumed to be distressed by a perceived loss of control over their current life circumstances and saw their actions as a way of regaining some control. The *'self-righteous' annihilator* seeks to shift blame for his crimes to the mother, whom he holds responsible for the breakdown of the family. The *'anomic' annihilator* sees his family success as the result of his financial success. When his economic success is threatened, he sees the family as no longer serving this function. The *'disappointed' annihilator* sees his family as an extension of his own needs, desires, hopes or satisfaction and believes that his family has let him down or acted in ways that undermine his vision of ideal family life. In some cases this becomes an 'honour killing'. Finally, the *'paranoid' annihilator* perceives an external threat – real or imagined – that may deprive him of his family (e.g. a legal threat or children taken into care). He sees himself as protecting his family by killing them.

John Sharpe doesn't fit neatly into any of these categories. He murdered his wife, child and unborn baby because he was not prepared to continue to shoulder his family responsibilities or to lose half of his assets in a divorce if Anna left him, which she had threatened to do when she became overwhelmed by the negative impact of his inadequacies.

Treatment

The most common treatments for people with an AvPD are group-based social skills training, cognitive behaviour therapy (CBT) and sometimes medication. CBT, which is designed to challenge exaggerated and unrealistic negative self-beliefs and beliefs about others and develop more 'rational' perceptions, has been shown to have a moderate degree of success. The primary purpose of social skills group training is for participants to learn and practise social skills while being observed and receiving feedback. This simulates real life and can encourage social confidence. Gaining and keeping a patient's trust is important, as people with an AvPD often avoid sessions if they distrust the therapist or fear rejection by them.

Many people with an AvPD are reluctant to practise the newly learnt ways of thinking and social skills between sessions. SSRI (selective serotonin reuptake inhibitors) medications such as antidepressants Zoloft and Aurorix may have some impact, but are less effective without appropriate counselling and training. Anti-anxiety medication used in specific situations may help, but relapse often occurs when the medication is discontinued. People taking SSRIs or anti-anxiety medication are usually advised to avoid alcohol as it can be a dangerous combination, and this can make some people with an AvPD reluctant to use these medications.

CHAPTER 1

ROBERT FARQUHARSON

The cast

Robert Farquharson: Drove sons Jai, ten, Tyler, seven, and Bailey, two, into a dam near Winchelsea

Cindy Gambino: Robert Farquharson's ex-wife and Jai, Tyler and Bailey's mother. She is now married to Stephen Moules and they have two sons together

Stephen Moules: Cindy's second husband; he also has a daughter and two older sons

Kerri Huntington, **Carmen Ross**: Farquharson's sisters. He also has a brother, Darrell

Bob and **Bev Gambino**: Cindy's parents

Faye and **Don Farquharson**: Robert Farquharson's parents. Faye died in 2002 and Don in 2010

Greg King: Farquharson's friend

Judi Fallon: Winchelsea Primary School principal in 2005

The motive

Robert Farquharson's main motive in killing his three sons was revenge: he sought to punish his estranged wife, Cindy Gambino, for leaving him and striking up a friendship with another man. Secondary gains would include ridding himself of his financial and parental responsibilities and attracting community sympathy as 'poor Rob who lost his children in a terrible accident'. He was anxious not to be seen as an inadequate man whose wife had left him.

Introduction

Winchelsea is a pretty town with a proud history. Nestled on the Barwon River, about forty kilometres south-west of Geelong in Victoria, it originally grew around the Barwon Hotel, which opened in 1842 as the Barwon Inn and still operates today. A nearby stone bridge was built in 1867, not long after the bluestone shire hall, which dates back to 1860 and is now a stately tearoom. A hub for surrounding farms and a charming place to raise a family away from the hustle and bustle of the city, this typical Australian country town has a population of around 2100 and a solid sense of community. It also has its heroes. Decorated war hero Albert Jacka, who won Australia's first World War I Victoria Cross following his 1915 Gallipoli efforts, was born on a dairy farm at Layard, just outside town, in 1893. Acclaimed opera singer Marjorie Lawrence was born in nearby Deans Marsh in 1907.

Those driving to Geelong from Colac, Camperdown or Warrnambool will pass the old schoolhouse, two pubs, the Globe Theatre (built by Marjorie Lawrence's father) and cafes and shops dotted along the highway as it snakes its way through the town, dividing it in two. If you look closely, about four kilometres past the town you will also see three white wooden crosses to the left on the road's shoulder. These simple but heart-wrenching memorials mark the lives of Jai, Tyler and Bailey Farquharson, three young brothers tragically lost on Father's Day in 2005. Aged ten, seven and two, the boys died soon after their dad Robert's car skidded off the Princes Highway and into a seven-metre-deep dam.

The deaths shook Winchelsea to its core and still haunt those left behind. The families of the boys' parents, Robert Farquharson and Cindy Gambino, have lived in the area for several generations. No fewer than nineteen Farquharsons are buried in Winchelsea cemetery, dating back to 1876 and including Jai, Tyler, Bailey and their paternal grandparents, Don and Faye. The black marble vault the boys share sits alone to the left of the cemetery proper, beside a long row of agapanthus lining the gravel drive, and features a photo of each child, three toy motorbikes, three sleeping angels and the carved letters J, T and B. The headstone has carved images of the Essendon AFL football club logo, an angel and Bob the Builder, whom little Bailey will never outgrow. The main inscription reads: *Much loved and cherished children of Robert and Cindy. Precious grandsons of Donald and Faye Farquharson, Robert and Beverley Gambino. We hold our children's hands for a while, their hearts forever. In God's hands until we meet again.*

It is a fitting tribute to three bright young souls – with one exception. Someone has tried to scratch off the name of their father, Robert, now twice convicted of killing them.

The lead-up to the crime

Father's Day is a time for sipping lukewarm coffee in bed, nibbling burnt toast prepared with tiny hands and opening homemade cards with stick-figure drawings of relatives and pets. It is a time for some dads to bond with their kids over a trip to the footy or a fast-food feast. In 2005, Father's Day was only half a day for Robert Farquharson. Separated from his wife, Cindy Gambino, he didn't see his boys, Jai, Tyler and Bailey, until the afternoon when he finished his morning shift at Cumberland Resort Lorne, where he worked as a cleaner. To Farquharson, juggling access to his boys was yet another humiliation he had suffered since his wife had ended their marriage ten months earlier.

Stephen Moules, a concreter who had moved to Winchelsea from Melbourne, had poured the concrete slab for the new house that Rob and Cindy were building before they separated. Stephen was divorced and had three children, two of whom were boys and ended up living with him. He was active in the Winchelsea community as a Cub Scout leader and a Sunday school teacher at his local church. Several months after Farquharson had left the family home, Cindy and Stephen became friends, and Farquharson was not happy about it. Before Cindy ended their marriage, they had appeared to have a solid relationship. Both were involved with the local football and cricket clubs and had attended working bees at the primary school. Winchelsea had no independent or Catholic school, so pupils with parents on welfare mixed with the offspring of wealthy landowners at the only local primary school. The Farquharson–Gambino family was somewhere in the middle, their boys well-mannered and popular. Rob and Cindy were not flush with cash, but lived comfortably enough.

Farquharson was a typical country bloke whose parents were locals; his mother Faye's family ran the Barwon Hotel for twenty-six years. After leaving school in Year 11, he scratched a living from a series of non-skilled jobs, most notably as a labourer with the local shire and more recently as a cleaner. A fairly quiet person, Farquharson enjoyed a drink and being part of a close-knit community. But he had his faults and grumbled about having to wait for access to his boys. Probably in an exaggerated attempt to elicit sympathy and make his estranged wife look bad, he would tell others he had arrived at Winchelsea Primary for Jai and Tyler as planned, only to find Cindy or Stephen had already picked them up. Farquharson also regularly blamed others if things went wrong. When one of his sons' footballs went missing, he stormed up to the school demanding that the then principal, Judi Fallon, confront the boy whom he was sure had taken it. The ball turned up in the school grounds the next day – it had simply been lost. Apart from his 'victim' mentality, Judi found Farquharson to be a solid citizen and 'by all accounts harmless'. 'He was great with the kids; he was quite a gentle man . . . a real country bumpkin type,' she says. '(But) he wouldn't be the sharpest tool in the shed.'

At 3 pm on 4 September 2005, Cindy drove Jai, Tyler and Bailey to Farquharson's place and watched as they gave their father his presents. It wasn't his access weekend, but Cindy had organised for the boys to be with their dad for Father's Day. She then left, confident her children were safe with a man who had never given any indication that he would hurt them.

Winchelsea did not have a KFC, so father and sons drove into Geelong for a meal of fried chicken. Next he took them to Kmart, where he bought a cricket bat for Jai and videos for Tyler and Bailey. They also saw Farquharson's sister, Kerri Hunting-ton, who worked there. On the way back they dropped in to Kerri's house in Mount Moriac, where they spoke briefly to her husband Gary.

What happened next still haunts people the world over.

The murders
Robert Farquharson and his sons left Mount Moriac at around 7.15 pm for the eighteen-kilometre trip home to Winchelsea, where Farquharson was to return the boys to their mother.

The section of the Princes Highway they were approaching was a two-lane, two-way undivided road with sealed shoulders and rumble strips outlining the shoulders. The speed limit was one hundred kilometres per hour, but Farquharson drove much more slowly. (He later claimed this was because he had the boys with him.) The road was straight and flat before rising over a rail overpass and then sweeping to the right towards Winchelsea. Just beyond the overpass, the car crossed to the wrong side of the road, turning right at an estimated thirty-degree angle as it left the highway and ran into a wire fence, clipped a tree and ended up in the dam (R v Farquharson, 2009).

Farquharson escaped from the sinking car, but Jai, Tyler and Bailey were all trapped, and they drowned. It appeared at first to have been a terrible accident.

Having made it to shore, Farquharson approached the road to wave down passing traffic. A car carrying two young men, Shane Atkinson and Tony McClelland, pulled over. It was now about 7.30 pm. Atkinson yelled, 'What the fuck are you doing, mate? Are you trying to kill yourself?'

Farquharson didn't answer but kept saying, 'Oh no, fuck, what have I done? What's happened?' He then said, 'I've killed the kids. They've drowned.' A few minutes later he asked, 'Can I grab a smoke off you, mate?'

Shane and Tony could not get much sense out of the short, stocky man who had flagged them down; Shane wondered if Farquharson's strange behaviour meant that he had an intellectual impairment. Farquharson first told them he must have 'done a wheel bearing', but soon added that he 'must have had a coughing fit and blacked out and just woke up in the water . . . and couldn't get the kids out'. He repeatedly said he had killed his kids and had to go home to tell his estranged wife Cindy that he had 'killed them'. He ignored Shane's repeated offer of the

33

use of his mobile phone to call police or an ambulance. Nor did he try to raise the alarm at a house not far from the dam, where a light was on. Instead, he insisted they go to Cindy's house to tell her what had happened.

Cindy had spent the afternoon with Stephen and was waiting with Stephen's nine-year-old son Zach for her boys to return. When a strange car arrived her heart sank.

When Farquharson had relayed the tragic news, Cindy called Stephen and arranged to meet him at the dam and then frantically drove there with Farquharson, and Zach. Shane and Tony alerted emergency services before meeting them at the dam. When they all arrived, one of the first things Farquharson did was ask Stephen for a cigarette. The car was fully submerged. Stephen, Tony and two emergency service volunteers tried several times to dive into the pitch-black freezing water to rescue the children, but they had little hope; the dam had originally been dug during roadworks and was seven metres deep. Still, they kept trying. Stephen dived in several times, only stopping when warned his own life was at risk from hypothermia. While all this was happening, Robert Farquharson stood watching. Those who were there noted that he did not participate meaningfully in the rescue attempt and his demeanour was unemotional. He asked several people for cigarettes and was happy to watch others conduct the search.

When Country Fire Authority volunteers and emergency services arrived, the search continued with a police helicopter hovering overhead, shining thin beams of light into the dark. Several hours later, a police diver found the car and the boys. Jai was face down across the front seats, partway out of the driver's door. Tyler's head was near a rear door with his legs between the front seats and Bailey was tangled in the straps of his car seat.

Farquharson, who had remained relatively calm, was eventually assessed in the back of an ambulance and taken to Geelong Hospital's emergency department for treatment. A physical examination revealed nothing untoward. He had no alcohol in his system and his blood pressure was normal, but his pulse rate was slightly raised (Garner, 2014). Due to his claim of having blacked out with a coughing fit, a doctor made a provisional diagnosis of cough syncope – a loss of consciousness due to coughing. Such fits are almost certainly related to serious infections or illnesses such as whooping cough, pneumonia or bronchitis, but there was no evidence of these during the examination and no signs of any wheezing or crackles in his lungs. No-one particularly noticed Farquharson coughing that night.

Farquharson later told police in his record of interview that he did not remember driving into the water. He recalled driving over the overpass and starting to cough. He then 'really, really' started coughing and remembered nothing further until finding himself underwater. He said he told the kids not to panic, but as Jai opened the front passenger door the car began to fill with water and nosedived slightly. Farquharson said he reached over and shut Jai's door then got himself out, after which the car sank further. He claimed that he then attempted to go around to the other side of the car but could not due to the water pressure. At one point he told police he had dived under three or four times before seeking help, but in other interviews he had to be prompted before repeating this claim (R v Farquharson, 2009).

Suspicions were raised immediately when Farquharson appeared to be more interested in his own welfare than his boys'. In 2013, Detective Senior Sergeant Jeff Smith, who interviewed Farquharson on the night of the crash, told journalist Andrew Rule: 'I had to break the news to Farquharson that his three kids were dead. I'll never forget his reaction. He said: "What's the scenario for me?" That set off a lot of bells.' When Jeff Smith called his investigator at the dam, before he could say anything about his suspicions, the other officer added: 'This is bulls---. He's driven into the water.' Smith replied: 'I was just going to tell you to have a good look at it' (Rule, 2013).

Yet Farquharson continued to insist the deaths of his children was an accident and he had no reason to kill them. He told police that, while their breakup hadn't been easy, he and Cindy had been on civil terms and he was learning to cope with life as a single man. On the night of the accident, he had been recovering from a throat infection that required antibiotics and about eight days off work. He claimed that it had left him with a troublesome cough that must have prompted the coughing fit. Cindy and his family believed him, as he did have a history of chest problems, but investigators had their doubts.

When police retrieved Farquharson's car they found the heater, ignition and headlights all turned off. The key was still in the ignition, suggesting the possibility that the driver was fully alert and turned the ignition off so that the car would not be observed when it went into the dam. There was no physical evidence on the ground to support Farquharson's claim of a car out of control due to the driver being unconscious. Nor did the tyre tracks appear to support his story. The Major Collision Investigation Unit's Sergeant Geoffrey Exton found the car could not have followed the path it had taken, particularly over the rough terrain, without some pressure at the steering wheel. He found the vehicle's path was consistent with the driver having conscious control.

As the school principal, Judi Fallon was called to the scene that night by a school parent. She remembers initially thinking that it must have been an accident. 'You think to yourself, "No-one could be capable of doing that,"' she says. However, when Judi arrived at the dam she quickly changed her mind when she saw that the car's route was not consistent with Farquharson's explanation of what happened. 'The way the road goes, there was no way a sneezing fit, coughing fit, whatever fit, you would have gone through that way.'

Judi also wondered why Farquharson had not gone out of his way to try to save his boys. As a mother who had once run several kilometres for help carrying her young daughter who had been kicked and injured by a horse, she could not understand his indifference. The deaths were big news around the world. As more facts emerged, many suspected foul play. Still in shock, Winchelsea locals were divided. Some, including Farquharson's sisters Carmen Ross and Kerri Huntington, could not believe that he had killed his children. Others were convinced he was guilty. The whole community is still traumatised.

The trials

In 2007, Robert Farquharson was found guilty of murdering his three sons and sentenced to life without parole. But Cindy Gambino and a number of others still believed he was innocent. In a segment aired on 28 October that year, Cindy told *60 Minutes'* Peter Overton that to think her ex-husband was a killer was 'too incomprehensible'. Cindy could not believe that Farquharson, who loved her and their children, would hate her enough to kill them.

Asked for her reaction to the verdict, including what she thought about the forensic evidence, Cindy said she wailed for both Farquharson and the honour of her children. Her estranged husband had been slowly starting to move on and she trusted him. Cindy told Overton she believed Farquharson was a devoted, protective father and the evidence presented in the case meant nothing to her as it was all a tragic accident.

That first trial heard that Farquharson planned the killings over a long period of time, with a phony excuse for driving the car into the icy water already prepared – a severe coughing fit that supposedly caused him to lose consciousness. Initially this ruse succeeded, even with Cindy. However the story began to unravel as evidence mounted against him.

Farquharson's defence claimed that he was a shy, timid and inarticulate man unable to handle an emergency, but not a murderer. His barrister, Peter Morrissey SC, said the case against him was circumstantial and questioned the evidence of Farquharson's friend Greg King, who claimed that the accused had earlier threatened revenge against Cindy. Several months before the boys died, Farquharson allegedly told King that he planned to pay his ex-wife back 'big time' by 'taking away the most important thing' to her, confiding he had thought about driving off a cliff or running into a tree. The controversial discussion occurred outside a Winchelsea fish and chip shop at about 6 pm on a Friday. In a police statement, King – who had worked with Farquharson at the local Shire and socialised with him – said his friend was inside the shop and when he came out Cindy pulled up and greeted them. Farquharson, he recalled, became angry.

The following is an extract from Greg King's statement to the police:

I said, 'Come on, Robbie, you have to move on.'

He said, 'Move on how, I've got nothing.'

Then he said, 'Nobody does that to me and gets away with it, it's all her fault.'

I said, 'What is?'

He said, 'Take that Sports Pack car I paid $30,000 for, she wanted it and they are fucking driving it. Look what I'm driving, the fucking shit one.' Then he started on about the house and said that she wanted the best of everything and 'we couldn't afford it'. 'Now it looks like she wants to marry that fucking dickhead. There is no way I am going to let him and her and the kids fucking live in my house together and I have to pay for it. I also pay fucking maintenance for the kids, no way.'

Then he said, 'I'm going to pay her back big time.'

I asked him how, he then said, 'I'll take away the most important thing that means to her.'

Then I asked him, 'What's that, Robbie?' He then nodded his head towards the fish and chip shop window where the kids were standing with Cindy and my kids.

I then said, 'What, the kids?'

He said, 'Yes.'

I asked him, 'What would you do, would you take them away or something?'

He then just stared at me in my eyes and said, 'Kill them.'

I said, 'Bullshit, that's your own flesh and blood, Robbie.'

He said, 'So I hate them.'

I said, 'You would go to gaol.'

He said, 'No, I won't, I will kill myself before it gets to that.'

Then I asked him how. He said, 'It would be close by.'

I said, 'What?'

He said, 'Accident involving a dam where I survive and the kids don't.' He then said it would be on a special day.

I asked him what day, he said, 'Something like Father's Day so everybody would remember it when it was Father's Day and I was the last one to have them for the last time, not her. Then every Father's Day she would suffer for the rest of her life.'

Then I said, 'You don't even dream of that, Robbie.' (R v Farquharson, 2009)

Farquharson's defence lawyers claimed he was not capable of murderous thoughts, plans or actions. Mr Morrissey told the court his client was simply shy and inarticulate, using terms such as 'a confused bloke' to describe him, emphasising his love for his kids and insisting that his behaviour leading up to Father's Day 2005 was not that of a man planning to kill his children. He urged the jury to 'walk in the shoes' of the accused, empathise with him, look him in the face and decide for themselves whether he could have been 'bubbling away like an evil stew' (Rintoul, 2010). According to his defence, Robert Farquharson was a man who had been stepped on by planet Earth. Everything had conspired against him – the dodgy old car, the supposed coughing fit and his inability to get his sons out of the car – to produce a tragic accident that was sheer bad luck.

But prosecutor Jeremy Rapke QC questioned claims that Farquharson was the innocent victim of a series of unlucky events. He told jurors that the evidence pointed to Farquharson being a murderer, not just 'a very unlucky, perhaps tragic, man'. In his closing address, Rapke urged the jurors to consider Farquharson's jealousy and outright hostility towards Cindy, as well as his moderate level of depression, a dangerous and volatile mix just waiting to be ignited. 'There was an antipathy or hatred by the accused for his former wife,' he said (Bice, 2014).

The jury agreed.

Given the guilty verdict, why did Cindy initially support the innocence of her ex-husband? Her actions were psychologically protective and essential to her survival. She knew there was no way that *she* could ever have harmed her children, so how could their father have done such a thing? How could *anyone* have done such a thing intentionally? It would also have been very difficult for her to accept that her decision to end the marriage, although perfectly reasonable and a decision many people have to make, had indirectly led to the death of her children, and that she had unintentionally handed them over to their killer. She was also determined not to have her children remembered as victims.

Cindy began to change her mind when Farquharson refused to see her in jail. She suspected that he didn't want to talk to her one on one because she would know if he was lying. Then a new witness, Dawn Waite, came forward to say she had seen Farquharson awake in his car at the time he said he had blacked out, driving erratically just near the dam. Once the realisation hit, Cindy, already deeply traumatised by what had happened to her children, became deeply depressed and endured several severe episodes of mental illness that required hospital treatment. She became addicted to sedatives and it took many years and the support of her new partner and her family to help her through. She still deals with the 'what ifs' to this day (Norris, 2013).

In 2009, Farquharson was granted a retrial on a number of technical grounds. Justices Marilyn Warren, Geoffrey Nettle and Robert Redlich quashed Farquharson's conviction and ordered a retrial after finding a number of errors in the 2007 trial. These included that prosecutors failed to tell Farquharson's defence team that King faced criminal charges for assault, and that the trial judge failed to properly instruct the jury on how it should consider parts of the trial evidence.

In 2010, the jury in the retrial heard Cindy's amended statement as well as the new evidence from Dawn Waite, who had not come forward earlier due to family stresses, including school exams, the recent loss of three relatives and, later, her treatment for lymphoma. Waite was also wary of becoming involved after a man she reported for dangerous driving in New Zealand several years earlier had died by suicide before the matter got to court. But she approached police in late 2009 after Farquharson was granted a retrial. Waite had been driving behind Farquharson's Commodore as it headed towards the dam. She saw it going slowly, braking, then speeding up, veering slowly from side to side, so erratically that she was reluctant to pass. The driver was not coughing or unconscious; he was upright. The three boys appeared to be in the back, contradicting Farquharson's version that had Jai in the front. Dawn said the headlights were still on as the car veered to the right (Hunt, 2010).

Cindy also gave police a second statement in time for the retrial, adding details that she hadn't mentioned in the first trial, including the fact that Farquharson had stalked her after the breakup and made angry threats towards her. When Farquharson was found guilty a second time, in October 2010, his sentence was reduced to a minimum thirty-three years. This was not enough for Cindy, who by then was convinced of his guilt. 'I don't believe it's enough; it's a life sentence for me, it should be a life sentence for him,' she said (Anderson and van den Berg, 2010). In December 2012, the Court of Appeal rejected another appeal by Farquharson based on key elements of the Crown case, including challenges to police reconstruction evidence and claiming that the conversation Farquharson had with Greg King was unreliable. The defence also claimed manslaughter should have been an option. In August 2013, Farquharson sought leave to appeal to the High Court, but failed to show cause. One of Australia's most notorious murder cases was finally closed.

Outside the court, Cindy, who cried as the three judges delivered their verdict, told reporters the case had taken a decade of her life, but her boys were finally at peace (Portelli, 2013).

It was a tragic end to a fourteen-year relationship that for the most part had seemed quite normal.

Robert Farquharson's background

The youngest of four children, Robert Farquharson was born in May 1969. A smaller than average child, he appears to have been overprotected by his mother and two older sisters, which is nothing out of the ordinary in those circumstances. Farquharson enjoyed a typical country Victorian upbringing, attending Winchelsea Primary School and then high school in Geelong until Year 11. As the 'baby' of the family he was somewhat spoiled and was rarely expected to take the initiative. There was always his older brother Darrell or one of his sisters to take charge, with Carmen and Kerri remaining protective throughout both of his criminal trials. When Kerri seized his arm and led him across the pavement outside court, author Helen Garner, herself the eldest of six, described it as 'a bossy big sister grip' (Garner, 2014).

In March 2011, Farquharson's oldest sister, Carmen, told the ABC's *Australian Story*, 'We were a little bit more protective of him than other kids because he was smaller for his age, he had poor coordination and . . . eyesight, but he is a very tough, tough little guy. He did all the normal things that kids do and he went to play football because he loved sport.'

After doing poorly at school and leaving when he was sixteen, Farquharson worked for the local shire as a labourer. Working with Cindy's father Bob Gambino, with whom he shared a birthday, Farquharson was part of a team responsible for tasks such as road maintenance and installing road signs. He could be a capable worker when he wanted to be, but was known to be a bit slack and to throw a tantrum if he couldn't get something to work properly and other people were watching. He was also perceived by some people as a 'bit of a bullshit artist'.

Farquharson met Cindy in 1990, when both were in their early twenties. She was living in Birregurra, halfway between Winchelsea and Colac, and worked at a supermarket in Winchelsea. Her new boyfriend had a reputation for being a bit of a whinger with a negative outlook on almost everything. But the young council worker generally seemed pleasant enough.

In the book *On Father's Day*, Cindy Gambino's story as told by Megan Norris, Cindy revealed that she was living independently when they met, but Farquharson was still living at home.

> Little Robbie was the youngest of [Faye's] four . . . She lovingly cooked and sliced his favourite food, miniature chickens, to make sandwiches for his work lunch box. Cindy wondered why he wasn't making his own lunch at the age of 24. Faye fussed over him, attending to his every whim, while he sulked like a spoilt child.
>
> Rob often behaved like a child too. Once, when his mother dished him up a meal of chops, he pushed his plate away, flatly refusing to eat the food his mother had laboured over. 'I'm not eating that shit,' he snapped. Faye hid her disappointment, but Cindy was shocked. She was also uneasy about Rob's attitude towards his father. (Norris, 2013)

In Helen Garner's book on the Farquharson trials, Bob Gambino described his son-in-law and colleague as 'a lazy little bugger'. 'If he didn't want to do something, well, he didn't,' Bob said. 'Not motivated – you know – a sook' (Garner, 2014). Cindy moved in with Robert and gave birth to Jai in October 1994. In July 1998,

Tyler was born. The pair married in 2000 and had Bailey on New Year's Eve in 2002, the year Faye died of cancer. Bailey's birth strained the couple's relationship. Cindy was keen to have another child but Farquharson didn't want the added responsibility. But Cindy was determined and won out (Kissane, 2007). Nor was Farquharson sure about building a second new house after Cindy was unhappy with the first one they had built.

He did try to be a good provider, but was clearly unsuited to running a business, holding down a decent job or getting promoted. After taking redundancy from the local council in 1996, he worked for Lidgerwood Seeds in Birregurra for a short time before purchasing a Jim's Mowing franchise. When that business failed in 1999, with debts of $40,000, Farquharson blamed clients who didn't pay him for his work. He then worked at Cumberland Resort Lorne as a cleaner until he was charged with murdering his children.

At home, Cindy usually took the initiative on most decisions, such as how many children they had and where they lived. She even assembled the bikes and Christmas toys. Her husband also lacked basic parenting skills. In her book, Cindy revealed that he avoided changing nappies like the plague, telling her it was her job. He whinged a lot, despite the fact Cindy did most of the work, and he taunted their children. This mild bullying was noticed by his parents, who asked him to stop.

> Rob had a habit of pouncing on the children when they were lying quietly or absorbed in a Nintendo game. With a smirk on his face, he'd start teasing them and calling them names. The two older boys would retaliate physically, and soon they'd be rolling around on the floor with Rob, who kept prodding them harder and harder. In no time, he'd have stirred them into a frenzy

of frustration, like some master tormentor on a mission. Jai, in particular, would burst into tears of rage and lash out at his father.

But Rob would keep going, smirking and apparently getting a perverse satisfaction from stirring his oldest son up, until Jai stormed off to lie on his bed. Then Rob would shrug his shoulders. 'What's wrong with him?' he'd ask. 'I was only playing.' But Cindy could tell Rob knew exactly what he was doing. His teasing was steady and purposeful, and he seemed to enjoy it. Did he get a sense of power from engineering conflict with the boys? He could escalate it at a whim, and his children were powerless to stop him. Everyone who watched him teasing the boys could feel his latent anger.' (Norris, 2013)

Cindy was also a target of Farquharson's passive-aggressive behaviour. Despite her protests, he'd also grab her breasts as she grappled with a saucepan full of hot vegetables, or grope her while she bathed the children, saying 'can't you take a joke'. He was not habitually violent, but once, after their separation, he shoved her into a wall and she contemplated calling the police. While there were days when he'd come home and play footy with the boys, 'there were many more when he'd swear and kick at the toys scattered around the back yard, screaming at Cindy and the children to clean up the place' (Norris, 2013).

Stephen Moules backed Cindy's assessment. His first impression of Farquharson was that he was happy to sit back as Cindy took care of everything; he was 'like a child, really'. Stephen formed the impression that Farquharson was a bit of a wimp and Cindy usually took charge because somebody had to.

Having suffered postnatal depression after the birth of Jai, Cindy suspected that her husband's mood swings and sleeplessness after Faye's death meant he too was depressed. He resisted help at first, insisting he was all right. By the time he agreed to seek help in late 2004, the marriage was over for Cindy as she realised she'd never truly loved him. Farquharson, who moved back in with his father, Don, later discovered Cindy had begun a friendship with Stephen that both insist did not develop into a proper relationship until after the boys died.

Farquharson took it hard and told people he was 'pissed off' that Cindy took the good car, a silver 2002 Commodore, while he got the 'shit car', a 1989 model. It appeared his efforts to build a dream home had come to nothing. While clearly upsetting for him, this was nothing out of the ordinary when it comes to family breakdown. Many people, rightly or wrongly, are left feeling that they got the rough end of the stick in asset division. In fact, Cindy went out of her way to ensure Farquharson was okay and offered to forgo some child maintenance so he could set himself up in his own place. She had already bought him a new set of saucepans, a quilt and quilt cover.

Eventually Farquharson sought help from a GP, who prescribed antidepressants. He also briefly participated in counselling sessions with a psychologist but claimed they were too expensive to continue. By mid-2005, it appeared that he had begun to settle into a routine and accept his new circumstances. No-one saw the murders coming and Farquharson clearly thought he was going to get away with his crime. But he did not count on the forensic evidence, the instinct of the police officers involved or the work of anti-violence campaigners like Phil Cleary.

A former independent federal MP, Cleary's sister Vicki was killed by an ex-partner in 1987. The perpetrator was convicted of the lesser charge of manslaughter after arguing in court that Vicki had provoked him. Cleary has since campaigned to give those affected by domestic violence a voice and to reform laws that allowed many men to effectively blame their victims. Cleary has no sympathy for Robert Farquharson. He has written many articles and several books on men who kill and warns that we should never 'entertain the myth' that those like Farquharson try to perpetuate about being loving fathers. 'When men act with such vengeance then lie, it's impossible to find compassion,' he says, adding that Farquharson showed his hand when he told Greg King he was going to get back at Cindy by killing her children. Just as Cindy struggled to believe her estranged husband could do that, Cleary says King, like most others, would naturally have struggled with the idea. For that reason, King didn't take his conversation with Farquharson that seriously at the time. It just seemed too crazy.

'For those of us who've had a sister or daughter murdered by an estranged partner, it's a different story,' Cleary says.

> The moment I heard about the boys in the dam I 'knew' it was murder. Like killing an estranged partner, it's what some men do. There will no doubt be the usual chorus of men telling me that women kill their children too. Yes, they do, but less frequently – 63 per cent of such killings are by men – and for far different reasons. Mad women, or women terrified about the safety of their children, have been known to kill. But rarely, if ever, are such killings an act of revenge against the father. Men have a monopoly on the revenge killing of women and children. And only men can put an end to these killings. (Cleary, 2007)

Spurned partners may fantasise about making life hell for their ex, but rarely do they take it out on their children. While there was some evidence of earlier mild depression, Robert Farquharson was not found to be mentally ill at the time of the crime. The court decided – twice – that he had murdered his children to spite his ex-wife.

Why?

Why did he do it?

According to the Australian Bureau of Statistics (2007), the divorces of 52,399 Australian couples were finalised in 2005. As a result, almost 105,000 people had to deal with the sadness, pain and loss involved in separating from a partner and starting a new life. Divorce is never easy and can be acrimonious. But most separating parents manage to set those feelings aside and put their children first when it comes to custody arrangements or choosing a school. They also try hard to keep the kids out of any arguments.

Not Robert Farquharson. He seethed with resentment. Rather than make the best of an unpleasant separation, he was consumed with exacting revenge. In his mind, whatever happened was Cindy's fault. So he killed his boys to pay her back and tried to pass it off as a horrible accident, hoping to forever be seen as 'poor Robbie', the loving father who lost his children after his wife dumped him for another man.

What could put such an idea into a father's mind? To most people he knew, the mild-mannered Farquharson's actions on the evening of 4 September 2005 were completely out of character. But when you dig deeper, it becomes clear why he acted the way he did. Genetic and environmental factors combined to produce this tragic outcome. These factors included a limited education, a relatively low level of intelligence, living in a small community, an overprotective upbringing and a personality disorder that left him unwilling and unable to cope with life's ups and downs.

As the youngest of four children, Farquharson was indulged and mollycoddled by his mother and older siblings. He lived at home until he met his future wife, and was comfortable with Cindy taking on most of the responsibility for their shared life. She took the lead in many of their life decisions, which suited a partner who was spoiled, immature, dependent and reluctant to take on adult responsibilities. On the surface he was a quiet, likeable country bloke, but underneath he was an angry and inadequate man with no confidence or resilience and few life skills.

Unable to run a successful business, Farquharson was the archetypal 'loser', hiding behind his more competent wife. It suited him to let the more socially outgoing and capable Cindy act as his 'shield'. For her part, Cindy probably felt she could help the apparently inoffensive and pliable Farquharson to become more like the kind of man she wanted. When it was clear that he was not prepared to act as a mature adult and left most of the work and responsibilities to her, she realised that she didn't love him and asked him to leave.

Robert Farquharson's pattern of behaviour is consistent with a diagnosis of an avoidant personality disorder (AvPD). People with an AvPD are painfully self-conscious, perceive that they are inadequate and inferior to other people, avoid jobs requiring significant interpersonal contact and unfamiliar social situations and are hypersensitive to actions or comments by others that could be seen as mocking, disapproving or rejecting. People with an AvPD often seek social situations that minimise potential embarrassment or rejection. Some who observed him socially said Farquharson sometimes gravitated towards playing with kids at social functions. Children make fewer social demands and it was safer for him than participating in sustained adult social contact and conversation.

Farquharson also had a background that research suggests is fairly typical of someone who develops an AvPD. As a child, he had limited athletic skills, was protected by older siblings, small for his age and had bad eyesight, as well as an awkward gait due to flat feet. As an adult he was chubby and a smoker. His mother appears to have shared some of his traits and may have used alcohol to cope with her anxiety. Farquharson probably started showing signs of a personality disorder while still at school, where friends say he regularly sniped at girls. Men with an AvPD are often especially angry at women and girls, whom they perceive to be easier targets.

Farquharson fits into the conflicted AvPD subtype (Millon et al., 2004). Such people seek out a stronger and more confident partner on whom they become dependent, but at the same time they resent this dependence. They tend to use passive-aggressive tactics to express their hostility. Some of Farquharson's many passive-aggressive acts included:

- Refusing to mind his children post-separation, even when Cindy needed to go to hospital.
- Planning to verbally provoke Stephen Moules into hitting him so that he could have him charged with assault (according to his psychologist, Peter Popko).
- Relentlessly teasing his boys and calling them names, even when his own parents told him to stop.
- Grabbing Cindy's breasts whilst she had a hot pot in her hands and then saying, 'Can't you take a joke?' when she objected.
- Complaining of unfair demands being made of him when this wasn't the case.
- Threatening, after the separation, to move to Queensland and have no contact with his children ('Then you'll be sorry').
- Failing to complete tasks or do his share of the work around the house.
- Sulking a lot like a spoiled child.
- Telling his children that Cindy loved Stephen's children more than them (in order to alienate them from her).

- Telling people his kids had told him they didn't like Stephen.
- Making threats towards Cindy and Stephen such as: 'I have contacts – don't underestimate me.'
- Exaggerating or lying about times when Cindy did not comply with agreed pick-up times in order to make her look bad in the eyes of other people.

He also lacked resilience, a common feature of most personality disorders. At one stage, Farquharson's own father actually thanked Stephen Moules when he told Farquharson to grow up and move on (Norris, 2013). Other signs that he lacked resilience included:

- Living at home until he was well into his twenties and having his lunch made for him.
- Wildly throwing a hole-digging tool at work when he couldn't operate it.
- Attacking a lawn mower when it wouldn't work for him and having temper tantrums.
- Avoiding having Bailey overnight so he didn't have to change nappies.
- Inappropriately crying on Stephen Moules's shoulder and complaining about his life after he and Cindy had separated (Norris, 2013).

When Cindy left her husband, the situation deteriorated. He had lost both of his 'shields': his mother and then his wife. When he no longer had Cindy to take responsibility and the initiative, he became lost and couldn't move on. He felt humiliated and angry at what he perceived to be the unfair division of their assets. His anger increased when he discovered that Cindy had started a new friendship with Stephen Moules. Living in a small town amplified this humiliation, because his family was quite well known and he could not hide. Farquharson's personality disorder reduced his capacity for dealing with the situation rationally or reflecting on his own behaviour. To him, it was all Cindy's fault for 'treating him like shit'. With little or no empathy for his boys, he probably assigned them some of the blame as well.

Everyone else was at fault except him.

In the lead-up to his crime, Farquharson cultivated the image of himself as a victim. He moped around town, arousing the sympathy of many locals, and began to complain of coughing problems, taking about eight days off work with a supposed throat infection. In one instance, he lay on the ground in front of a neighbour during an apparent coughing fit. All of this could easily be faked – there are many internet sites that show how easy it is to fake a cough. Farquharson even turned up in court on crutches on the first day of his appeal, having supposedly had a severe coughing fit in jail that made him fall of his chair and break his leg.

A work supervisor told the jury at his trial that two days before the boys died, Farquharson had a sudden coughing fit so severe that she feared he might be having a stroke. But he didn't pass out. That week he told a friend of thirty years that he had had a coughing fit while pulling into the local roadhouse in his car. When he came to, he said, his car had stopped. However, he later told police that his 'passing out' at the dam was the first time it had happened; clearly, he had real difficulties keeping his story straight and remembering to whom he had said what. He appeared to be setting the scene for his horrific plan to murder his children. By moping and playing the wronged husband and father, he made people feel sorry for him and take care of him, believing him incapable of murder. This strategy worked with some locals, but the jury saw through it.

In killing his boys, Farquharson believed he had come up with the perfect solution to his problems: he would pay Cindy back for humiliating him and leaving him to cope on his own, wreck her relationship with Stephen and dodge his parental and financial responsibilities. Farquharson appears to have gained enormous satisfaction from being the first person to see the look of horror on Cindy's face when she found out that her three sons were dead. It is very difficult to imagine any other motivation for his insistence that he be driven to Cindy's house before alerting emergency services.

Before he sentenced Farquharson to a life sentence without parole after he was found guilty at his first trial, Justice Philip Cummins said: 'You wiped out your entire family in one act. Only the two parents remained: you, because you had always intended to save yourself, and their mother, because you intended her to live a life of suffering.' (DPP v Farquharson, 2007)

Compared to other people, those with any type of personality disorder have a limited capacity for empathy. Farquharson's murder of his children was unbelievably cold-blooded and devoid of any empathy at all. As he planned his crime, he was able to remain calm even when imagining the terror and pain he would see on his children's faces. Did he picture this terror but decide to continue anyway? Or did he just smile at the thought of how Cindy's face would look when she found out they were dead? Did he revel in the thought of how much better he expected life to be without his responsibilities, while others took care of him in his 'bereavement'? It is beyond the comprehension of most to imagine how this man was able to plan all this and then watch as the car began to sink. Even then he did not change his mind, leading experienced coroner Dr Iain West to remark, 'In the 30-odd years I've been doing this job I have never, ever come across anything more horrific' (Norris, 2013).

Farquharson's limited capacity for empathy, coupled with his relatively low level of intelligence and education, also made it impossible for him to predict how somebody would react if they really had been involved in an accident that killed their children. Therefore his behaviour was totally inappropriate and signalled his guilt to others. Nor did he have the capacity to memorise his story and stick to it; his ever-changing versions of events was another clear indicator of guilt. He also failed to realise that Greg King might tell police about the specific threat he had made to kill his boys.

Almost two-thirds of people who kill their children also suicide (Liem et al., 2013). Those who don't are less likely to have a mental illness. Farquharson had no signs of mental illness. He simply continued his long-standing pattern of feeling inadequate and inferior and blaming others instead of looking inwards to see what personal improvements he could make to his behaviour and thinking patterns. Farquharson saw himself as the victim and created a 'show' designed to harm Cindy. In his eyes, it was her fault: 'Look what you made me do!' But he failed to anticipate that others would see through his story. Although they couldn't prove it, it was obvious to police and most others closely involved in the case that Farquharson had researched conditions he claimed to have experienced, such as 'cough syncope' and 'grey out'. He also failed to realise how thoroughly traffic accident investigators would research his car's movements into the dam.

Nothing added up and, in the end, two juries didn't believe his lies and saw fit to convict him. Robert Farquharson will forever be known as a man who killed his three sons.

While Jai, Tyler and Bailey will never be forgotten, the residents of Winchelsea are doing their best to move on. But locals are still haunted by what happened down the road from their historic main strip. 'That dam just gives you the horrors every time you look at it,' says one local. 'I would like to see it filled in. It just upsets me every time it comes up on the telly and all the kids' faces come up. It's still the same. You'll never, ever forget.'

ROBERT FARQUHARSON
DIAGNOSTIC CHART

Using DSM 5 indicators (APA, 2013), when four or more of these are present, a diagnosis of avoidant personality disorder (AvPD) can be made	Examples of Farquharson's behaviour that appear to be consistent with each indicator
Avoids occupational activities that involve significant interpersonal contact because of fears of criticism, disapproval or rejection.	Preferred to work basically alone, e.g. as a cleaner or franchisee.
Is unwilling to get involved with people unless certain of being liked.	Small circle of Winchelsea friends only.
Shows restraint within intimate relationships for fear of being shamed or ridiculed.	Not assertive or open with his wife. Behaved in a passive-aggressive manner rather than raise issues for discussion.
Is preoccupied with being criticized or rejected in social situations.	He regularly assumed, without any evidence, that other people were belittling him or disrespecting him and often made exaggerated statements to counter this e.g. he said to Greg King about Cindy: '*Nobody does that to me and gets away with it.*' He told Cindy and Stephen not to underestimate him because he had 'contacts'. School principal Judi Fallon found that Farquharson was often hypersensitive and readily took offence when it was not intended e.g. she tried to avoid making comments that reflected on his own limited education.

Using DSM 5 indicators (APA, 2013), when four or more of these are present, a diagnosis of avoidant personality disorder (AvPD) can be made	Examples of Farquharson's behaviour that appear to be consistent with each indicator
	He was prone to blame others when problems arose and often assumed that he was not being treated with respect e.g. he became angry when he incorrectly jumped to the conclusion that his son's football had been stolen. He stormed up to the school and demanded that the school principal ensure that it was immediately returned by the boy who had supposedly 'stolen' it. It had just been lost.
	He over-reacted when anyone witnessed his incompetence with a task, assuming that he was being mocked e.g. when he angrily threw a hole-digger on a work site when he couldn't make it work.
Is inhibited in new interpersonal situations because of feelings of inadequacy.	Insufficient information available to comment.
Views self as socially inept, personally unappealing, or inferior to others.	Judi Fallon described him as a 'country bumpkin'.
	His defence team described him, as 'shy', 'timid', 'retiring', 'placid', 'compliant', 'humble', 'innocuous', 'inoffensive' and 'emotionally inarticulate'. It is reasonable to assume that he probably recognised that many people in his community saw him this way and that he agreed with them. However this is speculative as Farquharson has not been directly asked about this.

Using DSM 5 indicators (APA, 2013), when four or more of these are present, a diagnosis of avoidant personality disorder (AvPD) can be made	Examples of Farquharson's behaviour that appear to be consistent with each indicator
Is unusually reluctant to take personal risks or to engage in any new activities because they may prove embarrassing. * Reprinted with permission from the Diagnostic and Statistical Manual of Mental Disorders, Fifth Edition, (Copyright ©2013). American Psychiatric Association. All Rights Reserved.	Lived with parents into his mid-twenties. Moved back in with his father when he and Cindy separated.

CHAPTER 2

JOHN MYLES SHARPE

The cast

Anna Marie Kemp: Victim and wife of John Myles Sharpe; Anna was pregnant with a boy when she was killed

Gracie Sharpe: Daughter of Anna Kemp and John Myles Sharpe, victim of Sharpe; nineteen months old

Lili Gebler: Anna's mother in Dunedin, New Zealand

Gerald and **Joe Kemp**: Anna's brothers in New Zealand

Constable John Woodhouse: Dunedin policeman who helped the Kemp family

John Myles Sharpe: The killer

Valerie and Myles Sharpe: Sharpe's parents

Barry Goldsmith: John Sharpe's neighbour

The motive

John Myles Sharpe wanted to rid himself of his family responsibilities in a way that enabled him to keep the assets acquired during his marriage. His wife, Anna, was threatening to leave him due to his inadequacies and a divorce would have meant reduced financial security for him.

Introduction

The first time Barry Goldsmith met John Myles Sharpe, who lived a few doors down from him in the leafy Melbourne bayside suburb of Mornington, Goldsmith told his wife: 'There's someone I wouldn't leave my kids with.' Goldsmith often saw Sharpe's wife Anna Kemp in the street with her young daughter Gracie and found her to be lovely, 'a beautiful person'. But he thought her husband John, who avoided making conversation with neighbours, was strange. 'He wouldn't talk,' Goldsmith says. 'He was just one of those neighbours who kept to himself. He always had a look like he was hiding something. He was seriously weird. Pretty much everybody who had anything to do with him was . . . "weirded out" by him. I don't think anybody really wanted to have anything to do with him.'

Goldsmith runs a business that catches and relocates Australia's infamous and deadly tiger, copperhead, black, brown and red-bellied black snakes, which are common throughout the peninsula. He tried to talk to Sharpe, but his neighbour never really wanted to engage. In contrast, Sharpe's parents Valerie and Myles were popular and well liked around Mornington from their days running a local chocolate shop. Goldsmith found them friendly and 'really nice to the kids'. But their son clearly found social situations uncomfortable. He wasn't obviously violent, Goldsmith notes, and lived a quiet life, rarely arguing publicly with his wife, who had moved with him into the pretty two-storey weatherboard cottage with a white picket fence in late 2003.

A pleasant beachside suburb a little over fifty kilometres from the CBD, Mornington's quiet, residential streets have a sleepy, almost semi-rural feel. Apart from families going about their business and visitors crowding the local foreshore in summer, not much happens here. However, that habitual calm was shattered in March 2004, when Anna and nineteenth-month-old Gracie suddenly disappeared.

For almost two months, Anna's Melbourne friends and her family in New Zealand had no idea where she was or what had happened to her or Gracie. There was no reason for Anna to leave. She was five months pregnant and anticipating the birth of her second child, which scans had revealed to be a boy. Desperately worried, Anna's relatives in New Zealand reported their disappearance to police.

In May 2004, almost two months after they were last seen, John Myles Sharpe appeared on Melbourne television pleading with his wife and daughter to return. Apparently fighting back tears, Sharpe explained Anna had left him for another man and taken Gracie with her, leaving him alone and devastated. Eyes downcast, Sharpe told reporters he had no idea where his partner and daughter were. 'Anna, our marriage may be over but I still love you and you are the mother of our beautiful daughter Gracie, whom we both adore more than anyone else,' he said. 'My biggest fear is being denied a part of Gracie's future' (Hadfield, 2014).

Sharpe insisted that he had not hurt Anna or Gracie: 'I haven't harmed my wife or my daughter. I haven't harmed either of them.' His parents, Valerie and Myles, even invited a *Herald Sun* newspaper reporter and photographer into their Mornington home for an interview. Valerie was left to do most of the talking, much like Sharpe's wife Anna did in their relationship, while her son – who had moved back into his parents' home – repeatedly left the room. 'He's now just getting more and more distressed,' Valerie told journalist Shelley Hadfield.

The anguish you can see in his eyes, just waiting for their return. We have got him home for that reason, so we can nurture him a bit. We love Anna very much, and Gracie, and we are desperately hoping to see them. It's important for Anna to know we would welcome her back, too. We don't want her to feel she can't come back to the family. (Hadfield, 2014)

Photographer Ian Currie recalls Sharpe constantly getting up to look furtively out the blinds shading the window of the neat suburban home and being comforted by his father during the interview. While the parents were friendly, Currie remembers feeling a bit uneasy around Sharpe, whose eyes darted around as he spoke; he rarely made eye contact. His behaviour was also strange, Currie recalls.

I got shots of his father and John sitting on the couch and the old man's got his arm around John's shoulder, more or less comforting him, while John's talking to us about what happened. He got up a couple of times in mid-sentence, while still talking, and just disappeared into the kitchen. I'm thinking, 'This bastard's going to come out with a knife or something.' It was a bit odd. He disappeared into the kitchen and then he came back. And then he's gone to the venetian blinds and was looking out of the venetian blinds, looking out on the road while we were talking . . . [He was] very on edge.

Those feelings of unease experienced by both Goldsmith and Currie in Sharpe's company were not misplaced. John Myles Sharpe was lying.

The quietly spoken husband and father stood in front of the television cameras and spoke to the newspaper reporter knowing that he had brutally murdered Anna, their nineteenth-month-old daughter Gracie and their unborn son. He then told the world that his wife was the one who had wronged him by running off with another man, to whom she was pregnant. But he couldn't maintain the charade.

When he was finally charged on 22 June 2004, Sharpe pleaded guilty to two counts of murder. In sentencing him to a minimum thirty-three years in jail on 5 August 2005, Justice Bernard Bongiorno of Victoria's Supreme Court described the crimes as 'perhaps, for many, too awful to contemplate' (R v Sharpe, 2005).

What emerged was a picture of a cold and calculating man who was prepared to 'erase' his entire family because, he explained to police, his wife was demanding and he didn't want a second child.

It was a disturbing picture and one that shocked those around him. Some of Sharpe's former work colleagues could not believe it. When he worked at the State Bank and then the Commonwealth Bank in the early 1990s, Sharpe was known as a quiet, unassuming worker who enjoyed a quiet drink with colleagues and treated others respectfully. He was not a womaniser and the worst his former colleagues could come up with to describe him was 'bland' and 'unobtrusive'.

How such a nondescript person could develop into a cold-blooded killer was a mystery to them and everyone else. But this tragic case demonstrated that some people, no matter how ordinary they may seem, are capable of committing truly horrendous crimes. Rather than trying to make the changes that would enhance his marriage or attempting to sort things out through discussion or counselling – or, if that wasn't successful, separating from his wife – John Myles Sharpe decided instead to kill his whole family.

Why?

The lead-up to the crime

John Myles Sharpe was twenty-seven when he met New Zealander Anna Marie Kemp, then thirty-one, a colleague at the Commonwealth Bank. They married in front of forty friends and family members in October 1994. They lived in, renovated and then sold several homes around the Mornington area before settling at their final address in late 2003. The profits from these renovations helped to make them financially comfortable.

The couple initially did not want children, but after a cervical cancer scare while in her thirties, Anna changed her mind (Suter Linton, 2012). Gracie Louise Sharpe was born on 13 August 2002, with dysplasia, a congenital hip problem that required orthopaedic treatment and a corrective harness for the first three months. While long-term problems were not expected, Gracie was, initially at least, somewhat unsettled. She cried often and had difficulty sleeping, and this may have strained her parents' relationship. Even after Gracie's harness was no longer needed, she had difficulties feeding and sleeping, for which Anna sought professional help. In November 2002, Anna attended Peninsula Health's Hillview Maternity Unit complaining of feeling anxious and being unable to cope. She had three in-patient admissions for respite with Gracie to try to establish regular sleeping and eating patterns and to allay her own anxiety.

Things were not easy, but these were all common problems that many young families face and work through. Children change lives and all parents have to learn to cope with their new situation. Initially, it seemed Sharpe and Anna were doing okay. Soon after Gracie was born, Sharpe – with Anna's support and encouragement – left his bank job after buying into a conveyancing business with an older former colleague. After purchasing and renovating several properties in the area, they could afford to branch out and support Sharpe in fulfilling his dream of working in his own business.

In November 2003, Anna fell pregnant again, which Sharpe later told police was a surprise to him. He had also reportedly told Anna's brother Gerald that he was angry that she had got pregnant again without his permission. When Anna had an ultrasound in February 2004 – which revealed she was carrying a boy – Sharpe, then thirty-seven, did not accompany her or even ask her about the result. 'She came home and she wanted him to say, "What's happened?" and he didn't,' Gerald told the *Herald Sun* newspaper. 'He was indifferent. He didn't bat an eyelid about what the results were. She got annoyed. He said, "You are going to tell me anyway." It was then that she gave him an ulti-matum, telling him that if he was going to be indifferent to this second child like he was with Gracie, she was going to leave him because she was fed up with his indifference (Hadfield, 2014).

After her honeymoon, Anna had reportedly told her mother, Lili Gebler, that her marriage was a big mistake. Gerald has also said that he believed Anna had married beneath her station. But Anna was resilient. A committed Catholic, she was determined to honour her vows and make the best of things. What devel-oped was a relatively functional relationship that, until Anna went missing, had appeared normal, though Anna's family was worried by John Sharpe's seeming lack of emotional commit-ment to both his wife and daughter.

Lili told the *Herald Sun* after Anna's disappearance that Sharpe was a cold man: 'There was no affection. I have never seen him cuddle Gracie and I never saw him put his arms around Anna.' Lili said Sharpe seemed indifferent to his daughter 'and when he carried Gracie it was like he carried a log'. 'It was as if he resented that Gracie was around.' Anna, who was a social welfare worker with the Salvation Army earlier in her career, had also sponsored two children in Africa. When she left work, Lili said Sharpe made her give them up (Hadfield, 2014). Shortly after Anna's second pregnancy was confirmed, Sharpe used cash to purchase a high-powered spear gun from a sports shop. The set only included one spear, but he purchased an extra one. He kept the gun at the family home, where he test-fired it in the backyard. He had never been interested in spear fishing and had no apparent use for this powerful weapon, later telling investigators that he was having thoughts of killing his wife when he purchased it.

The murders

On 19 March 2004, a female friend of Anna Kemp stayed overnight in the family's new home. She noticed no tension in the couple's relationship; indeed, she thought they appeared happy. On Sunday, 21 March, Sharpe, Anna and Gracie went to a picnic held at the park in nearby Moorooduc to celebrate Sharpe's nephew's birthday. Again, no-one noticed anything unusual.

The next day, Anna took Gracie to her Mornington childcare centre and returned for her at noon. That morning she also phoned her mother in New Zealand. She gave no indication either at the childcare centre or to her mother that anything was amiss. In the afternoon she arranged to meet a friend on the following Friday, 26 March and noted the date on her calendar. At 8.24 pm, another friend called Anna at home. They had a long and apparently normal conversation. At about 2 pm on Tuesday, 23 March, Anna phoned her private health insurance fund and asked about adding her unborn baby to the family's health insurance policy. It was to be her last known contact with anyone other than her husband and daughter.

From that point, sentencing judge Justice Bernard Bongiorno had to rely on Sharpe's confession, which he accepted with some concern about the accuracy of several details. Sharpe told police that on the evening of 23 March it was 'probable' that he and Anna argued, although he could not recall any specific subject of contention. They went to bed between 9 and 10 pm, and Anna went to sleep. Sharpe lay awake next to her, brooding about their unhappy marriage.

Eventually he went to the garage, retrieved the spear gun and loaded it with one of the spears. He returned to the bedroom and shot his sleeping wife in the left temple from only a few centimetres away. She did not stop breathing so he fired a second spear into her head, in the same area as the first. This killed her. Sharpe immediately covered Anna's body with towels so he would not have to look at her, closed the bedroom door and went downstairs to sleep on a foldout sofa bed. Meanwhile, Gracie was asleep in another room.

The next day, Wednesday, 24 March, Sharpe attempted to remove the spears from Anna's head. Unable to do so, he unscrewed their shafts (the rod to which the head attaches) leaving the metal spear heads embedded in her skull. On the Thursday, he took Gracie to and from childcare. That night, he wrapped Anna's body in the bloody bedsheets and a blue plastic tarpaulin, carried it downstairs and buried her in a shallow grave in their backyard. Then he began to act out an elaborate charade to cover his tracks. To explain Anna's disappearance, he told people that she had run off with another man to whom she was pregnant, leaving Gracie behind and planning to collect her at a later point. Nobody found his story convincing.

On Friday, 26 March, Sharpe took Gracie to childcare and told staff that he and Anna had separated so Gracie would not be attending anymore. He then phoned his mother-in-law in New Zealand in response to a message for Anna and told her Anna had left him for another man the previous Tuesday. He said he didn't know where she was and that he expected her to return to collect Gracie the following Sunday. All the while, Sharpe was deciding whether he should also kill Gracie to maintain this charade. With extreme callousness, he even took his little girl with him to purchase another spear for the gun he would use to kill her.

On the evening of Saturday, 27 March, Sharpe put his daughter to sleep in her cot and then drank several glasses of whisky and Coke to calm himself. Sometime between 9 and 10 pm, he collected the spear gun from the garage and loaded it with the new spear. He went to Gracie's bedroom, where she was asleep, and fired the spear into her head. It struck her on the left side and penetrated the skull. But Gracie did not die. She screamed loudly with the spear still embedded in her skull. Sharpe told police that he then went downstairs and retrieved the two spear shafts that he had removed from Anna's head. He returned to Gracie's bedroom and fired them into his child's head. But they didn't kill her either, so he pulled the first spear out and fired it again. Only then did the little girl die.

Sharpe returned to Gracie's bedroom the next morning, Sunday, 28 March, and pulled the spears from her head while holding a towel in front of his eyes as he could not bear to look at his daughter's lifeless face. He wrapped her body in garbage bags and a tarpaulin, bound it with black duct tape, then drove to the Mornington refuse transfer station, where he dumped Gracie along with the spear gun, spears and a few of her clothes and toys. At some point that day, Sharpe phoned his mother-in-law in New Zealand. He also made a call using Anna's mobile phone and made the first of several withdrawals from her bank account at an automatic teller machine in the nearby suburb of Chelsea.

On Monday, 29 March, Sharpe purchased a chainsaw, more duct tape and another tarpaulin. He returned home, dug up his wife's body from the makeshift grave in their backyard and used the chainsaw to cut it into three pieces. He used the duct tape and tarpaulin to wrap up the body parts and then disposed of them, the chainsaw and everything else he had used to kill his wife and child at the Mornington refuse transfer station, near where he had dumped Gracie. From there, in the course of the transfer station's operations over the next few days, the remains were taken to a landfill site elsewhere on the Mornington Peninsula.

That same day, Sharpe wrote an email purporting to be from Anna and sent it to her brother in New Zealand. It explained why she had not contacted her family and implied that she had ended her marriage to be with another man, whose baby she was carrying. She was well and happy, as was Gracie. Another email, again purporting to be from Anna and dated 5 April, read:

> Hi again. Just a quick message to say hello. I under-stand all of your concern but rest assured Gracie and I are fine and settling into our new life and surroundings. I just want a break from everything and I'm not trying to punish anyone. I'm obviously going through a lot of changes and still in an adjustment stage which I guess is normal. (R v Sharpe, 2005)

The emails only heightened her relatives' fears. Anna's mother soon reported her daughter missing to police in Dunedin, New Zealand.

Over the following days and weeks, Sharpe disposed of the bloodstained mattress from his bedroom, wrote letters to Anna's friends and sent more emails to her relatives pretending to be Anna. He continued to use her ATM card to make withdraw-als to give the impression that she was still alive. He arranged for flowers to be sent to his mother-in-law from his wife, with greetings for her birthday and Mother's Day. If the way in which Sharpe disposed of the woman he had vowed to spend the rest of his life with is horrific, his clumsy attempts to continue on with his life afterwards as if nothing had happened were even more disturbing.

Over the next two months, Sharpe continued the ruse that Anna was still alive. He made a number of calls using Anna's mobile phone and took other items associated with Gracie to the refuse transfer station to maintain the pretence that Anna had returned for her daughter and some of her things. Meanwhile, Anna's family back in New Zealand was becoming extremely concerned. On 20 May, after making their own inquiries following Lili Gebler's report, the police in New Zealand asked Victoria Police to investigate. When Mornington police visited Sharpe, he told them that his wife had left on 23 March, returning for Gracie the following weekend. He said he thought they were living in the Chelsea area but did not know the actual address.

Suspicions continued to grow. Covert police surveillance observed Sharpe retrieving a credit card from a plastic bag hidden in bushes near a toilet block in Mornington and discarding incriminating written notes containing key points in his cover story in a car park rubbish bin at Mount Martha South Beach. In mid-May, Sharpe declined to appear at a press conference calling for Anna and Gracie's safe return, leaving two of Anna's best friends to appear on his behalf, which struck many as odd. At the time, he told police he did not feel comfortable or able to face the media. Sharpe finally appeared on TV in late May, expressing concern for Gracie and saying he had spoken to Anna about a week earlier. He denied to journalists that he had harmed his wife or daughter.

On 10 June, police interviewed Sharpe in Mornington. He denied any wrongdoing. On 22 June, he was arrested by police and interviewed again, this time at the Homicide Squad's city headquarters. Initially he continued to deny any involvement, but after speaking to his family he finally admitted to both murders.

Sharpe told police that he had fantasised about killing Anna for several months before he decided to kill her. He complained that his wife was controlling and moody. Sharpe said he knew that what he did was wrong, but he couldn't stop himself from killing, claiming that when he finally murdered her he was effectively on automatic pilot. He described killing his daughter Gracie as an irrational act of madness.

Despite attempting to portray himself as not being in control of his thoughts and actions, Sharpe was not mentally ill. This was later confirmed by a forensic psychologist and psychiatrist.

Anna's and Gracie's remains were not recovered until July, four months after the killings, following a three-week landfill search by dedicated and determined police. It was a sad end to a horrific case that was almost impossible to comprehend.

The sentencing

After Sharpe pleaded guilty to both murders, he was described at his August 2005 sentencing as a man who could not cope with the stresses in his life and chose to address them by eliminating his entire family. Justice Bernard Bongiorno described his background, gleaned both from witness statements and forensic clinical psychologist Ian Joblin, as unremarkable. His parents were alive as were his four older sisters and a younger brother. None had any criminal or antisocial histories.

Sharpe did not apparently suffer from any serious health problems in the lead-up to the murders, but had consulted a general practitioner a few weeks earlier complaining of disturbed sleep patterns. He was prescribed two types of sleeping tablets, but he claimed that they did not have much effect. The doctor discussed the possibility of an underlying depressive illness and eventually did diagnose depression, but only after a consultation on 1 June 2004, during which Sharpe lied to him about Anna having left. The doctor found that Sharpe was agitated and suffering from poor memory and concentration. Justice Bongiorno later said this was not surprising given the stress he would have been under as a consequence of lying for more than two months about the fate of his wife and daughter and trying to maintain his complex charade.

However, Sharpe's depression was not considered to be serious. Forensic psychiatrist Dr Lester Walton examined Sharpe twice while he was on remand and described him in much the same way as his legal counsel did: a socially inept, dependent, passive and retiring individual who was unable or reluctant to confront problems in his life. Dr Walton found that Sharpe perceived irresolvable difficulties in his family situation and that he believed the only solution to these difficulties was to kill Anna and later Gracie.

Dr Walton believed the killings were 'irrational' but found no evidence that Sharpe was suffering from any psychiatric illness. 'I presume that by "irrational" he meant that you considered the killing of your wife and, later, your child were the only options you could see to relieve a state of desperation you considered yourself to be in,' Justice Bongiorno said in sentencing Sharpe.

As evidence of this irrationality, Dr Walton recounts your speaking of feeling 'threatened' by your daughter – a situation which is, of course, objectively absurd. Although you described to police a feeling of being 'another person' when you were committing these murders, Dr Walton considered that this was not a description of hallucinations indicative of psychosis, but a degree of what he termed 'dissociation of personality'. He thought that you were 'afflicted by a clinically significant depressive disorder prior to the killings, although seemingly not of very major proportions'. (R v Sharpe, 2005)

Forensic clinical psychologist Ian Joblin considered Sharpe to be an inadequate, isolated and withdrawn individual who had few appropriate social skills and few friends. He appeared to be very dependent on his parents and lacked the psychological resources to cope with the stresses in his life – marriage, parenthood and career change. Joblin found that Gracie's hip problems, coupled with Anna's announcement that she was pregnant again, led Sharpe to blame them for his problems. Joblin agreed with Dr Walton that Sharpe was not psychotic at the time of the murders, nor did he have an antisocial personality disorder.

Justice Bongiorno found that the two assessments indicated that Sharpe was not suffering from any psychiatric illness or any identifiable psychological abnormality when he killed his wife and daughter. But he was 'the subject of psychological stressors to which you reacted in an abnormal manner':

As Mr Joblin said, to have chosen the behaviour you did itself indicates abnormality. Such a conclusion neither justifies nor excuses your conduct. It throws but little light on the question of why an otherwise law-abiding member of society would do what you did when legal mechanisms, however imperfect, exist to settle matrimonial disharmony without recourse to violence. Your preparations for these crimes and your attempts to hide their perpetration, as well as the method you chose for carrying them out, strongly support a conclusion, for sentencing purposes, that you were at all times fully aware of what you were doing and that what you were doing was objectively wrong. (R v Sharpe, 2005)

In sentencing Sharpe, Justice Bongiorno said whether or not he had formed an intention to kill Anna when he purchased the spear gun and tested it in the backyard, he had certainly formed that intention when he went to his garage on the evening of the crime. 'Your killing your wife was no impulsive act of desperation,' he found. The method of the crime was also 'singular in its barbarity'.

Justice Bongiorno found Sharpe's complaints about Anna supposedly 'wearing the pants' in their relationship were far from an excuse for his shocking crimes. Other aggravating factors (i.e. that increased the likelihood of a more severe penalty), identified by the judge when he handed down his sentence included Anna being pregnant, the desecration of her body, the charade Sharpe engaged in to conceal the crimes and the cost to the state of investigating the disappearance. Justice Bongiorno did consider Sharpe's previous good character, lack of prior convictions and guilty plea, which prevented a lengthy and stressful trial. He also considered the expert reports about his psychological state, but was not convinced about Sharpe's remorse.

'Remorse is an elusive concept,' he said.

A confession and a plea of guilty will not always denote its existence. In your case, although your actions during and after the commission of these crimes would tend to suggest a lack of any concern for what you had done, at least until 22 June last year, Mr Joblin's assessment that you were well aware of the gravity of your actions indicate the commencement of a contrition process. No doubt in the coming years the gravity of your actions will weigh more heavily on you. You may reach a state of genuine remorse; it is to be hoped that you do. A positive finding that you have done so yet, however, cannot be made. (R v Sharpe, 2005)

John Myles Sharpe's background

John Myles Sharpe was born in Mornington in February 1967, and grew up in Melbourne's outer bayside suburbs. His parents ran a confectionery shop and he had four older sisters and a younger brother. Several members of his family, who have made it very clear that they do not support him, have described him as being indulged by his parents as a child and have characterised him as a sly, calculating, manipulative, sneaky and selfish person who always got what he wanted (Suter Linton, 2012).

Sharpe's childhood and early adult years were marked by social problems. He was not particularly happy at school and had few friends. These problems continued into his adult life and Anna had confided in members of his family that she had tried, unsuccessfully, to convince him to get help with his difficulties in coping with social situations. Sharpe completed Year 12 but did not pass his final examinations. After leaving school, he worked for the State Bank and then the Commonwealth Bank when it took over the State Bank in 1991. Sharpe stayed until 2002 when he resigned to go into a conveyancing business with an older business partner. The plan was to take over the business when the partner retired.

Those who worked with Sharpe at the bank and in his business were gobsmacked when they heard about the murders. It did not correspond in any way with their memories of the quiet young man who was part of the Southland branch of the State Bank team while in his early twenties. Sharpe was on the solemn side at times, but gave his colleagues no cause for concern. In the office he was courteous and, in those years at least, did not cause any trouble or stand out in any way. He was not a teller (cashier) but served at the counter when required. His position required him to interact with customers seeking financial transactions, but there was little need for extended conversation. He also spent quite a lot of time working on the bank's newly computerised ledger system.

During this period, Sharpe was single and, while he enjoyed a social drink with colleagues and had friends, he was far from a party animal. He was relatively quiet in the office and in social situations. When Sharpe started his conveyancing business, former colleagues trusted him enough to refer work to him. For that reason, those who had worked closely with Sharpe could not believe it when they learned he had murdered his pregnant wife and child. Nor has anyone come forward to say Sharpe was abusive towards Anna or Gracie. They appeared to have a relatively sound marriage. The murders came as a complete shock to everyone.

Why did he do it?

When John Myles Sharpe married Anna Kemp, he undoubtedly saw the positive potential of the relationship. Anna was extroverted and socially confident. Sharpe's defence described her court as strong-willed, vibrant, interesting and decisive, while her husband was 'dull'. Anna was competent and comfortable with taking the initiative when this was needed and with taking on and managing responsibilities. She could provide her husband with a sense of respectability within his family and local community and be his 'shield'.

Initially this probably worked well. Anna encouraged him to become a partner in the conveyancing business, which gave him more independence and responsibility. But Gracie was a difficult baby and Sharpe, who was indifferent to her, didn't cope. When Anna got pregnant again, he appears to have been overwhelmed by the implied responsibilities, workload and stress. Sharpe had not particularly wanted children and displayed ambivalence at best towards his unborn son. While most men in his position would have dealt with these perceived problems assertively, perhaps modifying their own behaviour or leaving the relationship, he just seethed and plotted.

Sharpe's behaviour pattern is consistent with his having an avoidant personality disorder (AvPD). People with AvPD find it difficult to cope with life's ups and downs. They feel hurt and angry if someone is even slightly critical or disapproving, and obsess about their perceived shortcomings. They want to be liked, accepted and respected, but believe that others treat them badly and/or see them as uninteresting, unappealing and inferior. They are socially inept and often feel threatened by social situations, fearing that they will embarrass themselves. Like Sharpe, most keep their fears of possible humiliation and rejection hidden. He hid this well by choosing relatively bland jobs and keeping a low social profile. The negative feelings really surfaced when Sharpe married and started a family. His plans for a quiet life 'hiding' behind his wife did not eventuate and he felt angry and resentful. He wanted to be rid of those who had placed him in an unwanted position of responsibility.

Like Robert Farquharson, Sharpe fits into the conflicted AvPD subtype (Millon et al., 2004). These people resent being dependent on their partner but also feel incapable of successfully running their own lives. Sharpe sought out a strong, sociable, confident and hard-working partner who enhanced his image and his life. She also helped him to achieve his goal of starting his own business. But he resented it when Anna wanted to achieve her goals too and moved in a direction he disagreed with. Instead of accommodating and adapting to the news of the second pregnancy, which Sharpe told police was unintended, he saw Anna as a 'dictator' who was intent on disempowering him. He decided his only option was to erase his entire family, thus removing all of his responsibilities.

Given Sharpe's calculating nature, he undoubtedly considered that he had much to gain financially if Anna died. The assets they had accumulated through buying older houses, living in them while renovating and then selling them at a profit, would all be his and undiminished by a divorce settlement that would award Anna a larger share as the children's primary carer (Suter Linton, 2012).

After Sharpe's conviction, *Herald Sun* journalist Kelvin Healey wrote that he had seen a copy of a letter reportedly written by a member of Sharpe's circle of family and friends, who claimed Sharpe had sexually abused her when she was a young girl and he was in his late teens (Healey, 2005).

If the sexual abuse allegations against Sharpe are true, they would fit in with his AvPD behaviour pattern. Several studies (e.g. Francia et al., 2010) have found that men imprisoned for child sex offences are highly likely to have an AvPD. Such offenders may be drawn to the relative powerlessness of children, their lack of assertiveness and the fact that they don't respond with contempt or criticism.

In the end, John Myles Sharpe came undone because his callous murder plan was poorly thought out and badly executed. His very low level of empathy made it impossible for him to convincingly act like a sad and worried husband and father. He was also unable to predict how people would interpret and respond to his behaviour. Many saw through the facade, including neighbour Barry Goldsmith, who was suspicious from the start. 'He wasn't easygoing or charming or any of those things,'

Goldsmith says. 'He was sort of a nerdy character. To pull that off [the murders] you've got to be a superb actor and John Sharpe could not do it.'

Whether Sharpe was acting or not, it is difficult to comprehend how such a nondescript man, who had hardly raised an eyebrow at work or in the community until then, could be a cold-blooded killer. Goldsmith found him strange, but those who passed Sharpe in the street would not have looked twice at him. For all intents and purposes he looked like what he was for many years – a mild-mannered bank clerk. Yet this man was prepared to kill his wife, daughter and unborn son simply to free himself from his parental responsibilities and protect his assets.

Due to the other prisoners' loathing and disgust, John Myles Sharpe reportedly spent most of his early days behind bars in isolation (Berry, 2005). After avoiding his life responsibilities for so many years, this prison pariah no longer has anyone to hide behind.

JOHN MYLES SHARPE DIAGNOSTIC CHART

Using DSM 5 indicators (APA, 2013), when four or more of these are present, a diagnosis of avoidant personality disorder (AvPD) can be made	Examples of Sharpe's behaviour that appear to be consistent with each criterion
Avoids occupational activities that involve significant interpersonal contact because of fears of criticism, disapproval, or rejection.	Wanted to have his own business and ultimately buy out his older partner and work alone. Worked in a position in the bank that didn't require more than simple routine business conversation with customers.
Is unwilling to get involved with people unless certain of being liked.	Minimal socialisation. Had hardly any friends throughout his life.
Shows restraint within intimate relationships for fear of being shamed or ridiculed.	Not assertive or open with his wife. Described by forensic psychiatrist Dr Lester Walton as unable or reluctant to confront problems and as having difficulty in expressing 'any sort of feeling'.
Is preoccupied with being criticized or rejected in social situations.	Tried to avoid many social situations.
Is inhibited in new interpersonal situations because of feelings of inadequacy.	Wouldn't talk to his neighbour; kept to himself.

Using DSM 5 indicators (APA, 2013), when four or more of these are present, a diagnosis of avoidant personality disorder (AvPD) can be made	Examples of Sharpe's behaviour that appear to be consistent with each criterion
	A newspaper photographer in Sharpe's home noted his 'odd' social behaviour (e.g. eyes darting around to check for how people were looking at him and what they were thinking, leaving the room halfway through a sentence etc.).
Views self as socially inept, personally unappealing, or inferior to others.	Forensic clinical psychiatrist Ian Joblin reported that Sharpe's childhood was marked by social problems and that he had few friends at school or in adulthood. Also described him as an inadequate, isolated and withdrawn individual. Anna encouraged him to get help to cope with his difficulties in social situations but he didn't do so. Dr Walton said he had few appropriate social skills, was socially inept, dependent, isolated, retiring, inadequate and passive. It is reasonable to assume that he recognised that many people in his life saw him as being socially inept, socially isolated, withdrawn and friendless and that he probably agreed with them. However this is speculative as Sharpe has not been directly asked about this.

Using DSM 5 indicators (APA, 2013), when four or more of these are present, a diagnosis of avoidant personality disorder (AvPD) can be made	Examples of Sharpe's behaviour that appear to be consistent with each criterion
Is unusually reluctant to take personal risks or to engage in any new activities because they may prove embarrassing. * Reprinted with permission from the Diagnostic and Statistical Manual of Mental Disorders, Fifth Edition, (Copyright ©2013). American Psychiatric Association. All Rights Reserved.	No evidence of his having travelled nor worked or lived very far from his parents.

Timeline of key events – John Myles Sharpe

Tuesday, 23 March 2004: At around 9–10 pm after Anna fell asleep, Sharpe shot her in the head with a spear gun.

Wednesday, 24 March 2004: Sharpe unsuccessfully attempted to remove the spears from Anna's head and buried her in the backyard. At some point after her death, he took Gracie to a sports fishing shop to buy another spear.

Thursday, 25 March 2004: Sharpe told Anna's mother in New Zealand that she had left him.

Saturday, 27 March 2004: At about 9–10 pm, Sharpe used the spear gun to kill Gracie.

Sunday, 28 March 2004: Sharpe pulled the spears from Gracie's head and dumped her body at the Mornington refuse transfer station.

Tuesday, 30 March or Wednesday, 31 March 2004: Sharpe exhumed Anna's body and dumped it at the Mornington refuse transfer station.

Why did they do it?

May 2004: Sharpe appeared on TV pleading for Anna and Gracie's return. Two of Anna's friends had done so several days earlier after he refused.

22 June, 2004: Sharpe confessed to Anna and Gracie's murders.

5 August, 2004: Sharpe was sentenced to a minimum 33 years in jail.

CONCLUSION

What we can learn from the murders committed by Robert Farquharson and John Myles Sharpe

Most of us find it hard to believe that someone could kill their own flesh and blood in the cold-blooded and calculating way that Robert Farquharson and John Myles Sharpe did. We know that we could never behave like this, so it is incomprehensible that other seemingly ordinary people could. When something awful like this happens, our first instinct is often to assume that they must be innocent or suffering from a mental illness. But some people can and do act like these killers. While most people are relatively resilient, adaptive and empathic, those with a severe avoidant personality disorder (AvPD), like Farquharson and Sharpe, do not cope well when faced with a situation that they find confronting or difficult to manage. They also show limited capacity for empathy. As happened here, the resulting frustrations and resentment can be extremely hard to spot. Many wear a 'mask' that is hard to penetrate.

Why did they do it?

Neither Farquharson nor Sharpe looked, spoke or acted like a callous killer in front of those they knew. But many people with an AvPD hide their true nature and cultivate a public image that makes them look better. There may be hints of anger and resentment in some of the small behaviours that they don't control well, such as negative talk and avoiding adult conversation, but most of their friends and family don't recognise the potential danger of these warning signs. As a result, those who have known anybody with an AvPD for a long time and have never seen them act violently can find it difficult to believe they are capable of killing.

Despite two murder trials finding him guilty, some people still believe Robert Farquharson is innocent, partly due to the 'victim' persona he projected. One Winchelsea man in his sixties who spoke to us on condition of anonymity remains adamant that Jai, Tyler and Bailey Farquharson's deaths was an accident. He insists that Farquharson loved his boys and idolised his wife. 'You saw how much he loved those kids,' he says, adding that Farquharson was a good, quiet, orderly fellow and a lot of the trouble was that his mother Faye was very quiet too. But, as two juries found, the evidence against Farquharson was overwhelming.

After his wife left him, Farquharson sought counselling and those around him thought that he was beginning to accept and cope with the situation; his friends, family and colleagues did not appear to notice anything in his behaviour that could have led them to predict the tragedy about to unfold. Nor did Sharpe emit any obvious signs of the growing rage he felt when his wife proceeded with a second pregnancy that he did not want. Sharpe also projected the persona of a harmless if boring man. He did not mope obviously in public like Farquharson, but he never displayed violent or aggressive tendencies. Former colleagues were aghast that the unassuming man they worked with in the local bank was capable of such violence.

Conclusion

Farquharson and Sharpe are among the small number of people with an AvPD who become ticking time bombs. Both fit into the conflicted subtype, which means they were both dependent on their partners but also unfairly resented them because of that dependence. In both cases this resentment turned into rage. Farquharson became enraged because, as he saw it, his wife had made his worst fears come true. By leaving him she had removed a source of support he had depended on and confirmed to him and others that he was inadequate. Sharpe appears to have kept his rage to himself for some time, making it even harder to spot. He was probably a bit more intelligent and measured than Farquharson, making his motives less obvious. As he saw it, Anna was forcing him to take on unwanted extra responsibilities. He did not want the personal, social or financial responsibility of being a parent and was determined to keep the assets he shared with his wife for himself. He feared his family and acquaintances would criticise him if he abandoned his pregnant wife and didn't want access to his children, but reasoned others would nurture him if they believed Anna had simply left.

Most people with an AvPD can have successful relationships if they recognise the importance of appreciating and accepting the social and emotional support they receive from their partner, while trying to give back as much as they get. But some don't and that's where the trouble can start. Those who have a partner they suspect has an AvPD should look for warning signs. These might indicate that the relationship is in trouble and that counselling should be considered, or that there is some potential danger. Such signs include:

- Acting in very emotionally immature ways.
- Being chronically negative, always complaining, blaming everyone else for what happens to them.

- Often feeling mistreated or hard done by without justification.
- Expecting their partner to do most of the work and take on most of the responsibilities (especially if they also feel resentful and angry about it and complain about their partner's 'controlling behaviour').
- Not being prepared to discuss and resolve relationship issues.
- Mocking or putting down their partner in public (especially men in front of other men).
- Using aggressive non-verbal expressions in discussions, such as baring teeth, jaw-jutting, aggressive staring, snarling and smirking.
- Using a lot of passive-aggressive behaviours (see page 358).

Women whose partners have an AvPD and continually act passive-aggressively, resenting her strength and confidence yet still relying on her to behave that way, should not be complacent. They should directly discuss any issues that arise and not ignore them. If violence occurs, a partner should consider leaving the relationship and be vigilant about custody conditions. They need to walk a fine line by taking threats from an ex-partner seriously without 'overreacting' in ways that make their former partner feel more powerful each time they make a threat. If you think someone in your life might have this personality disorder, consider talking to a psychologist about it. See the appendix on page 347 for suggested contacts for those who may need professional help to deal with their situation.

PART II

NARCISSISTIC PERSONALITY DISORDER

INTRODUCTION

Narcissistic personality disorder (NPD): It's all about me

Most of us have some narcissistic traits. We might boast about a small success, exaggerate our contribution to a project, act in a slightly selfish way or occasionally enjoy being the centre of attention. Some highly 'successful' individuals will display even more narcissistic traits. They may enjoy being recognised and awarded, regularly seek to be the centre of attention or surround themselves with admirers. But an individual does not have a narcissistic personality disorder (NPD) unless these traits become an inflexible, maladaptive and persistent behaviour pattern that causes problems or distress in their relationships, workplace and everyday life. An NPD is generally characterised by a pervasive pattern of grandiosity, a constant need for admiration and a lack of empathy for others. It begins by early adulthood and is evident in a variety of situations.

Rosa Caruso and Allison Baden-Clay were two very different women killed by men with an NPD. Peter Caruso and Gerard Baden-Clay were narcissistic and controlling men and Rosa and Allison both made the fatal mistake of trying to stand up to them. Rosa was an elderly Italian woman living her dream retirement in a leafy Melbourne suburb when her husband Peter bludgeoned her to death when she threatened to leave him. It appears likely that Gerard Baden-Clay murdered his wife Allison after she threatened to expose him for the narcissistic fraud that he was.

Keli Lane and Roger Dean also have an NPD. Lane killed her two-day-old daughter Tegan after hiding the pregnancy from family and friends, simply because the baby was an inconvenience. Dean, a nurse, started two fires at Quakers Hill Nursing Home that killed fourteen residents and injured many more in order to cover up his theft the previous night of prescribed medications.

Recognising someone with an NPD

Diagnosing a personality disorder is difficult and requires some professional knowledge. However, an examination of the criteria that have been identified can help to give us a general picture. The DSM 5 (APA, 2013) describes an NPD as 'a pervasive pattern of grandiosity (in fantasy or behavior), need for admiration, and lack of empathy, beginning by early adulthood and present in a variety of contexts', as indicated by five (or more) of the following:

1. Has a grandiose sense of self-importance (e.g. exaggerates achievements and talents, expects to be recognized as superior without commensurate achievements).
2. Is preoccupied with fantasies of unlimited success, power, brilliance, beauty or ideal love.

3. Believes that he or she is 'special' and unique and can only be understood by, or should associate with, other special or high-status people (or institutions).
4. Requires excessive admiration.
5. Has a sense of entitlement (i.e. unreasonable expectations of especially favorable treatment or automatic compliance with his or her expectations).
6. Is interpersonally exploitative (i.e. takes advantage of others to achieve his or her own ends).
7. Lacks empathy: is unwilling to recognize or identify with the feelings and needs of others.
8. Is often envious of others or believes that others are envious of him or her.
9. Shows arrogant, haughty behaviors or attitudes.

Those with an NPD often gravitate towards careers and businesses that have the potential to provide wealth, status, power or celebrity, such as business, finance, the military, the entertainment industry and politics.

Prevalence
It is estimated that up to 6.2 per cent of the population has an NPD (Dhawan et al., 2010) and, according to DSM 5, 50–75 per cent of them are male. However, there is some evidence that NPD rates may be increasing, at least in the USA. Researchers such as Professor Jean Twenge, co-author of *The Narcissism Epidemic* (2010), have identified a general trend in which today's young people are developing more narcissistic personality traits than earlier generations. Twenge suggests that this is due to a combination of more permissive parenting, an over-focus on developing children's self-esteem by stressing how 'special' they are, and the development of celebrity culture, the internet and

social media. In line with these findings, another study found that only 3.2 per cent of those aged over sixty-five had experienced an NPD during their lifetime, compared to 5.6 per cent of people aged forty-five to sixty-four, 7.1 per cent of those aged thirty to forty-four and 9.4 percent of those aged twenty to twenty-nine (Stinson et al., 2008).

Comorbidity (other disorders that often co-occur with NPD)
About 21 per cent of people with an NPD also have an antisocial personality disorder (Blackburn et al., 2003), while 37 per cent also have a borderline personality disorder (Stinson et al., 2008). (See pages 351, 352 for a detailed explanation of these disorders.)

Typical behaviours of someone with an NPD
As with other personality disorders, the severity of NPD can range from mild to extreme. Two people with an NPD may also behave differently in some ways, depending on which criteria they meet, other factors in their lives and which subtype they fit into. Four main subtypes of NPD have been identified – elitist, amorous, compensatory and unprincipled (Millon et al., 2004) – and help to explain some of the small variations in the behaviour of those who have it. A person may fall entirely into one subtype, or have a combination of traits from several.

Elitist: Characterised by a narcissistic pattern of behaviour that arises from a desire to be seen as superior to other people, plus their fear of being ordinary. They strive to find ways in which they are better than others, drawing on aspects such as their family background, their wealth, and what school or university they went to. They self-promote, boast and lie about or exaggerate their achievements and often exploit others while doing so. Many are 'social climbers' who will do whatever it takes to be seen as having high status. Their belief in their own superiority often results in their ignoring the suggestions, advice or concerns of others.

Amorous: Characterised by a narcissistic pattern of behaviour that arises from a constant need for admiration and a sense of their own superiority that makes them feel entitled to the sexual favours of others. They usually engage in multiple sexual conquests as a way of reinforcing their overinflated self-image. They often play their game of sexual and romantic seduction with several people simultaneously. They usually exploit and discard each conquest, moving on to the next one. They often falsely imply the possibility of an exclusive relationship but have very limited capacity for genuine intimacy and connection.

Compensatory: Characterised by a pattern of unstable, narcissistic behaviour that arises from an underlying sense of insecurity and weakness rather than genuine feelings of self-confidence and high self-esteem. They strive for recognition and prestige to compensate for their basic lack of self-worth, which often arises from 'wounds' experienced early in life such as the effects of a traumatic or disadvantaged childhood. They usually have ongoing aspirations for status and prestige, a tendency to exaggerate and boast, and are hypersensitive and over-react to criticism or slights.

Unprincipled: Characterised by a pattern of unscrupulous and antisocial behaviour in an arrogant way. They may steal, defraud or con others.

Initially many people with an NPD seem charming and appealing with their apparently buoyant mood and optimistic outlook. But their true colours eventually emerge when they do whatever it takes to preserve their 'superior' status, often harming others in the process. Many men with an NPD are misogynistic, seeing women as sources of admiration and support for them and their self-image. Both men and women with an NPD tend to dress in a way that attracts attention and admiration. For example, they may wear expensive designer clothing or jewellery or 'extreme' clothing that shows off biceps, cleavage and tattoos. They may not be as good-looking as they think they are, but their way of dressing, coupled with their self-belief, can make them seem attractive. They enjoy being photographed or having their children photographed and enthusiastically share these pictures on social networking sites, such as Facebook, where they work to boost their self-image by developing many contacts and online 'friends' rather than creating a sense of intimacy with real friends. They will find as many ways as they can to promote themselves positively (Buffardi and Campbell, 2008).

The life approach of someone with an NPD is often more like a 'fantasy' of success than a realistic process involving goals, hard work, persistence and willpower. As a result, aspects of their life resemble a house of cards that in some cases is easily knocked over or simply falls down. The following are some of the typical behaviours of someone with an NPD:

- Looks for friendships or romantic relationships with people they believe can potentially contribute to their success and their 'successful' public image.
- Has limited capacity to love anyone but themselves. Any relationship is based mostly on *their* wants, needs and expectations. They have very little sensitivity to, or concern about, the needs of their partner or children and are not interested in participating in a mutually nurturing and supportive intimate relationship.

- Often uses emotional and/or physical abuse to establish power and control over an intimate partner. This may involve pushing, shoving or punching, mocking, belittling and humiliation, sulking, withdrawal or creating self-doubts. They hide this abuse to preserve their public image. Their victim may get used to the abuse and see it as less controlling than it actually is, gradually losing trust in their own perceptions and judgments.

- Lacks realistic insight into their own behaviour and tends not to learn from mistakes. Blames other people when things go wrong and excuses their own shortcomings by claiming that others are pressuring them or imposing unrealistic expectations. Hides any 'failure' where able to do so.

- Expects to be catered to and may become angry when this does not happen. For example, they may assume that they do not have to queue up like other people, or that their priorities are so important that others should defer to them.

- May act in ways that are arrogant, rude and patronising, especially towards those they perceive to be of 'lesser status' (e.g. waiters). They do this partly to show off to others and partly to display their superiority.

- Tries to present an image of themselves as powerful and all-knowing. Often overestimates their abilities, exaggerates accomplishments, minimises limitations and seems boastful and pretentious. They assume that others see them as they see themselves and are surprised and sometimes shocked when this isn't the case. They get irritated when others fail to assist with their 'very important work'.

- Often acts vengefully towards people who they think have not supported them or who have acted against them.

- Uses charm and confidence about their future success to convince people to lend them money or invest in their ventures. This money is often lost.

- May insist on having the 'best' (e.g. the best – and most expensive – car, house, computer, clothing brands and school for their children).
- While playing up their self-assessed abilities, dismisses and undervalues the abilities, work, successes and contributions of others, looking for opportunities to undermine those they see as competition. Doing so helps them to feel superior.
- Tends to be a rather boring conversationalist as they are not very interested in what others have to say. They often monopolise the conversation, talk about themselves, lecture others, show off and interrupt to regain control of the conversation.
- Often hurts people in their lives with insensitive or unkind remarks.
- Is oversensitive to what they perceive as slights and quickly take offence.
- Has difficulty coping with feelings of embarrassment and shame and with the frustration that arises when they can't have what they want.

People with an NPD tend to be oversensitive to criticism and struggle to cope when their self-image is threatened by their own actions or someone whose words or actions makes them feel powerless, ashamed, embarrassed, defensive or exposed. This can happen if they make a mistake or a wrong move, or if someone they rely on as part of their 'public image', such as a partner, criticises them, disagrees with them or threatens to leave them. Many avoid working in teams, unless they can manipulate the situation to make it look like they are the star performer, even if they are far from it. When a person with an NPD believes that something or someone has threatened their inflated view of themselves or their positive public image, they suffer what has been described as a 'narcissistic injury'. For example, a shop assistant may rebuke them for trying to jump the queue and tell them to wait their turn, or their partner may stand up to them after years of emotional abuse.

A narcissistic injury can then spark a 'narcissistic rage', an angry verbal and/or physical attack on the person whom they perceive has 'injured' them (Kohut, 1972). They might direct verbal abuse at the shop assistant for daring to challenge them, or physically attack their partner for daring to criticise them. Depending on the nature of the narcissistic injury, these rages can vary from short and minor to prolonged and severe and, in some cases, can include murder. Both Peter Caruso and Gerard Baden-Clay appear to have murdered their wives whilst in a state of narcissistic rage.

What causes an NPD?

Genetic and environmental factors combine to create an NPD. The heritability of NPD – the degree to which genetics plays a role in developing a disorder – is estimated to be .77 (Torgersen et al., 2012). This means that 77 per cent of the differences between those in research studies who had an NPD and those who didn't were due to genetic differences between them. But research has not yet clearly identified exactly what specific genetic predispositions are inherited. A number of studies have suggested that some people with an NPD have a deficit in serotonin, a brain chemical that regulates mood. A serotonin deficit can also lead to depression and sometimes aggression.

It seems likely that limited capacity for emotional empathy might be one of the genetic factors. Although results from research studies into NPD and empathy are mixed, they have generally found that people with an NPD display lower levels of emotional empathy (feeling the feelings of others) but normal levels of cognitive empathy (reading and interpreting the feelings of others) (Ritter et al., 2011; Baskin-Sommers et al., 2014). One 2014 study concluded that people with an NPD are capable of responding emotionally to the feelings of others, but are more able and willing than others to switch off this 'emotional empathy' when it suits them or it isn't in their best interests (Baskin-Sommers et al., 2014). For example, they may use this type of self-serving 'empathic disengagement' when they don't want to emotionally respond to the distress of someone they are mistreating or trying to control, or when they themselves are trying to stay in control and not appear vulnerable.

Many people with an NPD develop and talk about a mythical 'perfect childhood' as part of their self-image. Parenting does appear to play a role in the development of an NPD, especially when parents give a child excessive praise, fail to set clear behavioural boundaries or let their child misbehave without consequences. This type of parenting can give a child unrealistic messages about who they are and what is acceptable behaviour. If children don't experience and learn to manage 'moral emotions', such as compassion, embarrassment, humility, guilt and shame, it is more difficult for them to be resilient, respect the rights of others, develop behavioural boundaries and behave well. If they get almost everything they ask for easily, they don't learn that setting realistic goals, working hard and making sacrifices are the keys to success. If a parent gives a child what they are demanding in order to calm them down during a temper tantrum, the child learns that they can use negative emotional pressure to extract things from others. Overindulgence and/or a lack of parental supervision can also send the child a message that they can do and have whatever they want and denies them opportunities to learn to tolerate the frustration when they find this isn't the case.

Parents have an important role to play in helping children to learn about their ability strengths and character strengths, but they also need to help their child to understand their limitations. A child raised in a family that rates status and success extremely highly learns that the types of qualities that contribute to a grandiose self-image are highly valued and learns to prioritise them in their own life. Telling a child too often how 'special' he or she is and how everyone expects them to excel and outshine others can also contribute to an unrealistic sense of self. Such self-illusions are difficult to maintain in the world outside the family and as they become independent young people. It is also important for parents to teach their child to respect the strengths of others and to value teamwork.

Treatment

Individuals with an NPD rarely seek treatment. They are usually unwilling to acknowledge the disorder and unable to admit that their weaknesses have had a negative impact on others. Many of those who do agree to undertake treatment, often at the urging of a partner, soon drop out as they usually find the process too exposing to cope with and most are not genuinely interested in changing. Some try to manipulate the therapist into acknowledging their superiority. Treatment, which usually involves cognitive behaviour therapy (see glossary), is more likely to be successful in cases where an individual with an NPD may also have an associated depression. Taking SSRI (selective serotonin reuptake inhibitors – see glossary) medication, may be helpful under these circumstances in some cases.

Peter Caruso, Gerard Baden-Clay, Roger Dean and Keli Lane are all extreme examples of people whose behaviour patterns are consistent with a diagnosis of an NPD.

CHAPTER 3

PETER CARUSO

The cast

Rosa Caruso: The victim, wife of Peter

Peter Caruso: The killer, Rosa's husband

Santo Caruso: Rosa and Peter's son (Santo also has a non-identical twin brother who prefers not to be identified by name)

Patty Braumueller: Santo's long-term partner

Costantina and **Giuseppe Pallante**: Rosa's parents, who are buried next to her

Maria Pallante: Rosa's sister, who lived in Melbourne and died of cancer in the 1980s

Matteo (Mac) Pallante: Rosa's brother, who lives in regional Victoria

Julie Pallante: Mac's wife

Antoinetta: Rosa's surviving sister, who stayed in Italy

Tina Paganella: Rosa's cousin, who lives in regional Victoria

Pat Paganella: Tina's husband

Joe (Giuseppe or Zio) Caruso: Peter Caruso's brother who moved to Australia and died soon after Rosa of leukaemia. Another brother and sister stayed in Italy.

The motive
Peter Caruso wanted to prevent his wife from leaving him in order to keep all of their assets and preserve his image and social standing within Melbourne's Italian community.

Introduction
The exclusive, tree-lined court is one of many in leafy Templestowe, an eastern suburb in Melbourne where families enjoy privacy and a comfortable lifestyle on large blocks with stately homes and manicured gardens. The popular residential area borders the Yarra River and retains some of its charm from the days when cows roamed on dairy farms and orchards grew apples, peaches, lemons and pears. It was here that Peter Caruso and his wife Rosa were enjoying their retirement and approaching their fiftieth wedding anniversary. What better place for an Italian-born fruiterer than an old orchard?

With their two sons no longer living with them, Peter and Rosa had their immaculate home, set on an acre of well-tended gardens, to themselves. The single-storey brown-brick dwelling was large but not flashy; a steep driveway looped at the top and led to the double garage with a separate entrance into the house that they used most of the time. High on a hill, the property offered privacy and pleasant views beyond their small cul-de-sac. Caruso mowed the lawns and trimmed the bushes, which were framed by towering conifers, as he refused to pay someone else to do it. At the base of the steep driveway a low brick fence welcomed visitors, without the security gates installed by some of their neighbours.

Like so many Italian women of her generation, Rosa did most of the cooking and cleaning. The house was spotless, as was Caruso's garage, where he tinkered with cars. The couple was financially comfortable due to hard work and clever property investment, so they had the means to do as they pleased. As a result, Rosa enjoyed the good things in life. She wore high-quality clothes and make-up, and decorated her home with expensive furniture. Life appeared to be good – until this petite seventy-two-year-old woman was bludgeoned to death with thirty-six blows from a hatchet.

The shocking crime occurred sometime after 4.30 pm on 1 July 2008. Rosa's killer covered her face with a cloth and left her to die face down in the hallway, surrounded by her stylish furniture and treasured belongings.

A flustered Peter Caruso, who called his son Santo's partner, Patty Braumueller, before alerting emergency services, later told police he had returned from the local shops to find Rosa dead or seriously injured and the house ransacked by burglars. He told Patty their home had been robbed, and Rosa was on the floor. Jewellery was also apparently missing. At first glance, it appeared to be a burglary gone wrong. Robbers had apparently entered the house and, after Rosa disturbed them, attacked her on impulse. They had then fled, unseen by neighbours returning from work.

It did not take long for police to become suspicious as inconsistencies emerged in Caruso's story, which changed several times. Police found no sign of forced entry and Rosa had been hit many times, which wasn't consistent with a bungled burglary. In this case, the perpetrator clearly wanted her dead. Nor was the house ransacked in the usual way favoured by burglars. Drawers were pulled open and cushions removed from couches, but not much was disturbed. Serious crooks usually 'trash the joint' as they search for valuables. But not in this case. Stranger still, Rosa's handbag was in one of the bedrooms with the wallet clearly visible. Why didn't the offenders take it or any other valuables? It made no sense. As the investigation progressed, it became clear that Caruso had killed his wife.

Almost everyone was stunned. Most of their friends and family knew of no violence between Peter and Rosa Caruso, who were upstanding members of Melbourne's Italian community. By all accounts this was a happy couple; their marriage appeared solid, with no suggestion of relationship or financial problems. Even if Caruso had killed his wife, they reasoned, the crime was completely out of character. He must have simply 'snapped'. The full truth did not emerge during the much-publicised trial, which saw the accused murderer unsuccessfully try to portray himself as a 'doddery old man' unable to speak English and physically incapable of violence. Our research, however, has revealed that his narcissistic reign of terror over Rosa almost certainly started many years earlier.

The lead-up to the crime

Outwardly, Peter and Rosa Caruso were a happy couple. They generally kept to themselves, but remained close to some of their Italian relatives. Caruso was known to have a bit of a temper but was not known to be violent, and Rosa seemed unafraid to argue with her husband, and, according to relatives, could stand up for herself.

Few saw any cracks in their long marriage, not even their son Santo. During his father's trial there were constant references to the vicious attack being 'out of character'. But there were several simmering issues and a likely history of control and violence by Caruso towards Rosa. There was also some violence towards the Carusos' second son, who had a long history of mental illness, was on a disability pension and had been written off by his father as a 'bludger'. Rosa wanted to help support him financially but her husband refused. Caruso considered him to be a 'blot' on the perfect life he had created for himself. But none of this was raised at his trial; it was probably not necessary due to the convincing forensic evidence.

Peter and Rosa had appeared content in their impressive home, which cemented Caruso's status in the Italian community as a successful businessman. Rosa's cousin, Tina Paganella, says Rosa loved Templestowe's peace and beauty, but her husband was becoming tired of mowing the lawns and maintaining the large grounds. He also thought Templestowe was too far from the city. Tina's husband Pat recalls that, in 2008, Caruso said he wanted to sell their house, then valued at more than $1.3 million, and convert two of the three small Brunswick units that they owned and rented out into one larger unit to live in. But Rosa wanted to stay in Templestowe and her husband would not consider living apart; in his eyes that would lessen his status in the Italian community. Everyone who knew him knew that money and status were everything to Peter Caruso.

Pat and Tina agree that Caruso was capable of underhand tactics to keep his money. 'If he spends a dollar he wants to recover it three hundred per cent,' Pat says, adding that when they went out to dinner with him, at the end of the meal Caruso would often go to the toilet to avoid paying his share of the bill. In Caruso's case his money was not used for flashy cars, clothes or overseas holidays; it gave him a feeling of control. 'It's in his blood,' Pat says. Adds Tina: 'He would sell you an apple for a pear. That's the type of person that he is.'

Not long before she died, Rosa told Tina that she and her husband had been discussing their wills. Tina knew that if they ever had a problem, money was usually involved. In this case, Rosa wanted to leave something to their second son, whose significant mental health issues made it difficult for him to work. Caruso didn't want to leave him anything and had always objected to Rosa giving him small amounts of money towards his rent and food to supplement his disability pension. If any of this troubled Rosa, she didn't let on – 'Her private life was her private life,' Tina says –but the subject appears to have been a source of growing tension.

During her final weeks, Rosa made occasional visits to her son Santo's sports bookshop, which was then in the city and where she and Caruso had sometimes worked voluntarily for many years, though less often as they grew older. She seemed pale and tired, and one acquaintance saw bruises on her face, which she had tried to cover with heavy make-up. But Rosa didn't complain and continued to defend her husband, who could be curt with Santo's customers. She continued to tell people that deep down he was 'a good man'.

Santo's brother believes that at times his mother avoided going out in order to hide bruises and marks of physical abuse:

> I used to see marks on her and she'd tell me that she either fell down the stairs or fell over or hurt herself in the garden. When she got hurt and she was bruised up she wouldn't go out. She'd have weeks when she wouldn't go to the shops. Whatever was going on up there for twenty-odd years, she just didn't tell anyone. She didn't tell me. She was the greatest actress that I ever came across.

Rosa's son often encouraged his mother to leave the marriage, but she would say, 'No, no, he's changed.' He now believes she was trying to prevent him from confronting his father. 'I used to tell her, "Walk, because this psycho's going to kill you" . . . She used to say . . . "I've got a way to control it." In hindsight, obviously she was copping a lot for years. I didn't realise how much Mum copped . . . no-one knew.'

At the time she died, Rosa was on the verge of inheriting money from her mother, Costantina, who died in 2007. Rosa stood to gain about $290,000 from the sale of her parents' Heidelberg Heights house after giving her two siblings and a granddaughter nominated in Costantina's will $25,000 each (Ross, 2008). If she did decide to leave her husband, she would have been able to support herself. But Rosa did not tell anyone about Caruso being violent or express any desire to leave him. She did tell Tina a few months earlier that when her husband got 'upset, wild', he'd once said that 'one day he's going to kill me'. At the time, Tina thought nothing of it; it's the kind of thing people say when they're angry. Then, on the morning of the day she died, Rosa told Patty that something was not right, but didn't elaborate. Says Santo: 'Patty asked her how she was and she said, "Oh I'm not too well, something's got to change here, something in Templestowe, something's got to change."'

Santo's father killed his mother that afternoon.

The murder

Rosa Caruso's final day – 1 July 2008 – probably began with her eating breakfast as usual with her husband in the kitchen. It seems that an argument ensued – possibly over their wills, the money from Rosa's mother's estate, or Caruso's insistence that they sell their house and move closer to the city. Caruso's rage would have grown as Rosa refused to submit to his demands as she always had in the past. Based on the forensic evidence, it is likely that an angry Caruso struck her forcefully on the forehead with the tin snips he used while gardening.

This early altercation probably left her shocked or slightly concussed and might explain why she was still wearing her dressing gown and slippers later in the afternoon. Patty later told police that Rosa 'wasn't herself' when they spoke. At that stage, it is likely that she had decided she was no longer safe and had to leave her husband. She was probably hoping to stay with Santo and Patty for a while before deciding where to live.

During the day, Rosa made several calls to Santo, most of which were brief as he was very busy in the shop that day, and Patty, who was home on a day off from her job in the city. It appears likely that Caruso, having overheard Rosa making a number of calls and saying she would call back later, may have assumed, probably correctly, that she was planning to leave him. If she did, his assets and social status would be threatened. Santo and Patty would disrespect him and tell other relatives what he had done to his wife. Rosa might also reveal any other secrets about his money – he was quite wealthy for someone who had run a fruit shop. At some point that day, he must have planned how he would murder her and stage it as a robbery gone wrong.

Rosa rang Santo at his shop at around 4.30 pm, but they were only able to speak very briefly as he was busy with customers. While she was hanging up the phone, Caruso ambushed her, hitting her on the head thirty-six times with a hatchet. She fell to the ground face down and died, still clutching the cordless phone. He then cleaned himself up, changed his clothes and tried to stage a burglary by opening drawers and moving items around in the house. He poured car oil on the driveway to make it look like robbers had parked a car there and went to the local shops to provide himself with an alibi, returning to 'discover' his wife's body.

Police found blood on the kitchen floor tiles and on the kitchen wall phone and handset, making it likely that Rosa was attacked as she hung up the phone or soon after. Rosa had thirty-six 'incised defects' to the scalp consistent with the hammer face of a hatchet. The autopsy also found a diamond-shaped wound on Rosa's forehead different to the blows that killed her, probably inflicted earlier in the day with the tin snips, prompting Rosa's morning call in an attempt to speak to Santo (R v Caruso, 2010).

In death Rosa lay with her feet towards the front door, face down in a partial foetal position. When she was turned over police found the cordless phone under her stomach. Cushions had been removed from chairs in the lounge and kitchen drawers were open, but nothing had been thrown around. Her handbag was in one of the bedrooms, apparently untouched and still containing her money and credit cards. When police arrived, Caruso claimed he had been to the local shops and returned to find his wife seriously injured in the hallway. He said the house had been ransacked and jewellery taken, pointing out a 'new' oil spill in the driveway from the robbers' vehicle. He also claimed to have seen a dark-coloured car that supposedly drove off with two people in it.

But it was soon clear that Caruso's story did not add up. For a start, he had called Patty before calling emergency services. When he did call 000, he was transferred to an ambulance call centre operator who asked him to try to help his wife until an ambulance arrived. But he refused to touch her. Caruso made no attempt to save Rosa, claiming he was too traumatised to help. Or did he want to be sure she died?

Rather than showing distress, one of the first things the newly widowed husband did when two police officers arrived at his house was to hand them a receipt to prove he was at the shops buying milk, bread and fish and chips when the crime occurred. Not only did his unprompted producing of the receipt seem strange, there was a pot on the stove in preparation for a meal.

Caruso literally had blood on his hands, which he told police was from a cut he suffered while changing a car battery. When police found bloodied clothes in the garage – which were later found to contain his and Rosa's DNA and no-one else's – he claimed that the burglars must have worn his clothes to commit the robbery and the murder, then changed back into their clothes, leaving his clothes behind to frame him. Rosa's jewellery was also found in a bag hidden in the garage. Although the lower bottom pane of glass in the back door had been kicked in, this would not have helped anyone to reach the inside door handle and gain entry. Police believed the robbery was staged and charged Caruso with Rosa's murder the next day.

Santo initially believed his father's story, though he found it odd that none of his parents' expensive artworks or plasma TVs were gone. When Caruso was granted bail two weeks later, he went to live with Santo and Patty until the trial, reporting to police three times a week. Caruso told people that he visited his wife's grave every week, washing the headstone and leaving flowers.

Santo tried to give his father the benefit of the doubt. He simply could not believe that he would kill his mother and dutifully put up his father's $100,000 bail. There was nothing to suggest that their relationship was troubled and he did not think his father was violent. Before long, however, Santo and others were forced to reassess everything they knew about this elderly man who was in all likelihood a calculating and violent killer.

When Rosa died, her cousins Tina and Pat were in Italy visiting relatives, including Rosa's sister Antoinetta. Initially they thought it was a random killing, but within a week had changed their minds. Pat says Caruso's story never added up and he made mistakes 'all the way along'. Tina adds that when Caruso was at the police station the night his wife died, he tried to impress them with his coffee-making skills. 'He tells the cops, "You can come to my place, I'll make you a beautiful coffee" . . . I mean, you're wife's dead! Hey!'

In another strange twist, Caruso instantly began planning Rosa's funeral and within days of her death was disposing of her clothes and possessions. Soon after, he appointed a real-estate agent to sell their house. Tina and Pat received nothing, although Santo and his brother managed to secure a few keepsakes. The furniture was gone within weeks. 'Peter didn't ring me at all,' Tina says.

While Rosa's loved ones grieved, Caruso continued on with his life as if nothing had happened. He kept volunteering at Santo's bookshop, which appalled those who could not believe he would show his face in public while on bail. The situation changed when Santo realised his father was guilty. Caruso had continued to protest his innocence and three months later, out of the blue, he brought home to Santo the bloody tin snips in a rolled up newspaper, saying, 'Look what I found, the killers used this.' He told Santo he had gone back to the house and found the tin snips near the neighbour's fence. He urged Santo to take them straight to the police. But in his heart, his son knew that there was no way all the detectives and forensic experts who had combed the property could possibly have missed them. Caruso had hidden them, possibly somewhere near the shops, after using them to hit Rosa.

Later, when Santo noted that the case was taking a while to get to court, his father seemed unconcerned. When Santo pushed the point, Caruso told him to forget his mother. Santo recalls saying, 'Pa, look, you know, what's happening in court, let's get things moving here, it's been a year now.' His father replied, 'No, no, I've got all the time in the world. I don't care if it takes five years. Mum's gone now, she's rubbish, she's gone now, forget about her.' Shocked, Santo immediately withdrew the $100,000 bail he had provided. Rather than pay it from his own substantial assets, through his lawyers Caruso asked the recently widowed wife of his brother, 'Zio Joe', for the bail money. Santo says that when his aunt said she did not have $100,000 in her pension account, his father had asked if they could use her land title. Luckily her daughter was there at the time so they refused. 'That's desperation,' Santo says. 'Why harass a woman who's just lost her husband? That's rat cunning. The stupid thing is he's not a pensioner. He's got over one million dollars in different accounts.'

The trial

In May 2010, a Supreme Court jury heard hours of complicated forensic evidence that left little doubt that Peter Caruso was the only person with his wife when she died. His DNA and no-one else's was on their bloody clothes and the murder weapon. There were no other suspects or witnesses.

Yet Caruso maintained his innocence, even when his story continued to change and unravel. The keen gardener and handyman, who was seventy-four at the time of the crime, presented in court as a 'bumbling old man'. He adopted a shuffling gait to accentuate his age, implying he was not physically or mentally strong enough to kill his 148-centimetre wife, who weighed just 48 kilograms. His English was also apparently so bad after nearly sixty years of living and running a business in Melbourne that he needed an interpreter.

None of this fooled the jury.

The trial before Justice Betty King heard that on 1 July 2008, Santo arrived at his bookshop just before 9.30 am. Patty had called Rosa around 9.10 am, but she didn't answer so Patty left a message. Patty rang again twenty minutes later and this time spoke to Rosa for just over seven minutes. Patty asked Rosa how she was and Rosa said, 'Good, darling.' But, Patty told the court:

> She sounded flat. She's always very excited if I speak to
> her. She was quite sad, quite down and I just said, 'What's

113

wrong?' I just thought it might have been because she was upset about Zio [Caruso's brother, who was ill]. And she said, 'Something has to change.' And I said, 'What do you mean?' She said, 'Nothing darling, nothing, it's nothing.' And I said, 'Do you want me to come around?' . . . And she said, 'No, no, you're too busy. You call me after six.' I said, 'All right, I'll call you after six.' That was the end of the conversation. (R v Caruso, 2010)

Rosa called Santo between 10.30 and 11 am, but he had a customer with him so told her to call back. At 1.46 pm, Patty rang Rosa again and they spoke for just under a minute. Rosa called Santo again at around 4.30 pm, but, as was often the case during business hours, he was busy with customers, and the call lasted a little less than a minute and a half. Santo had no reason to suspect that anything was wrong, so he then closed his shop and went to the gym and the movies.

Caruso had told police that he left home sometime after 4.30 pm to buy milk and bread at the supermarket and then fish and chips at The Pines shopping centre in Doncaster East. This would have taken a little under an hour. CCTV footage at the fish-and-chip shop showed Caruso rubbing his hands, which he later claimed was to clean off blood after cutting himself while changing a car battery. When he got home, he said, he found the garage door open. He also noticed two small oil patches on the driveway that were not there when he left. He then saw his wife on the floor, apparently alive. The house had been trashed, presumably by burglars.

Caruso said he tried to give Rosa some water and she moved her eyes, but she didn't answer. At one point he claimed that she was moaning. Yet before the ambulance arrived, he put a cloth over her head. At about 6.20 pm, before calling 000, he rang Patty and told her, 'They've killed Mum; there's been a robbery.' Patty said Caruso appeared to be confused. 'He said her fingers were moving . . . her eyes and her fingers were moving,' Patty told the court. After dropping her dog at her mother's place in Airport West, Patty went to Templestowe and travelled with Caruso in the police car to the station. Santo, who was at the movies and still unaware of what had happened, did not arrive until later.

After he called 000, police called Caruso back on his home phone at 6.36 pm. Two female police officers arrived at 6.42 pm. He said, 'We've been robbed', and, 'I got home six minutes ago'. Caruso told the officers that he and Rosa had been robbed four times before: 'They think we have money.' He was shaking slightly, held the female officer's arm and seemed distressed. Ambulance officers expected shock symptoms such as low blood pressure and light-headedness, but found Caruso's blood pressure and heart rate normal. He complained of chest pain, which later changed to 'not pain, I just feel upset'. Most people in such a dreadful situation would experience stress-related symptoms, but Peter Caruso's readings were that of a man going about his everyday business.

Soon after the police arrived, Caruso told them he had been to the shops and immediately produced his supermarket receipt, which had 5.57 pm printed on it. There was some confusion in court over whom he told, when and how, but Caruso definitely offered the receipt unprompted at some point, an extremely unusual act for someone whose wife had apparently just been murdered.

Summing up, prosecutor Christopher Beale highlighted the inconsistencies in Caruso's story and the overwhelming evidence against him. For example, the accused had initially talked about seeing one dark car in the court, then added that he had also seen a light-coloured car. He had told police he saw two people in the car, but later said there was no-one in the car. 'And it was like, "Ah, that's a problem", and that's when he introduces the white car,' Beale said.

Beale also noted that Caruso was insistent on handing over his shopping receipt and that CCTV footage at the fish-and-chip shop was highly suspicious. The DNA evidence was also damning. 'There's no DNA from an unknown contributor confirmed to be present on objects likely to have been touched or worn by the offender,' Beale stated. 'The objects . . . include the hatchet, tin snips, because remember they were found to have blood on them, and there were also hairs wedged into the tin snips, and the blood was tested for DNA and there was a match with Rosa Caruso.'

Caruso clearly had no idea how advanced DNA testing was.

Beale told the jury nothing was smashed or damaged and where drawers were open nothing was disturbed. Valuables were untouched and nothing was stolen. Peter Caruso's blood, however, was on the hatchet, his grey trousers, his windcheater and his slip-on shoes. Initially he had denied the clothes were his. 'You will recall what he said about those items in cross-examination when they were shown to him,' Beale told the court. 'The pants are much too big for him. Windcheater, never seen it before, or the pants. But he reverted later on in re-examination, admitting they were his, saying he just got confused. So there's no dispute either that that windcheater and those grey trousers were his.'

The inconsistencies kept coming.

Beale reminded the jury that Caruso had indicated that when he got home Rosa was still alive. 'He says he thought she moved her eyes and made a moaning noise. If that's right and he's observed these signs of life shortly before he gets on the phone, shortly before he calls the police operator, shortly before he receives a call from the ambulance operator, what's he doing putting a cloth over her head?' Caruso had refused to follow the emergency operator's instructions to turn Rosa over and tilt her head back, and offered several different versions of how Rosa was lying when he found her. The oil he said was freshly spilled in the driveway was also tested and found to be 'consistent with' a tin of oil in his shed. The evidence was damning.

It took the jury just four hours to find Peter Caruso guilty of murder. The whole situation was overwhelming and distressing for Tina, Pat and Santo, who attended the trial. Tina and Pat sat through two weeks of evidence, largely to keep Rosa's sister in Italy, Antoinetta, informed. Having already lost her husband and a son to murder during a 1990s property dispute, Antoinetta was beside herself with grief.

In sentencing Caruso to eighteen years jail with a minimum non-parole period of thirteen years, Justice Betty King described Rosa's death as 'brutal and horrific' and completely motiveless. 'There was no evidence of violence or even disagreement between you and your wife,' she said. 'I have no information that would assist me in determining why you decided to kill your wife and particularly in this quite gruesome manner. You have been a decent hard-working man your entire life. This offence is totally out of character for you and for the demonstrated relationship that you had with your wife' (R v Caruso, 2010).

It now seems that Peter Caruso's actions were not out of character at all. Santo, who was shocked to discover what his father was capable of, could not believe his reaction after being found guilty. 'I'll never forget,' Santo says. 'He just stood up, gave me his bag and cap, and said, "See you later." If you think you're genuinely innocent, [you would have said], "You [are] wrong, I didn't do it, I want to prove you wrong." He just said, "Here you are, here's my bag, see you later. I'll ring you next week." Like, oh, okay, big deal.'

On 11 October 2011, the Victorian Court of Appeal dismissed Caruso's application for leave to appeal against his sentence. Then, in June 2012, an attempt to appeal his conviction on the grounds of 'fundamental procedural irregularities' – namely that he was not arraigned in front of the full jury during his trial – also failed. What this calculating murderer didn't reckon on was DNA evidence and police officers expert in identifying suspicious crime scenes. He may have been a canny businessman, but Peter Caruso was hopelessly out of his depth when it came to current forensic technology and modern policing. Nor was he a very good actor.

Rosa's sister-in-law, Julie Pallante, was far from convinced by the 'doddery old man' act. Married to Rosa's brother Matteo, known to all as Mac, Julie says her brother-in-law was fit for his age and easily scaled the steep hill at Rosa's funeral. 'He was on the ball,' she says. 'He was down to the gravesite that quick, kissing the coffin. I nearly slipped down the hill. I thought to myself, "Doddery old man, my foot."' Julie also thinks it is ridiculous that Caruso asked for an interpreter in court, as his English was perfect. Rosa had not confided in Julie, but she says Caruso was very controlling and the time could have been right for Rosa to leave as Rosa's mother who liked Caruso, had died. 'After her father died and then her mother, I think she would have had the courage,' Julie says.

Peter Caruso's background

Peter Caruso was born in October 1933 in the small Sicilian town of Ramacca, in a mountainous region about 140 kilometres south-east of Palermo. At nineteen, Caruso joined the many post-war European migrants heading to Australia for a better life. He arrived in Melbourne in 1953, settling in Westgarth Street, Fitzroy, and listing his occupation as a labourer. His first job was selling shoes out of a van. During his trial, Caruso said he also worked at the Dunlop rubber factory in Richmond before opening a small fruit shop in Brunswick in 1964.

Peter Caruso met Rosetta Pallante after her family arrived from Foggia, Italy, in 1956. Peter and Rosa married in September 1958, and had two sons. Neither parent had attended high school, but they were financially savvy and hard-working, running a fruit shop in Brunswick at a time when thousands of post-war migrants were making the most of the freedom and opportunities Australia provided. They worked long hours when the boys were young, relying on babysitters as they built up the business. In her later years, Rosa worked in school canteens and as a seamstress.

Initially the Carusos lived in North Fitzroy, not far from their shop, but later moved to Bulleen and then, in 1988, Temple-stowe. Santo says his father was a successful businessman. 'He made a fair bit of money out of that,' he says of the shop. 'I think he bought some properties around Bulleen, Templestowe. He was always canny with money. He didn't flaunt it with the flash car, the gold watch, the necklaces and all that. He . . . looked like a cleaner or something. He wasn't flamboyantly dressed.'

Some close relatives believe Caruso's fast-growing fortune may have had sources other than the fruit shop over the years. Police investigated a possible mafia link, in case Rosa's murder was related to the deaths of her brother-in-law and nephew in Italy, but did not find anything. Regardless of how he earned it, Caruso was extremely tight with money to the point of annoying relatives and friends.

To most people, Caruso appeared to be the archetypal family man. He worked hard and lived an ordered and predictable life. He kept his garage immaculate, even while tinkering with cars. If something spilled, he cleaned it immediately. Nothing was left lying around. The garden was perfectly pruned, the hedges trimmed and the lawn mown. Caruso did it himself, partly because he didn't trust anyone else to get it right. Rosa was also houseproud and kept her home spotless; on this much she and her husband agreed. He didn't drink or smoke and hugged and kissed his wife in front of their sons. But he did not show any sense of love or concern beyond duty.

Family meant everything to Rosa, a slightly built but physically and emotionally strong woman. She doted on her sons and was close to her parents, visiting her mother daily during her final years in a nursing home. Rosa was devoted to her family but was feisty at times, unafraid to debate her husband. However she was mostly affectionate towards him and never pushed to the point of major disagreement. Although they argued occasionally, they seemed happy. Santo only saw his father 'lose it' twice – when he pushed Rosa aside during an argument and when he slapped Santo's brother on the face as a teenager.

Rosa's other son, who left home at sixteen, saw another side of Caruso, whom he says hit both he and Rosa on other occasions when Santo was not around. He says his father, whom he refuses to name and calls 'the convicted murderer', came close to killing him several times, including one incident during which Caruso tried to drown him in the bath as a young child until he screamed and Rosa disturbed them. This son says he saw his father hit his mother 'a couple of times' and suspects this was the tip of the iceberg. Santo was oblivious. As a 'good boy' who worked hard and made his father proud, he did not attract Caruso's wrath. Santo had lived at home on and off until he was thirty-six because he was on 'such a good wicket' and due to two bouts of cancer, which he survived with the help of his family. Rosa's other son, however, had substance abuse and significant mental health problems. He spent fifteen years working as a storeman, but has been unable to work for about twenty years. This made his relationship with his unforgiving father worse and his angry reaction to his father's violence led people to believe that he was more troubled than he really was. 'A lot of people thought I was an annoying kid and playing up for no reason,' he says.

Rosa's cousin Tina was among her closest friends. They grew up in the same Italian town, where their grandmothers were sisters, and both moved to Australia as teenagers. Tina and her husband Pat have lived about four hours drive away in regional Victoria for forty years, but remained close to Rosa and Peter. Pat says from a young age Caruso treated Santo's brother badly as he was less compliant and much more active, which his father had no patience for.

All Rosa wanted was for both her sons to be happy, marry and have children. Not being a grandmother was a big disappointment to her, but she loved her sons and got on well with Patty. 'I was probably the daughter that she didn't have,' Patty told Caruso's trial. 'She would have loved us to be married and have half a dozen children. She was always wanting to buy us things, always. She was very loving. My observation was that [she and Caruso] were a loving couple. She was terribly affectionate. She'd always . . . give him a kiss before she went to bed and squeeze his face' (R v Caruso, 2010). These shows of affection may have been among the strategies Rosa used to keep herself safe from her husband.

As they lived in regional Victoria, Rosa's main female confidants, Tina and Julie, were not in a position to notice small clues about physical or emotional abuse. Patty told Caruso's trial that she spoke to Rosa weekly and her relationship with Caruso, who did odd jobs for her and Santo, was 'normal'. She said Rosa 'drove Santo nuts' ringing him every day and telling him he was too thin. But they had a very loving relationship. Meanwhile, Caruso played the dutiful husband and drove Rosa everywhere. Rosa did

121

get her licence at some point, possibly when she was in her sixties, but her other son says that after taking him on a few trips she stopped as her husband did not want her to drive. Instead, when Rosa's mother was in a nursing home, Peter drove his wife to visit nearly every day. But money was always his main motivation and he used it to maintain control in his life and over his family. He had several investment properties and loved talking about financial issues. Part of his disappointment with his second son stemmed from his lack of interest in money.

Rosa's brother Mac and his wife Julie lived a three-hour drive away, but Mac, who got on well with Caruso, spoke to his sister every week. Julie says Caruso was a 'tight arse' and obsessed with money. She recalls a time when she and Mac were going to buy an old freezer that Rosa and Peter had been storing in the garage for about five years. Despite its age, Caruso wanted almost what he had paid for it new. Mac and Julie refused and eventually he relented, giving it to them more cheaply. 'He was always like that,' Julie says, adding that she would not be surprised if the murder motive was financial: 'It would have been over the money because Peter was the biggest tight arse. I never liked Peter, never.' Julie says Caruso worked hard in his fruit shop, often seven days a week, so probably earned his money honestly. But it grated on her that he pretended he was struggling when he was much wealthier than they were. She and Mac were shocked when Caruso was charged with murder, but within a couple of weeks Julie decided he had done it and not very well: 'I said to Mac, "He's not a really clever man. He's clever with money but he's not very clever."'

Trust was also an issue, even before the murder, and it often came back to money. Caruso was suspicious of other people's motives and quick to question browsers in the bookshop. While a family friend who worked with them described Rosa as friendly, she said Caruso 'had that arrogance; you couldn't have a conversation with him'. She continued, 'He didn't trust anyone. I often said to [Rosa], "If you can't trust anyone, it means you can't trust yourself."'

Santo says that apart from speeding fines, his father appeared to be law-abiding. 'That's what makes it worse,' he says. 'When they arrested my dad, I thought, "This is wrong, this is a mistake." I hardly ever saw him lose his temper. I'd love to . . . say right, he had a girl in Doncaster or he had a gambling problem or he bumped [Mum] off for the insurance. I'd love to get a reason.'

Rosa's other son thinks the reason for her death is relatively simple. After years of abuse, she had probably decided she'd had enough. He believes Rosa's mother's death proved the catalyst and gave her the courage to act. 'She'd stand up to him, she wouldn't back down,' he says. 'This is what I reckon; he used to beat her because she wouldn't back down. I reckon she was literally just packing and was literally going to walk. She was going to walk out the door.'

Why did he do it?

All couples have their differences. Most argue occasionally and some will separate, often acrimoniously. But no matter how serious the fallout, such conflict rarely ends in violence. Everyone is capable of being enraged by a loved one, but only a small percentage will hurt or kill them. What tips that person over the edge? Peter Caruso was controlling, cunning and arrogant. Combined with a lack of empathy, these characteristics enabled him to kill his wife and to believe that he could get away with it. He also mistakenly thought that he was smarter than police and could fool them into concluding that his wife's death was the result of a burglary gone wrong.

Why?

Peter Caruso's behaviour pattern is consistent with a diagnosis of a narcissistic personality disorder (NPD), which is characterised by an inflated view of one's own importance and cleverness. Those with an NPD think they are superior beings whose needs should always come first. They crave admiration and have limited capacity for empathy. Caruso had always had an inflated view of himself and felt superior to those around him. He certainly craved excessive admiration, felt entitled, was preoccupied with fantasies of success and power, lacked compassion and took advantage of others.

In pursuing the 'trappings' of success, Caruso was happy for Rosa to dress well and buy the best of everything as it made him look important and like a good provider. He thought he was superior and clever when he regularly stole bread rolls from the hotel supplies sitting on the footpath near Santo's shop and when he disappeared into the toilet to avoid his share of a restaurant bill. To do so without guilt or shame, he had to regard himself more highly than others.

Caruso was convinced that he had the right to control his wife and children and always put his needs first. Rosa largely allowed this charade to continue by defending him when people doubted his character. This all fed his ego and allowed him to control her and others, but it may also have been another of Rosa's strategies for protecting herself and her son from her husband's violence and ensuring that her son didn't attack his father while protecting her and end up on an assault charge.

Like others with an NPD, Caruso almost certainly defended his view of himself as clever, successful and powerful by flying into a narcissistic rage and attacking Rosa when she wouldn't accede to his wishes about the wills and her mother's estate. He had clearly physically attacked her in the past and Rosa had managed to keep the bruises hidden from others or explain them away. It is highly likely that Caruso also regularly emotionally abused her, as both types of abuse tend to co-occur in violent husbands. But when he injured her with the tin snips – probably the first time he attacked her with a weapon – he almost certainly crossed a line; Rosa would have feared for her safety and her actions suggest that she had made the decision to leave.

Caruso fits into the compensatory NPD subtype (Millon et al., 2004; see pages 94–95), which includes those who have suffered wounds early in life, such as a traumatic or disadvantaged childhood. They then try to 'compensate' by seeking status, recognition or prestige through gaining qualifications or awards, becoming a celebrity, becoming wealthy or having a high-status job. Arriving in Australia as a poorly educated non-skilled Italian migrant from a poverty-stricken background, Caruso worked hard to build his business and his status as a successful and wealthy businessman within the local Italian community. He would have been enraged by Rosa's decision to leave him as it threatened everything he had worked for – his money and status and his reputation. He didn't want anyone to know about the violence he had been inflicting on her. Additionally, if she divorced him, she would also have been entitled to a significant proportion of their assets.

Beneath all this bravado, as someone with an NPD, Caruso lacked resilience and coping skills when dealing with stressful situations. This made him a potentially dangerous person who would stop at nothing to protect his image and wealth. Once he had become enraged and seriously injured Rosa with a weapon, he could think of no other way to manage the situation than to kill her and stage a robbery gone wrong. The possibility of Rosa leaving would have been excruciating for him and the resulting loss of face unbearable. It would also damage his reputation and possibly expose him to family and friends as an abusive husband.

There was never empathy for Rosa in Caruso's cunning plan, only concern for himself. He viewed his wife as one of his 'assets', who helped to promote his self-image as a wealthy Italian businessman with a loving wife. He showed her no genuine affection and clearly felt no distress when he murdered her. To him, she was disposable – like 'rubbish', as he told Santo. All he cared about was getting away with his crime. He might have done so, too, if he had been smart enough.

All this gained Peter Caruso entry into a notorious club – spousal killers.

Research shows that those who kill their life partner are more likely to use excessive violence or 'overkill'. Dutton and Kerry (1999) found this excessive force included two or more separate actions of stabbing, cutting, shooting or a very severe beating. Stabbing or cutting were most common. The range of 'excessive force' was five to twenty-five blows or stabs. Dutton and Kerry also found the most common motive was recent or imminent abandonment, as was the case here. Homicidal husbands often make threats first, their abandonment rage causing a combination of anger and anxiety that builds up and explodes, leading to 'overkill'. In these cases, it is not uncommon for the killer to continue his attack after the victim is clearly dead (Crawford and Gartner, 1992). Peter Caruso did not need thirty-six blows to kill his wife; he was clearly determined not just to end her life but to punish her for not putting his needs first.

None of this offers much comfort to the Caruso and Pallante families, but it might give them some answers and help them to move on.

Despite everything, Santo still speaks to his father, who calls him from jail every week. Santo is gentle and loving, a very different man from his father. Although he cannot forgive him for murdering his mother, he still regularly visits him in jail.

Santo's brother refuses to have anything to do with his father. To this day, Caruso still denies everything, even though Santo has told his father many times that he knows he is guilty and that the evidence is overwhelming.

Santo also regularly visits his mother's grave at Templestowe cemetery, a tranquil, tree-lined resting place close to her home. The large, double headstone in dark pink marble with a black background sits on a hill with angels watching over her. Statues of Mary sit on either side below. At the front, large black marble vases hold the flowers Santo brings. Next to Rosa's grave is the smaller, black marble headstone of her parents, Giuseppe and Costantina. Santo wants to keep their memories alive and connected after all that his family has been through. He is determined to honour Rosa's legacy and says there is no way his father will join her in that double grave, despite Caruso's insistence that he will. 'As long as I'm alive, my father can't be buried here,' Santo says.

Even in jail, Peter Caruso is looking out for number one — and not always successfully. In 2012, his obsession with money saw him ripped off by a fellow prisoner. The *Herald Sun* reported that triple killer Gregory John Brazel swindled $37,000 from Caruso after promising to find him a solicitor who could get him out of jail in two weeks. 'The $37,000 was allegedly deposited by Caruso,' the newspaper reported. 'The account name was later found to be bogus and the money has not been recovered' (Buttler, 2012). Once again, Caruso was nowhere near as clever as he thought.

PETER CARUSO
DIAGNOSTIC CHART

Using DSM 5 indicators (APA, 2013), when five or more of these are present, a diagnosis of narcissistic personality disorder (NPD) can be made	Examples of Peter Caruso's behaviour that appear to be consistent with each indicator
Has a grandiose sense of self-importance (e.g. exaggerates achievements and talents, expects to be recognized as superior without commensurate achievements).	Continually tells son Santo (when Santo rings or visits him in jail) how to run his finances and criticises him if he doesn't continually seek the highest interest-bearing bank accounts. Frequently boasted about his wealth and financial success. Just hours after Rosa died, he told the police he would make the police a beautiful coffee at his home with his fantastic coffee machine.
Is preoccupied with fantasies of unlimited success, power, brilliance, beauty or ideal love.	Told a family friend his life was 'perfect'.
Believes that he or she is 'special' and unique and can only be understood by, or should associate with, other special or high-status people (or institutions).	
Requires excessive admiration.	Expected Rosa and the people with whom he associated to admire 'his' achievements.

Using DSM 5 indicators (APA, 2013), when five or more of these are present, a diagnosis of narcissistic personality disorder (NPD) can be made	Examples of Peter Caruso's behaviour that appear to be consistent with each indicator
Has a sense of entitlement (i.e. unreasonable expectations of especially favorable treatment or automatic compliance with his or her expectations).	Expected Rosa to obey his wishes.
Is interpersonally exploitative (i.e. takes advantage of others to achieve his or her own ends).	Went to the toilet to avoid paying his share of a restaurant bill. Would 'sell you an apple for a pear', according to relatives. Was dishonest and cunning and you couldn't believe what he said, according to relatives. Allowed Santo and Patty to house him when he was released on bail, even when it became extremely uncomfortable. Tried to get his brother's widow to loan him bail money. Stole bread rolls from a hotel near Santo's shop and boasted about it.
Lacks empathy: is unwilling to recognize or identify with the feelings and needs of others.	Unconcerned about Rosa's second son's mental health issues. Instead insulted and mistreated him and refused to help him.

Using DSM 5 indicators (APA, 2013), when five or more of these are present, a diagnosis of narcissistic personality disorder (NPD) can be made	Examples of Peter Caruso's behaviour that appear to be consistent with each indicator
	Probably refused to leave that son any money in his will and tried to force Rosa to follow his lead.
	Did not care that Rosa was happy in her home; he was insisting that they downsize and move closer to the city.
	Was able to hit Rosa in the head with a hatchet thirty-six times.
	Quickly sold or dumped Rosa's possessions without offering them to her relatives.
	Sold their house as soon as he could.
	Told his son Santo to forget his mother as she was 'gone, like rubbish'.
Is often envious of others or believes that others are envious of him or her.	
Shows arrogant, haughty behaviors or attitudes. * Reprinted with permission from the Diagnostic and Statistical Manual of Mental Disorders, Fifth Edition, (Copyright ©2013). American Psychiatric Association. All Rights Reserved.	Was arrogant and rude to customers who browsed, but did not buy, books in Santo's shop. Labelled his mentally ill son a useless bludger.

CHAPTER 4

GERARD BADEN-CLAY

The cast

Allison Baden-Clay: The victim and Gerard Baden-Clay's wife. Their daughters were aged ten, eight and five when she died

Priscilla and Geoff Dickie: Allison's parents

Ashley Dickie: Allison's brother

Vanessa Fowler: Allison's sister

Kerry-Anne Walker: Allison's close friend

Gerard Baden-Clay: The killer, and great-grandson of scouting movement founder Lord Robert Baden-Powell. Baden-Clay was a director at the Westside Century 21 Real Estate agency in an outer suburb of Brisbane

Nigel and Elaine Baden-Clay: Baden-Clay's parents

Olivia Baden-Walton: Baden-Clay's sister

Adam Baden-Clay: Baden-Clay's brother

Toni McHugh: Baden-Clay's lover at the time of the murder; formerly worked at Westside Century 21 Real Estate

Phillip Broom and **Jocelyn Frost**: Baden-Clay's business partners in Westside Century 21 Real Estate

Bruce Flegg: Former Queensland state government minister and acquaintance of Gerard Baden-Clay

The motive

Probably during a heated argument with his wife, Allison, over his continued affair with Toni McHugh and his deception about it, Gerard Baden-Clay appears to have lost control and violently struck Allison. Realising that he had caused her a serious injury, he probably then decided to murder her to prevent her from exposing him as an abusive husband, while enabling him to access her life insurance policy to rescue himself from the serious financial difficulties that were threatening his image as a successful businessman.

Introduction

Gerard Baden-Clay's world was crumbling. The smooth-talking real-estate agent appeared to have it all – the picture-perfect family, status as a successful local businessman, respect as a community leader and an impeccable bloodline to his great-grandfather Lord Robert Baden-Powell, the British Boer War hero who founded the scouting movement. Then his wife Allison, a former beauty queen and the mother of his three girls, disappeared from their home in the pretty outer Brisbane hamlet of Brookfield.

Baden-Clay told police that Allison had a history of depression and he had no idea where she was; she must have slipped out for a late-night or early-morning walk while he was sound asleep. The clear implication was that his wife had wandered off in the middle of the night and either died by suicide or had a terrible accident. Allison Baden-Clay's disappearance came completely out of the blue and transfixed Australia. Model mums from stable families in upmarket communities didn't go missing every day. Where was she?

It didn't take long for police to raise their eyebrows at Gerard Baden-Clay's story; within hours they were on his scent. His calm demeanour, the way his bed was so neatly made, new scratches on his cheek and his claim that Allison went for a long walk early in the morning, despite having a conference to attend that day, just didn't gel. They were right to be suspicious. The man with the carefully crafted public image that borrowed much from his famous ancestors and who brazenly puffed himself up at the expense of his long-suffering and devoted wife was about to be caught out as a murderer.

Before his world came crashing down, the then forty-one-year-old ran the Westside Century 21 real-estate franchise in Brisbane's outer west with two business partners. He liked to remind people of his link to Lord Baden-Powell. Baden-Clay boasted of the connection on his real-estate blog and used it in talks to students and other groups. While imparting his wisdom to Kenmore State High School's 2008 school leaders, he quoted his famous ancestor, a very successful man by any measure, who had emphasised that the most fundamental element of good leadership was to lead by example. But Gerard Baden-Clay was nowhere near as successful as his forebears, either in business or in life. He was a narcissistic man preoccupied with self-glorifying fantasies of unlimited success, who always put himself first and, in the end, became a convicted killer.

In 2008, the year he gave that school talk, the self-appointed community leader started an extramarital affair – not his first – with colleague Toni McHugh. The affair would last almost four years. While outwardly playing the role of the perfect husband, family man and successful businessman, Baden-Clay cheated on Allison, cheated on Toni and borrowed large sums of money from friends and family (who were never paid back) to prop up his ailing business. When this carefully constructed personal and business charade began to crack, he killed his wife.

Baden-Clay's 2012 arrest and 2014 murder trial created a media sensation. People queued outside the court every day, desperate to secure a seat inside. Some parents brought their children as a school holiday excursion. Journalists live tweeted proceedings and wrote thousands of words each day for newspaper websites. Why? Why did this case create such feeling when murder trials are regularly held around Australia? A number of factors combined to transfix the nation. Many people related to this middle-class outer suburban family who could have lived next door to any of us. The successful and popular Allison Baden-Clay could have been a mum at any of our local primary schools. But her husband attracted attention for the wrong reasons. The self-proclaimed successful real-estate salesman was a bit too cool and calm the day his wife was reported missing and avoided taking part in the search for her. His link to scouting royalty and his infidelity added to the intrigue, which later turned to anger when it became clear that Baden-Clay had killed Allison and dumped her body on a lonely creek bank.

The case was baffling and difficult to understand. Gerard Baden-Clay appeared to have the perfect marriage, three perfect children and the perfect setting in which to bring them up – a semi-rural middle class suburb outside Brisbane. Why would an apparently upstanding member of a close-knit middle-class community kill his devoted wife, who had given up a high-flying corporate career for her family?

The lead-up to the crime
In 2011, Gerard and Allison Baden-Clay's fourteen-year marriage was hanging by a thread. His real-estate business was in serious

financial trouble and his affair with employee Toni McHugh was causing increasing tension in the office.

Baden-Clay's business partner at the time, Jocelyn Frost, later told police that the situation was 'diabolical'. She said that in 2010 she discovered that the business owed $150,000, which shocked her and fellow business partner Phillip Broom, given the huge amounts of money it was turning over. As 2010 had been such a success, they wondered where all the money had gone. When the three met to discuss the financial situation, the affair with Toni McHugh was raised. Baden-Clay cried and insisted he was only having a sexual relationship with her for the sake of the business, arguing that she was a good salesperson and they needed her. After his business partners made their displeasure clear, Baden-Clay agreed to tell all the agency's employees about the affair (Sutton, 2014).

Things did not improve with the business's expensive relocation to nearby Taringa, increasing staff numbers to about twenty-five just as the devastating Queensland floods hit in January 2011. Baden-Clay managed the move badly, leaving the business unable to afford the associated expenses even before the floods decimated local property values. The rent was twice as expensive, the business had more staff to pay and the new office did not have the passing foot traffic of their old location. Police alleged that by early 2012, Baden-Clay owed more than $1 million, including $275,000 that he had borrowed from three friends, $200,000 owed to a former business partner, $335,000 as guarantor on a mortgage, $45,000 on his credit card, $75,000 to the CEO of Century 21, various business loans and $58,000 to his parents, Nigel and Elaine (Remeikis, 2014). He had also tried to borrow several hundred thousand dollars from MP Bruce Flegg, who refused.

As their financial situation deteriorated, Allison had moved to reduce her life insurance cover. She and Gerard had a teleconference with their financial adviser about both of their life insurance policies in late March and discussed the possible need to reduce their premium and potential payouts. Payments were overdue and Allison's cover was due to expire on 19 May 2012. On 17 April she had called an insurance broker to investigate possible reductions. At that stage her death cover was $364,651. Combined with her superannuation fund, the total payout on her death would be more than $900,000 (Sutton, 2014). After her death, federal police ended up holding almost $800,000 from her life insurance policies in trust.

A court also heard that the couple had made no payments on their Westpac credit card, which had a minimum repayment of $2406 owing, from 24 January to 30 May 2012 (Wilson, 2014).

The couple's financial problems were compounded by Baden-Clay's repeated and continuing infidelity. Despite the public image he projected of a devoted family man, he had cheated with another agent at a previous job before starting his affair with Toni, a former teacher, when she joined his Century 21 franchise in 2008. The union caused much angst at work as his business partners knew but Allison didn't. At one point Baden-Clay even cheated on Toni, arranging for another woman to spend the night with him at a Sydney real-estate conference before Toni was due to arrive to be with him the next night (Baskin, 'Day 5', 2014).

Baden-Clay ended his relationship with Toni in September 2011, when Allison found out about the affair. Toni then resigned from the business, angry and hurt, and he failed to return her many calls. Their separation was brief. After returning to her in December 2011, Baden-Clay promised he would end his marriage so they could pursue an 'unconditional relationship'. On 3 April 2012, he emailed Toni under the alias of Bruce Overland to give her a commitment that he would be separated by 1 July, which happened to be Allison's birthday.

In April 2012, Allison was easing her way back into working in her husband's business after many years at home with their three young daughters. Friends later said that she was excited about returning to work and asserting herself more, that she had recovered from the depression she had experienced earlier in her marriage and had learned to stand up for herself. Allison was also working hard to help save her husband's struggling business and their troubled marriage, issuing him with an ultimatum to choose between her and Toni. Toni later said that Baden-Clay had told her that Allison had warned him that if he left their marriage 'it wouldn't be pretty' and that she would fight to keep custody of their daughters and gain control of their assets.

Before going into the office for a four-hour training session on 19 April, Allison spoke to her friend Fiona Christ about a sleepover for her children, a school Mother's Day stall and Baden-Clay's new baby nephew in Canada. Gabrielle Cadioli, who worked for Baden-Clay and attended the training session, later told the jury in Baden-Clay's trial that Allison was happy, in a great mood and joking around with them (Sutton and Crane, 2014).

When Allison left the office that day, others noted that she was very positive about growing the business. She later went to the hairdresser to have her hair coloured and blow-waved in preparation for a real-estate conference the following day. That afternoon, Toni, by now working for another real-estate agency, realised after talking to Baden-Clay that she and Allison would both be attending the same conference. He had told neither and later said the potential clash did not concern him. But Toni felt sick, thinking Allison deserved to know, and vented her anger at him on the phone when they spoke for about thirty minutes around 5 pm.

That morning, Baden-Clay had been to a Chamber of Commerce meeting before watching his daughters' school cross-country carnival and heading to work. At 3.45 pm, he had a parent–teacher interview, so his parents collected the children from school and took them to their place. Baden-Clay joined them for an early dinner, then took the girls home. Allison returned from the hairdresser at around 7 pm. The girls, who were aged ten, eight and five, went to bed between 7 and 7.30. At 8.30 pm Allison spoke to her sister-in-law, Olivia Baden-Walton. It was the last anyone saw or heard from her apart from her husband (R v Baden-Clay, 2014).

What happened next may never be fully known, as Gerard Baden-Clay has continued to deny killing his wife.

The murder and search

Baden-Clay later claimed that after the girls went to bed on the night of 19 April 2012, he and Allison discussed the cross-country, the parent–teacher interview and the sleepover plans. As part of the fifteen-minute discussions a marriage counsellor had recommended to enhance their marriage, he says Allison asked about what happened on Toni McHugh's birthday and whether he regretted the affair or just being caught. He says he reiterated how much he appreciated her strength and forgiveness and was very remorseful. The mood was apparently 'perfectly normal' and 'certainly civilised' before he went to bed around 10 pm, leaving his wife on the couch watching *The Footy Show* (R v Baden-Clay, 2014).

What actually happened was quite different.

Sometime that evening, Baden-Clay murdered his wife and disposed of her body near the Kholo Creek Bridge, about thirteen kilometres from their Brookfield home, on a sloping creek bank covered in thick mud.

Based on the available forensic evidence, the most likely scenario is that he did not plan to kill Allison that night, but had probably thought about it in the previous few days or even weeks. The murder was more opportunistic than premeditated as he hadn't prepared himself with a weapon. Things most likely came to a head when he was forced to tell Allison that Toni would be attending the same conference the next day. This probably occurred in the privacy of their bedroom so as not to wake or alarm the children. Allison undoubtedly became very angry after realising her husband was still in a relationship with Toni, despite his earlier reassurances that he had ended it, and might well have told him exactly what she thought of him and his deceitful behaviour. It is probable that he became enraged by her critical words and angry voice. He'd already been on the receiving end of angry and critical comments from Toni McHugh earlier that evening and had dealt with his increasing feelings of shame and humiliation in reaction to the two encounters by converting them into anger. It is highly probable that he became enraged and lost control. At the time, he may have felt irrationally justified in this act of 'retaliation' against someone who was threatening to destroy his 'sense of self' (Malmquist 1996).

The autopsy report later identified a chipped tooth and probable bruising on Allison's head and chest consistent with blunt force trauma. This suggests that at some point her husband probably punched her in the face or used an object to hit her in the face and then hit her on the head with an object or pushed her against bedroom furniture. These blows would have caused a non-bleeding head injury that probably stunned and frightened her.

Most women are not used to physical fighting, so Allison wouldn't have automatically known how to defend herself or retaliate against an attack. If it occurred in the bedroom, the most likely location, she probably lay on the bed to recover and considered what she should do next. Realising he had gone too far and now faced with the possibility of Allison exposing him as an abusive out-of-control husband and maybe even leaving him – an image in stark contrast to his 'perfect' persona – Baden-Clay had to quickly work out how best to control the damage and turn the situation to his advantage. If he murdered Allison, he had some chance of minimising his substantial business losses through her insurance policy, which she was in the process of reducing and possibly cancelling. He could also access her super-annuation fund, giving him almost $1 million to keep alive his image as a successful businessman.

Once he decided to act, Baden-Clay probably sought some-thing to strangle or smother Allison with and settled on the jumper that was found wrapped around her neck when her body was finally recovered. Described in the autopsy report as a 'Bonds XL (extra-large)', it would have had very long sleeves and was probably made from a lightweight material. Next, Baden-Clay may have approached his wife on the bed and pretended to apologise for his loss of control. He probably then straddled her to immobilise her, seized her arms, kneed her forcefully in the chest and either strangled or smothered her, or both. The coroner noted that although Allison's larynx and hyoid bones were not broken, strangulation did not always cause such injuries, espe-cially if a soft broad ligature, such as an item of clothing, had been used.

There is a slight possibility that this took place outside, as Allison was found with a number of leaves and twigs in her hair. However it is more likely that it happened inside and Baden-Clay then dragged her through the garden on the way to the car. Wherever the murder happened, she clearly fought for her life, screaming for help and inflicting two deep scratches on her husband's cheek and a number of small wounds on his upper body. But he was now committed to killing her.

With Allison dead, Baden-Clay had to devise a plan to dump her body and cover his tracks. Kholo Creek Bridge was close to a rental property he had let and which had been the subject of several disputes and police evictions. Before leaving, Baden-Clay probably attempted to dress Allison as if she was going for a walk. But he didn't do a very good job with the jumper; when she was found, it was partially inside out and both the neck and the waistband remained around her neck. The autopsy also found that the laces on one of her shoes were tied tightly but the other side was loose, possibly indicating that someone else tried to tie them up. It isn't easy to dress someone who is deceased. At seventy-two kilograms, Allison wasn't tiny and would have been a challenge to move to the car, so her husband probably dragged her down the back steps and across the backyard garden to where their Holden Captiva was parked before lifting her into the boot.

After dumping Allison on the banks of Kholo Creek, Baden-Clay probably returned home at around 1.45 am, as his phone was plugged back into its charger at 1.48 am.

A number of residents who lived near the Baden-Clay home later testified that on that night, sometime between 7.30 and 10 pm – many were not sure of the exact time – they heard what they described variously as either arguing and screaming, yelling, a startled exclamation cut short, an urgent yell, the scream of a female in distress and a loud dull thud followed by a car leaving. One witness said that the thud she heard was about fifteen to thirty minutes after the woman's scream. One resident who lived near the Kholo Creek Bridge testified that he heard noises between midnight and 1 am the next morning, including thuds and the sound of a car door being shut (R v Baden-Clay, 2014).

While all this was happening, Baden-Clay claims he was fast asleep.

The following morning, 20 April, he texted and rang Allison's mobile phone several times before calling his father at around 6.30 to tell him she was missing. Nigel and his daughter Olivia headed to Baden-Clay's Brookfield home. He rang emergency services at approximately 7.15 am to report his wife missing after supposedly taking a short drive to look for her. He did not call her parents until 9.45 am. A uniformed officer arrived at the Baden-Clay home around 8 am and noticed several scratch marks on Gerard's face, which he calmly explained had happened while shaving as he had been in a rush to get his children ready for school. The officer looked through the house and did not see blood or any sign of a struggle. A sergeant who arrived soon after noticed that the bed in their bedroom had been neatly made. He questioned Baden-Clay with another sergeant at around 8.20 am.

Baden-Clay told them that his wife's state of mind was pretty good but she had suffered from depression in the past, which was managed by medication. He said he did not know if Allison had slept in the bed as he was a heavy sleeper and she sometimes went walking at around 5 am. When an officer told him the marks on his face looked like scratches, he again said he had cut himself shaving. He told the police that he and Allison were having marriage counselling and mentioned that their finances were 'pretty tight'. But he insisted nothing untoward had happened the previous evening, when Allison discussed a list of questions she had for him about his affair with former colleague Toni McHugh, which he had recently resumed despite telling Allison it was over.

Police were immediately suspicious and started a meticulous investigation, involving dozens of officers and volunteers, within hours of Baden-Clay's 000 call. Within twenty-four hours, Allison's disappearance had also become the subject of a media frenzy. Young mothers in this upmarket part of Brisbane's west did not simply 'go missing' and, as many women wondered out loud, why would someone who had had her hair done the night before a big event risk spoiling it on an early-morning bushwalk? Nor were police suspicions allayed by Baden-Clay's behaviour. He hired a lawyer almost immediately, appeared cool and calm throughout, refused to give a formal statement and was reluctant to give full answers to their questions. He did not join the official search, telling people that police had told him not to participate and that his main priority was to continue his daughters' routine. While playing the concerned husband during the search, Baden-Clay also admitted his affair with Toni McHugh to the police. As they were analysing his car, he borrowed a friend's and crashed it into a pillar on a straight road, which police later suspected was an attempt to cover up facial and chest injuries that Allison had inflicted as they struggled. Baden-Clay was also caught using a phone borrowed from local MP, Bruce Flegg, whom he knew through the local Chamber of Commerce, to make secret calls to Toni.

Baden-Clay's explanations were at best confusing and often evasive. He told several conflicting stories about Allison's walking habits and claimed that some of the marks on his body were from a caterpillar bite. A cut on his hand supposedly happened while he was helping a friend with renovations. Baden-Clay also refused to appear at a media conference calling for his wife's safe return, leaving it to her parents. His only appearance during the search was when cornered outside his home by a Channel 9 TV news reporter. Baden-Clay's voice cracked as he told of his concern and how he was helping police as best he could. Flanked by his sister Olivia, he looked worried but nervous. And he should have been. Police were already investigating him as a possible killer. Baden-Clay told the reporter that was trying to look after his three young children and that he and his family trusted that the police were doing everything they could to find Allison. At no stage did he appeal for his wife's safe return.

Allison Baden-Clay's body was found on 30 April, ten days after she was reported missing. The next day, before the body had even been formally identified, Baden-Clay contacted his wife's insurers (Wilson, 2014).

The trial

On 13 June 2012, Gerard Baden-Clay was charged with murdering Allison and interfering with her corpse. Considered a 'flight risk', he was denied bail and remanded in custody. The couple's three daughters were put into the care of their maternal grandparents, Priscilla and Geoff Dickie. The local community – and the rest of Australia – was stunned. Baden-Clay was a well-known real-estate agent and community leader, a former president of the Kenmore and District Chamber of Commerce, vice-president of the Brookfield State School PandC volunteer group and a kindergarten board member. To observers, his marriage had seemed strong. But as more details emerged, it became clear that this man wasn't what he seemed. Far from a devoted family man, he was a liar, a serial cheat, not a very good businessman and now possibly a murderer.

Baden-Clay appeared calm for most of his trial, which ran for five weeks from 10 June 2014. However he was not averse to breaking down at opportune moments and appearing stoic when it suited. Baden-Clay did not waver from his story about Allison disappearing while he was sound asleep, probably after going for a walk. He and his defence team spent much of the trial painting a picture of his wife as dependent, depressed, reliant on drugs and possibly suicidal. The implication was that she had either died by suicide or become disoriented after taking too much of her antidepressant SSRI medication Zoloft, falling into a local creek. It didn't matter that the body was found thirteen kilometres from home, making it unlikely that Allison had walked there and almost impossible that she had fallen into the creek near her home and drifted there. Nor did it appear to matter that Baden-Clay's phone had been connected to a charger at 1.48 am on the morning she went missing, despite his claim that he had slept through the night. The struggling would-be entrepreneur, whose business was failing, also stood to gain enough from his wife's life insurance and superannuation to wipe out his debts.

The evidence against him was strong, but largely circumstantial. Dozens of small details added up to paint a clear picture of what happened.

Crown Prosecutor Todd Fuller QC told the court that behind the picture-perfect facade, Gerard and Allison Baden-Clay were both desperately unhappy, with Gerard leading a double life and 'looking for a way out'. Experts also testified that Allison had recovered from earlier bouts of depression and was definitely not suicidal. 'On the surface, to so many of these witnesses, the Baden-Clays seem like the perfect couple,' Mr Fuller said. 'But it was just a facade. A facade which had been carried on for a long period of time' (Baskin, 'Day 5', 2014).

The court heard that Allison was trying to save her marriage and, three days before she disappeared, she took her husband to see Relationships Australia counsellor Carmel Ritchie. Allison told Carmel that Baden-Clay had high expectations of her and the children, and didn't understand her depression. She also felt she was not good enough for him. On meeting Carmel, Baden-Clay was quick to list his achievements and try to impress her. 'He said he worked in real estate, was the president of the Chamber of Commerce, vice-president of the P&C and was in the Real Estate Institute of Queensland,' she told the court.

When the counsellor told Baden-Clay he had to let Allison ask questions about his affair during fifteen-minute evening discussions at home, he was resistant, arguing that it was 'in the past'.

Excerpts from Allison's journal were read to the court and revealed that while she described her marriage in earlier years as loving and with great sex, her husband now often belittled her and no longer wanted to make love to her. She noted, too, her dismay about the affair. Allison also wrote of her anger when she felt she was treated unfairly. She said that if her relationship ended, it would be because Gerard had had enough and didn't love her anymore (R v Baden Clay, 2014).

Allison's family and friends told the court that while she had suffered depression in the past, a side effect of the anti-malarial drug Lariam, which she had taken while overseas in the late 1990s, in the weeks leading to her death she was happy and confident. A psychiatrist and psychologist also testified that those issues were in the past. Psychiatrist Dr Tom George treated Allison in 2003 when she was troubled by anxiety, panic attacks and a worsening mood. He had found she was prone to transient suicidal thoughts, but in the six years he saw her she did nothing to self-harm.

Allison's parents, Priscilla and Geoff Dickie, told the court of their unease when they arrived at Allison's Brookfield home on the morning she was reported missing. Geoff noticed scratches on his son-in-law's face, and Priscilla found him a bit too calm. 'I couldn't believe it, he had a pink-striped shirt on and a tie . . . just calm as a cucumber,' she said. 'He just came over and said g'day Dad, g'day Mum and gave me a bit of a hug . . .' Priscilla said Baden-Clay offered her a cup of tea and she went into the kitchen but 'the place was just sterile'. She said the usual cups of tea in mugs were replaced that day by tea served in cups and saucers. She went into the main bedroom and the bed was made.

'There was something about the place that wasn't quite right,' she said (Calligeros, 'Gerard Baden-Clay trial', 2014).

Priscilla was also inclined to disbelieve Gerard's story about Allison staying up to watch *The Footy Show* the previous night when he went to bed, because she knew her daughter didn't even like the show (Kyriacou and Murray, 2014).

In his defence, Michael Byrne QC told the court that Baden-Clay's only deception was having a lengthy affair. He had no history of violence and was 'not a person who would cold-bloodedly kill his wife, the mother of his children'. Byrne said Allison was a known 'conflict avoider' and could have taken her antidepressant medication, changed into her walking clothes, put her husband's phone on charge at 1.48 am and gone for a late-night walk to clear her head. He argued it was possible she became disoriented by 'serotonin syndrome' or greater than usual side effects and at some point ended up in the river (R v Baden-Clay, 2014).

Accused murderers don't often take the stand, but Baden-Clay was determined to have his day in court and seemed sure that he would impress the jury. He sobbed openly while giving evidence to his defence counsel, but remained dry-eyed when questioned by the prosecution. He seemingly broke down while watching a video of his daughters discussing their mother, when he talked about Allison finding out about his affair with McHugh and when he recounted his call to emergency services to report Allison missing. Several times he sobbed into his handkerchief while telling the jury he had been unfaithful. 'I just wanted sex,' he said, dabbing his face. 'And Allison and I hadn't had any physical intimacy for years. It's not an excuse but that's why' (Baskin, 'Day 12', 2014). The internet has many sites for drama students that explain some effective ways to make yourself cry.

Baden-Clay admitted to a four-year affair with Toni McHugh and briefer affairs with two other women, blaming his infidelity on a lack of intimacy with his wife. He alluded to other affairs, 'many of them concurrent'. After ending the affair with Toni in late 2011, he was soon seeing her again and they had sex at least two more times. 'Yes there were a number of women that I went to for sex,' he told the court. 'But Allison and I had recommenced our physical relationship and were rebuilding that. I'd had a number of infidelities over the years. The difference with Toni McHugh to the other women was that she worked together in the office with us. That made life a lot more challenging' (Kyriacou and Murray, 2014).

While admitting infidelity, Baden-Clay also falsely portrayed himself as the glue that kept his family together. He said that at times, due to her depression, Allison would collapse on the couch and sleep during the day. Their sex life was non-existent for years and he often did all the housework and organised the girls at night. 'Most occasions I would do the majority of that routine, on many occasions Allison would go to bed pretty much as soon as I walked in the door,' he told the court (Baskin, 'Day 12', 2014). Her family and friends knew this was largely untrue.

Baden-Clay told the court that his conversation with Allison on the night she disappeared was 'perfectly normal'; when he woke around 6 am she was gone. When she failed to return, he texted and called her but there was no reply. Baden-Clay said he put Allison's hot rollers on in the bathroom and started getting his girls ready for school. He claimed that, by then in a rush to get his daughters ready, he cut himself shaving several times (R v Baden-Clay, 2014).

The forensic evidence told a very different story. DNA taken from a bloodstain found in the boot of the family's car matched Allison's and four fingernail experts gave evidence that the scratches on Gerard Baden-Clay's face were consistent with fingernail scratches and not, as he had claimed on the day

Allison went missing, shaving cuts. The DNA found under Allison's fingernails was not hers but couldn't formally be identified because it had become degraded due to the length of time it had been exposed to the environment.

Crucially, an exhaustive investigation by Queensland Herbarium director Dr Gordon Guymer discovered six different varieties of twigs and leaves in Allison's hair, on her arms and on the jumper she was 'wearing'. Dr Guymer testified that all six varieties were growing in the garden of the Baden-Clay house, many along the back verandah and the carport area where their car had been parked. An extensive search of Kholo Creek and surrounding areas failed to locate all six species in the one spot. Microscopic algae expert Dr Jacob John also testified that the absence of any diatoms (microscopic algae) in Allison's body showed that her death was not due to drowning (R v Baden-Clay, 2014).

Other forensic evidence was inconclusive due to decomposition, but supported the theory that Baden-Clay killed his wife during a struggle. There was some evidence that Allison had been thrown off the bridge soon after her death. Her body was severely decomposed and the facial features unrecognisable. This destroyed or concealed any clear-cut evidence of the cause of her death, but forensic pathologist Dr Nathan Milne, who conducted the autopsy, concluded that Allison died of an unnatural cause. He was also able to say that there was no evidence of drowning and that the possibility that she had been smothered or strangled could not be excluded.

On 15 July 2014, no-one was more shocked than Gerard Baden-Clay when a jury of five women and seven men found him guilty of murder. Towards the end of the trial he had reportedly told prison guards he would soon be free. At the same time, media reports claimed his family was negotiating media deals

149

worth up to $600,000 should he be found not guilty. The bereaved husband also would have collected up to $1 million from his wife's insurance policies and $440,000 from a Gold Coast investment property he owned with her (Murray and Kyriacou, 2014). Baden-Clay secretly sold the property, which was registered in the name of his and Allison's company but also jointly-owned by Allison's brother and his wife (Sandy, 2012), three months after his arrest, while in jail, to fund his legal costs. This was despite Geoff Dickie having control of all of Allison's assets. When this happened, Dickie had to reapply for control of them (Calligeros, 'Gerard Baden-Clay guilty', 2014).

Handing down a mandatory sentence of life in prison with a fifteen-year minimum non-parole period, Justice John Byrne found the killing was probably not premeditated, but it was violent. 'That night, you were under considerable stress,' he said.

> Your financial circumstances were, as you confessed to police, dire. Your domestic circumstances were no better. You had resumed your affair with Toni McHugh. You kept telling her that you loved her. You led her to understand that you intended to leave Allison and to be with her. Allison knew nothing about the resumption of the affair. If the two women were to meet the next day, the consequences could have been dramatic, as you realised. (R v Baden-Clay, 2014)

Justice Byrne said that while Allison was doing her best to save the marriage, her husband continued to betray her and, the evidence suggested, smothered or strangled her when the pressure became too much, driving her body to Kholo Creek, where he disposed of it in an undignified way, dumping her over a ledge to leave her lying in mud, exposed to the elements, insects and wildlife. 'You have insinuated that mental illness may have led to drug overdose or suicide,' he said.

> And besmirching Allison's memory in that way is thoroughly reprehensible. You have no criminal history. But you are definitely not of good character. You are given to lies and other deception: so much so that whatever you may say on any application for parole, 15 years or more hence, will need to be assessed with considerable scepticism . . . You took a devoted, loving mother from her three girls, blighting their lives.

Allison's family and friends cheered. The Baden-Clay family was stunned. Gerard Baden-Clay put his head in his hands, shook uncontrollably and appeared to have trouble breathing.

Within two days, he had appealed his conviction.

Gerard Baden-Clay's background

Embellishment already ran in the family when Gerard Baden-Clay's famous great-grandfather was born in England in the mid-nineteenth century. Two respected biographers (Jeal, 2007; Rosenthal, 1986), found that Robert Baden-Powell's mother, Henrietta, was an extremely socially ambitious woman who exaggerated and lied about family connections to foster her social image and gain financial advantages. She was unrelenting in her aspirations for her children's success and helped some of her seven living children to prosper financially and attain public success through the likes of political position and membership of an exclusive regiment. She once wrote in a letter that she only ever wanted to make new friends if they were 'very choice people indeed' (Jeal, 2007).

Why did they do it?

Lord Robert Baden-Powell became a British hero after the Boer War, and he founded the scouting movement in 1907. But Baden-Powell was a complex character. Both biographers concluded he was most likely homosexual. In school and army concerts he specialised in performing the female roles and had no emotional relationship with a woman until, at the age of forty-seven, he proposed to eighteen-year-old Rose Gough and was turned down. In 1912, aged fifty-five, he married twenty-three-year-old Olave St Clair Soames, confirming in a letter to his mother that the generous dowry offered by Olave's father was part of his motivation for the marriage, as it would enable him to support his mother's lifestyle as well as confer respectability on him as a world youth leader. In those days, it was not unusual for gay men to live closeted lives. Robert and Olave Baden-Clay had three children but slept in separate bedrooms during most of their marriage. Olave made a valuable contribution to both the Scouting and Guiding movement and was of great assistance to Baden-Powell with administration and paperwork and correspondence.

Gerard Baden-Clay's father, Nigel, is Lord Baden-Powell's grandson. Born Nigel Clay to Baden-Powell's daughter Betty, whose married name was Clay, he added 'Baden' to his surname when he moved his family, including wife Elaine and children Gerard, Olivia and Adam, to Australia from Zimbabwe in 1980. Nigel Baden-Clay did not lack confidence and sported number plates on his car reading 'Bwana', Swahili for 'boss' or 'master'. In an online profile, written when he worked for his son's real-estate business, the former financial planner and insurance salesman described himself as an 'avid big game hunter and conservationist'. His profile also highlighted his heritage, suggesting that his personal history made him a desirable dinner party guest and that his role as financial director of one of Century 21's most successful businesses was not surprising given the name made famous by his grandfather Lord Robert Baden-Powell.

Gerard Baden-Clay is a complex and contradictory character. As an adult he used the family name when it suited and was quick to take any road that made life easier for him, promoting an image of himself as successful in every endeavour. He also displayed a sense of entitlement by suing an earlier employer, Flight Centre, for making him redundant, and later borrowed large sums of money from friends and family, most of which he never paid back. Yet his upbringing was largely unremarkable, despite the family's colourful origins. Born in Bournemouth, England, on 9 September 1970, Baden-Clay spent his younger years in Rhodesia (now Zimbabwe). He was ten when his family moved to Australia. They lived in Melbourne for eight months before settling in Toowoomba in 1981. Gerard completed primary school at Gabbinbar State School and attended the all-boys Toowoomba Grammar School until 1987, completing Year 12 with a respectable tertiary entrance score of 900.

Toowoomba Grammar School was a private school with 400 day students and 400 boarders, some from wealthy rural families. A school friend of Baden-Clay recalls that, despite its privilege, their school was 'a great leveller'. After graduating, Baden-Clay, who represented Toowoomba in hockey, completed a Bachelor of Business degree, majoring in accounting and computing, at the Darling Downs Institute of Advanced Education, now the University of Southern Queensland. At the same time, he spent three years with the Army Reserve as a training officer for the University of Queensland's Gatton Regiment. While at high school and university, Baden-Clay supplemented his income chipping onions and picking potatoes and strawberries in the Lockyer Valley and working as a waiter at Squatters restaurant.

At university, he 'did okay', according to his former school-mate, though he got into trouble during his basic training with the Army Reserve for 'snogging one of the female officer cadets'. 'After two weeks of running around the scrub without a shower this was considered a miracle by the other blokes. There were less entertaining ways to lose a day's pay.' This friend finds it hard to reconcile the unassuming student he knew then with what later happened to Allison.

From 1991 to 1993, Baden-Clay, who did not complete his chartered accountant qualification, worked in the audit division of KPMG Peat Marwick. For about twelve months, he worked as a company accountant for Designer Workwear, and from 1994 to 1997 worked at Flight Centre. Later, he worked as an office and recruitment systems manager.

Baden-Clay cried in the witness box as he described meeting his future wife in 1995, when they both worked at Flight Centre in Brisbane. 'I fell in love with her,' he said. 'I fell in love with her pretty well straight away and I had had a couple of girlfriends previously but I felt a level of emotional attachment to Allison that was far deeper than ever before and because of that I knew she was the one.' During their post-marriage travels, Baden-Clay worked in London as a financial systems consultant with Block-buster International for six months while Allison worked with Dale Carnegie Training. He also spent three months as a volunteer in the project department of Kandersteg International Scout Centre in Switzerland and worked as an assistant director of the International Scout Centre for twelve months.

While they were travelling in South America, Allison developed depression as a side effect of the antimalarial drug Lariam. She subsequently required medication on and off, and took the antidepressant Zoloft for a number of years. Baden-Clay claimed that she was sometimes unable to function, but her friends and family insist she coped well and was fine in 2012. The couple returned to Australia in 1999 and in March 2000 Gerard returned to Flight Centre as part of a team attempting to harness online booking technology. They failed and he was made redundant after less than six months. He took legal action against them.

In 2003, Baden-Clay worked at Raine and Horne in Kenmore for ten months, obtaining his real-estate agent's licence in early 2004. He took the job on condition that his parents, Nigel and Elaine, join him. After his employer was reluctant to take on Nigel and Elaine, Baden-Clay agreed to subcontract them so they could work with him. All three ended up leaving after less than a year to start a rival agency – Century 21 Westside – next door. Baden-Clay started as principal and managing director, and retained that position until his 2012 arrest. In the business's early days, Baden-Clay hung a portrait of his famous forebear, Lord Robert Baden-Powell, in the office and embarrassed colleagues by calling his parents Mummy and Daddy (Murray, *The Murder of Allison Baden-Clay*, 2014).

The franchise initially thrived in a strong market. It won a number of minor awards and Baden-Clay took on two business partners, Jocelyn Frost and Phillip Broom, when his parents retired. Baden-Clay's blog boasted that his business embraced superior standards of training and recruitment, while his personal philosophies of ethical excellence and team loyalty were derived from his lineage as Lord Robert Baden-Powell's great-grandson. He also talked about his keen support of the local scouts and girl guides, his contribution to a school chaplaincy service and his involvement in the Chamber of Commerce. The apparently devoted family man even insisted that he enjoyed 'chick flicks'.

At one point, the personable businessman was touted as a future Liberal Party politician. He was friends on Facebook with a number of Liberal MPs, and while Allison was missing former Liberal MP for the Queensland federal seat of Ryan, Michael Johnson, told the *Courier Mail* he thought Baden-Clay was 'definitely a future state government minister'. 'He has a very strong pro-business background and that is the DNA of the Liberal Party.' Others in the party were aware of Baden-Clay's community networks, but didn't believe he was lining up for endorsement (Chamberlin, 2014).

Baden-Clay's image was certainly enhanced by Allison. A former Miss Brisbane and Australian Youth Ballet dancer, she excelled academically and had studied three languages. While in high school, she travelled to Denmark as an exchange student and was deputy head girl in her final year at Ipswich Girls' Grammar School. She also spent a year in Japan teaching English. While at Flight Centre, first in Ipswich and then Brisbane, Allison quickly rose to become human resources manager and then global human resources manager, overseeing three thousand workers in six countries and winning a Young Businesswoman of the Year award. She also worked as a staff recruiter at the International Scout Centre in Switzerland, earned an arts degree majoring in psychology and had started a master's degree.

When Allison had previously been engaged to scuba diver Ian Drayton, whom she met while working on Heron Island, she eventually chose Baden-Clay after some indecision. They settled in the upmarket and semi-rural Brookfield and Allison stayed at home when her children were young. But she sold health products, taught a resilience program at the local school and was in the process of returning to work at her husband's business before she died. In the early years the marriage appeared solid. Allison's friends say she was smitten with her handsome husband, who was confident, eloquent, charming, and 'very convincing'. But some of her friends never warmed to him. To them, he appeared too confident, arrogant, not authentic and too controlling. This control was not as obvious early on but it became apparent to some as time went on (Murray, *The Murder of Allison Baden-Clay*, 2014).

While Allison initially idolised her husband, he increasingly isolated her, criticised her, controlled her finances and cheated. She found this difficult to cope with, more so when her depression recurred. Allison sought professional treatment that made a significant difference to her mood and capacity to cope. Outwardly nothing changed as Baden-Clay continued to cultivate a respectable public image. Appearing personable, self-deprecating and empathic, he wrote glowingly about his family on his blog, which was peppered with personal anecdotes and reflections. When Allison had a week away for her fortieth birthday in 2008, he wrote a 'Mr Mom' piece about his newfound respect for homemakers like his wife.

In reality, the marriage was increasingly troubled and Allison, whose mental health had stabilised, was working hard to save it. Around 2010, Baden-Clay told his wife he no longer loved her. She was devastated but refused to give up. Priscilla later said Allison was always trying to please her husband. She said her daughter was 'very down' after Christmas in 2011 and told her mother she wanted to be a better person. 'Because she wanted to be what Gerard wanted her to be . . . she tried everything she could for that man,' Priscilla said (Baskin, 'Gerard Baden-Clay trial forces shattered families together', 2014).

Allison had always been anxious, even as a child. As a high achiever, she pushed herself in every endeavour, constantly worrying about whether she lived up to her husband's lofty expectations. This was not helped by his attitude to her depression and complaints that her medication was affecting her weight and reducing her libido. While Gerard denied ever hurting Allison physically, Priscilla told police that she once saw bruises on her daughter's body, which could have indicated that he had physically attacked her at least once before. 'I was at Allison's house, Gerard wasn't home,' she said. 'Allison showed me some bruising . . . I have never known Allison to be an easy bruiser' (Calligeros, 'Gerard Baden-Clay, consummate salesman', 2014).

The picture-perfect marriage that Gerard Baden-Clay used to bolster his public image and further his business interests was clearly far from it. He even visited swingers' websites in search of more sexual 'action', using the pseudonym Bruce Overland to describe himself as 'married but don't want to be' and looking for extramarital sex. Then, when the chips were down, he besmirched Toni's name in court, responding with, 'I don't know', when asked if she was involved in Allison's disappearance. He downplayed Toni's role in his life, telling the court that he intended to end their relationship and couldn't even remember her birthday ('The Baden-Clay story', 2014).

Before she died, Allison was beginning to assert herself and planning to return to her husband's office as general manager. In a long letter to her husband written at the end of 2011 – and obtained by Channel 7's *Sunday Night* program – she clearly and calmly articulated her feelings, revealing her despair about his affair and largely blaming herself. But she told him how hurt she felt and how determined she was to make things work. The letter also made it clear that Allison was unhappy that Baden-Clay had been unsympathetic about her depression, disrespectful towards her, selfish and deceitful (Bath, 2014).

Allison made a list of demands, which included a date night, lunch and flowers every week, one Saturday off per month and a weekend every three months. She also asked for support in her counselling and expressed her need for reassurance about her physical appearance. She wanted to be treated with dignity and for her husband to accept that he had to work hard to re-gain her trust.

Far from curled up in foetal position, Allison Baden-Clay was fighting back. But she was not to know that it wouldn't make any difference.

Why did he do it?

Gerard Baden-Clay was a very ordinary businessman who cheated on Allison with at least three other women, controlled and belittled her until she lost all confidence and killed her when she challenged his deceitful behaviour and he saw that he could benefit from her death. It was the ultimate betrayal of a woman who had done nothing but lovingly support him for seventeen years.

Why?

Baden-Clay's life was in freefall, and when everything was about to come crashing down he decided the only way to preserve his carefully crafted – and false – public image and sense of superiority was to kill his wife and make it look like she had taken her own life. As a result of his self-serving actions, his daughters were left without a mother or a father (with him in jail), his mistress's reputation was damaged and his and Allison's family, work colleagues and friends were incredibly bereft and distressed.

Baden-Clay was able to do all this because his pattern of behaviour is consistent with a diagnosis of narcissistic personality disorder (NPD). This led him to display a pervasive pattern of grandiosity, a strong need for admiration, a sense of entitlement, a willingness to exploit others for his own purposes and a lack of empathy for others. He fits into two of Millon's NPD subtypes – elitist and amorous (Millon et al., 2004; see pages 94–95). Like others in the elitist subtype, Baden-Clay desperately wanted to be seen as superior and constantly drew on his family background to highlight that he wasn't just an ordinary person. He shamelessly self-promoted and created a false facade of success and integrity that most people fell for and was prepared to do whatever it took to preserve this 'status'. Baden-Clay's belief in his own superiority meant he ignored the suggestions, advice and concerns of others and created an even greater divide between his self-created false image and reality.

His many affairs, often simultaneous, were also typical of someone who fits into the amorous NPD category. Baden-Clay felt entitled to betray his wife and to charm as many women as he could into a sexual relationship. During his trial he alluded to 'many' affairs on top of the three detailed in court, including one when his wife was pregnant (Murray, 'Accused wife killer Gerard Baden-Clay created web of lies', 2014; Baskin, 'Day 17', 2014). He also deceived Toni McHugh into believing he desired an exclusive long-term relationship with her, behaviour typical of those in the amorous subtype. Essentially, Baden-Clay used all of his affairs to bolster his inflated view of himself. He saw himself as irresistible to women, whom he thought admired his power, success, looks and sexual prowess. He believed he was entitled to exploit as many as he could for his sexual needs and to bask in their admiration and love without giving anything in return. So deluded was he, this average looking man in his gold blazer, described by author David Murray as 'boyishly handsome with soft, almost feminine features', probably even believed that other men envied his looks and so-called seductive powers (Murray, 'Allison Dickie had to choose between two men', 2014).

Baden-Clay even put his need for control ahead of his children's need for healthy development. In his book *The Murder of Allison Baden-Clay*, Murray, who covered the trial for Brisbane's *Courier-Mail*, revealed that Baden-Clay literally controlled his daughters with the use of military-style 'field signals'. Colleagues would see them touch their father on the knee when they entered his office, waiting for a signal before they could speak. When he held his hand to his head the girls would come running. When they were small their father also had a baby monitor in the kitchen while he worked in the garage so he could hear Allison talk to them and their visitors. In court Baden-Clay claimed he had rigged it up in case she needed to call him for help.

An NPD, like all personality disorders, is the result of a combination of genetic and environmental factors. In Baden-Clay's case, both probably contributed. His great-great-grandmother, Henrietta Baden-Powell, mother of Lord Baden-Powell, was obsessed with the social advancement of herself and her children. Evidence suggests Gerard Baden-Clay grew up believing he was special and superior to others, partly due to these family connections. This may have interacted with what appears to be a genetic predisposition for a deficit in emotional empathy. In the end, Baden-Clay's arrogance and grandiose self-illusions became boundless – until the facade started to crumble.

People with personality disorders are less resilient than others and, because they don't tend to learn from their mistakes, they keep repeating the same maladaptive behaviours. Given the mess he had created for himself, Baden-Clay's lack of insight, resilience and empathy set him on a path to disaster. That fateful night, Toni McHugh had already inflicted a narcissistic injury upon him when she confronted him about not telling Allison they would be at the same conference the next day. Allison's angry criticism was a second blow to his self-image and proved to be too much. He then lashed out in a narcissistic rage and decided to kill her, stage it as a suicide and turn the situation to his advantage. Maintaining his image in the eyes of others was always the only thing that really mattered to him.

In stark contrast to his actions, honesty and integrity were topics Baden-Clay constantly revisited in his blogs, his company profiles and in his capacity as a real-estate industry leader. In a story published while Allison was still missing, the *Courier-Mail*'s Kate Kyriacou referred to an interview he gave in 2008.

'In business, it's simple: never lie,' Baden-Clay reportedly told the paper. 'For starters, it's the wrong thing to do but secondly you will always get caught out and usually when you least expect it. There are just too many people, too many personalities, too many trails . . . and too much to lose' (Kyriacou, 2012).

Gerard Baden-Clay should have taken heed of his own advice as well as that of his famous forebear, Lord Baden-Powell, who urged others to leave the world a better place than they found it. Baden-Powell's great-grandson could not have moved further away from this admirable ethos.

GERARD BADEN-CLAY DIAGNOSTIC CHART

Using DSM 5 indicators (APA, 2013), when five or more of these are present, a diagnosis of narcissistic personality disorder (NPD) can be made	Examples of Gerard Baden-Clay's behaviour that appear to be consistent with each indicator
Has a grandiose sense of self-importance (e.g. exaggerates achievements and talents, expects to be recognized as superior without commensurate achievements).	His whole life was a facade; he had few assets and the business was going badly. Used his position in the Chamber of Commerce to boost his importance. Put wife Allison down and told others he had to 'look after her', making himself appear superior.
Is preoccupied with fantasies of unlimited success, power, brilliance, beauty or ideal love.	Believed that he was the 'best' according to his blog and school talks. Criticised other agents on his blog, accusing them of underhand tactics.
Believes that he or she is 'special' and unique and can only be understood by, or should associate with, other special or high-status people (or institutions).	Associated with local MP Bruce Flegg. Was Facebook friends with several Liberal MPs. Joined the Chamber of Commerce in order to mix with important and influential businesspeople.

Using DSM 5 indicators (APA, 2013), when five or more of these are present, a diagnosis of narcissistic personality disorder (NPD) can be made	Examples of Gerard Baden-Clay's behaviour that appear to be consistent with each indicator
Requires excessive admiration.	Used his blog to talk up his character and achievements. Had several affairs going at the same time and advertised for sex on a 'swingers' site. Put Allison down so she lost self-confidence and allowed him to take control and be 'the boss'.
Has a sense of entitlement (i.e. unreasonable expectations of especially favorable treatment or automatic compliance with his or her expectations).	Used his family links to Lord Robert Baden-Powell to boost his public image. Expected Allison to do everything his way and put his needs first. Expected mistress Toni McHugh to promote his needs above her own. Paid himself a large salary from the company despite poor performance.
Is interpersonally exploitative (i.e. takes advantage of others to achieve his or her own ends).	Claimed he only kept sleeping with Toni McHugh because of the business and said in court that he told her whatever she wanted to hear. Borrowed money and never paid it back. Admitted that he was a man who would say anything to avoid the consequences of his actions.

Using DSM 5 indicators (APA, 2013), when five or more of these are present, a diagnosis of narcissistic personality disorder (NPD) can be made	Examples of Gerard Baden-Clay's behaviour that appear to be consistent with each indicator
	Was prepared to kill his wife to solve his perceived problems.
Lacks empathy: is unwilling to recognize or identify with the feelings and needs of others.	Juggled at least three affairs. Totally ignored Allison's needs. Belittled Allison during their marriage and spoke about her in a derogatory fashion after her 'supposed' disappearance. Disposed of her body in an undignified way and showed no remorse for what he did to her. Was prepared to leave his daughters without a mother. Kept telling Toni McHugh he was leaving his wife but never did.
Is often envious of others or believes that others are envious of him or her.	
Shows arrogant, haughty behaviors or attitudes. * Reprinted with permission from the Diagnostic and Statistical Manual of Mental Disorders, Fifth Edition, (Copyright ©2013). American Psychiatric Association. All Rights Reserved.	Bragged about his time as president of the Kenmore and District Chamber of Commerce, vice-president of the Brookfield State School PandC volunteer group and a kindergarten board member. Complained on his blog about the unethical conduct of some other real-estate agents.

CHAPTER 5

ROGER DEAN

The cast
Roger Dean: The killer
Dean French: Roger Dean's ex-partner, with whom he was still sharing a unit at the time of the killings
Peter Arnold: Roger Dean's neighbour
Luneta Mateo: Quakers Hill Nursing Home clinical manager
Deepa Kunwar: Agency nurse
Lang Reid: Roger Dean's Bible studies teacher/friend
Rev Geoff Bates: Quakers Hill Anglican Church senior minister

The motive
Roger Dean was desperate to cover up evidence of his theft of prescription medication from the nursing home where he worked as a registered nurse. If found guilty of theft, he would be deregistered as a nurse and, despite having nearly completed a law degree, be prevented from practising as a lawyer.

Introduction

Roger Dean was impulsive. The Vietnamese-born Sydney nurse once had a pattern tattooed around his belly button, only to declare three weeks later that he no longer wanted it and start laser treatment at a local shopping centre to have it removed. He also spent money he didn't have and expected others to drop everything when he wanted company. Peter Arnold, Dean's former neighbour, remembers him as friendly but self-absorbed. Most conversations usually ended up revolving around him. 'It was more focused on him; me, me, me,' Peter says, noting that, after some initial flattery, Dean was quick to bring the conversation back to himself.

Dean, a registered nurse who worked at Quakers Hill Nursing Home as a night shift nursing manager on Wednesday and Thursday nights, was generally friendly to his neighbours but occasionally lost his temper. Peter once saw him overreact when someone parked in a no-standing area outside the shop of his ex-partner, Dean French. Rather than simply ask them to move, Dean started yelling. 'He [verbally] abused the person,' Peter says. 'It was way over the top. He's done that a few times to people as I understand it.'

Dean had developed an addiction to prescription medication following a car accident. He also had relationship and money problems. He was separated from French, but they still lived together. At one point, Dean told his neighbour he was $80,000 in debt, which Peter did not doubt was due to Dean's tendency to waste money. After crashing his car, despite the debt, Dean purchased a new Ford, which would have cost at least $25,000, if not substantially more. 'He came to me and said, "Do you like my new car?"' Peter recalls. 'My first thought was: "How can you afford something like that when you're in extensive debt?" To me it just seemed pretty odd. There were some real issues

167

going on in his life. A couple of times I really wondered how he was going to deal with [them].'

Another time, Peter was gardening at the front of the units when Dean asked him to go out for lunch. Peter declined because he had already eaten and, being on a limited income, saw going out for lunch as a luxury, but Dean persisted and Peter relented, partly because he knew Dean was depressed to some degree and probably needed someone to talk to. When they arrived at the Vietnamese restaurant, Peter was shocked when Dean ordered dishes totalling about $45. 'That was his impulsiveness,' Peter says. 'He would do things, but he didn't really think through the consequences. I don't think he thought it through.' According to Peter, Dean was often impulsive and 'over the top'. French once came home to find no bread in their unit and voiced his displeasure. After an argument, Dean went to the shops and returned with seventeen loaves.

But never did Peter think his neighbour's eccentric behaviour would turn sinister. 'He seemed very odd on occasion,' he says. '[But] he was pretty friendly with me. It's not like you think . . . "he's going to commit a murder".'

But Roger Dean is a mass murderer.

That impulsive nature and chronic self-focus compelled him to light several fires at Quakers Hill Nursing Home to cover up his theft of prescription painkilling medication from the nursing home's medicine storage room. Those fires on 18 November 2011, killed eleven elderly nursing home residents and injured another eight, causing untold pain to their families and nursing home staff. Three more residents died after Dean was charged, taking the total fatalities to fourteen. At the time Dean tried to blame his actions on the devil, telling police that he loved the residents but it was like Satan had told him he should do it (Hoerr, 2013).

After initial denials, Dean confessed to lighting the fires when it became obvious he was responsible. He said he hadn't realised the blaze would take hold, despite lighting one fire in a room with two empty beds and another in a room where two residents slept. When cornered, he admitted using a colleague's cigarette lighter to set the fires as a distraction. He told police he wanted to start a fire and the empty bed just happened to be there.

It was a desperate act with horrendous consequences and gave Roger Dean the distinction of being the worst mass murderer in New South Wales history.

The lead-up to the crime

Roger Dean lived in the outer western Sydney suburb of Quakers Hill with his former partner, Dean French. Their unit was in a complex of neat single-level orange-brick 1970s-style dwellings just 500 metres from Quakers Hill Nursing Home, where Dean began working the night shift two nights a week in September 2011. The nursing home and the Quakers Hill Anglican Church, where Dean had been part of a Bible study group, were both an easy walk from where he lived.

At the time of the crime, in November 2011, thirty-five-year-old Dean had been working at the nursing home for two months, after leaving another aged-care facility under a cloud. He told Peter Arnold he was victimised by a manager, but did not reveal much more. 'He said he had some falling-out with one of the managers,' Peter says. 'He was painting that he was the victim, obviously from his point of view.'

In the months before the fatal fire, Dean told friends in his Bible study group that he was gay and worried about the possible fallout. Lang Reid, who befriended Dean in 2010 when he was referred to classes she and her husband ran, told his sentencing hearing that he stopped seeing her family about three months before the crime. After he came out as gay, Dean was concerned that Lang would tell the other parishioners and worried that others were gossiping about him (Gardiner, 2013).

Dean was also stressed and anxious when he needed hospital treatment after a car accident. Lang worried that he was depressed and possibly suicidal when Dean talked about suicide in his Bible study class (Gardiner, 2013).

Partly as a result of his car accident, Dean had become addicted to prescription medication. On the night before the fires, Wednesday, 16 November, he was caught on CCTV footage entering the nursing home's treatment room multiple times. The Schedule 8 medications (S8), which are drugs of addiction, were stored there and dispensed using strict protocols. These included that both the registered nurse on duty and an assistant nurse be present when S8 drugs were collected and dispensed. A written entry also had to be made in the Drug Register each time an S8 medication was collected, showing the time and date, who collected it, the name of the patient and why they needed it. Each entry also required the signature of the registered nurse on duty and the assistant nurse who helped. This Drug Register was kept with the S8 drugs in a locked cupboard in the treatment room.

By the end of his shift at 7 am on Thursday, 17 November, Dean had stolen 237 Endone tablets (oxycodene) and one capsule of the morphine drug Kapanol. At about 7.30 pm on 17 November, the nursing staff who audited the S8 drugs discovered that a lot of medication was missing (R v Dean, 2013).

The clinical manager, Luneta Mateo, was called in and conducted a re-audit of the S8 medications, confirming the missing drugs. At about 10 pm she rang the Quakers Hill police station to report them missing. When Dean arrived for work at 10.23 pm that Thursday, nurse Deepa Kunwar told him that police were coming to interview everyone about the previous night's drug theft. Mateo had instantly suspected Dean, as it was the first such incident and he had just joined her staff. But the nursing home was desperate for a registered nurse who would work those night shifts and she needed to be cautious about jumping to conclusions.

When two police officers arrived at around midnight, Mateo gave them a partial report but the officers were called away after seventeen minutes to attend an unrelated and more urgent domestic violence incident elsewhere. Mateo then reviewed CCTV footage from the previous night, which showed Dean entering the treatment room and locking the door behind him thirty-six times. An hour or so before Dean started the fires on the morning of Friday, 18 November, she rang the police again and asked them to send over an officer, but they advised her to go home as it was the end of her shift. She locked the stolen pills' blister packs, CCTV footage, audit documents and computer records relating to the theft in the manager's office, to which only she and the facilities manager had the key. It remained locked until a police officer opened it after the fire. Mateo left at 3.43 am. Police did phone back later, at around 4.50 am but decided not to attend as the manager was not there. No-one could possibly have predicted what happened next.

At 5 am, Mateo was called at her home and told the nursing home was ablaze. She later said staff had had a gut feeling something terrible was about to happen before she left. They hadn't wanted her to leave and she had spoken to a police officer, but was told to go home as she was overtired and emotional (Marcus, 2013).

Nursing assistant Lence Darley later told the Coroner's Court that she had complained about Dean three times, including on his final shift before the fire. Although she was worried about her patients, Darley could not imagine a registered nurse stealing medication and then starting a fire (Crawford, 'Supervisor knew Roger Dean had stolen painkillers', 2014).

The murders

The sun had not yet risen on the morning of Friday, 18 November 2011 when Roger Dean, who was on duty as the night nurse manager with three assistant nurses/carers, in charge of eighty-eight residents, many of whom suffered from dementia, committed his deadly act. He encouraged two of the nursing assistants to take an unscheduled break, stole a cigarette lighter and lit two fires, the first at 4.53 am, in an empty room, and the second at 5.02 am, in a room where two elderly residents slept. He disposed of the lighter in a bathroom sanitary bin. The automated fire alarm went off at 4.53 am and the first Fire and Rescue officers arrived at 4.59 am. Staff directed them to the fire in room 19 in A2 wing, and the officers extinguished the fire. But they were unaware of the second fire, which was in A1 wing, and it quickly took hold.

Chaos ensued, with black smoke billowing from the windows and residents in a state of panic. More than one hundred firefighters fought the blaze while they and others desperately tried to rescue immobile residents, some of whom were bedridden. Many residents were wheeled or walked to a makeshift triage centre out the front, but others succumbed to the smoke and flames.

Dean was filmed encouraging some elderly patients to leave the building. But he initially walked past the room where he had lit the second fire, ignoring the pleas of another resident to save those inside, who could not escape on their own. After the woman implored him to get them out, he grabbed her arm and told her not to worry as others were on their way to save them. Both the residents in that room would die. As emergency services, staff and neighbours evacuated the building, Dean was again caught on camera, watching the horrific scene with no obvious emotion, almost as if he were fascinated by the drama he had caused. He was also seen watching the clean-up from a police mobile command centre across the road.

In sentencing Dean, Justice Megan Latham recounted how he then selfishly diverted the attention of several firefighters from extinguishing the flames and rescuing residents as he attempted to reach the office containing evidence of his drug theft, which he had lit the fires to cover. The Drug Register was still in the treatment room when the fires started.

Between 5.20 am and 6.10 am, the offender made three concerted efforts to enter the nursing home through the front doors. On each occasion he was rebuffed by a Fire Brigade officer or police officer. On the last occasion the offender said to a Fire Brigade officer, 'I need to go inside to get the drug books, I need to get in there.' The offender showed a Fire Brigade officer the two lanyards that operated locks to the treatment room and the cabinet. The offender was given permission to enter the building and retrieve the drug books.

The offender accompanied two fire fighters into the building and went with them to the treatment room. He gave the keys to one of the officers, explained the location of the cabinet and described the two books. He said, 'We need them. We need to get these out.'

The offender remained in the corridor away from the treatment room and outside the scope of the CCTV cameras. When the Fire officers were unable to open the door they invited the offender to assist. The offender appeared reluctant and complained that he was an

asthmatic. He ultimately approached and unlocked
the door to the treatment room, entered the room and
unlocked the S8 drug cabinet. He removed two drug
register books, put them into a yellow shoulder bag and
left the building. He said, 'I need to go home, I need to get
Ventolin. I live close by and I really need my Ventolin.'
(R v Dean, 2013)

As he left the building and was confronted by a TV camera crew,
Dean had the gall to claim some credit for the rescue effort. His
image was beamed across Australia as he portrayed himself as a
hero. 'I'm Roger and I'm one of the nurses and just, there was
a fire and I just quickly just did what I can to get everyone out
and the smoke is just overwhelming but you know we got a lot
of people out so that's the main thing,' he said (Cooper, 2013).
Dean then went home, tore up the two S8 registers and disposed
of them in a rubbish bin some distance away.

As the investigation began into the cause of the fire, suspicion
soon fell on the new nurse, who had been captured on CCTV
footage stealing strong prescription medications the previous
night. At 7.50 pm on the night after the fire, Roger Dean was
arrested and cautioned. At 9.50 pm he confessed. Dean told
police he was having severe nightmares, had been suffering from
depression for two years and had attempted suicide 'by taking
a lot of medication all at once'. He had been taking the antidepressants Aropax and Lovan (both SSRI medications) and the
antipsychotic Seroquel, but had taken only Lovan before the fires
(R v Dean, 2013).

While acknowledging the consequences of his actions, Dean
appeared not to grasp the gravity of what he had done. He
insisted that all he had wanted to do was create a diversion from
his theft; he had no idea the fires would be so serious. He said he

loved the residents and felt terrible that so many had been killed or injured. Speaking dispassionately, he told police that he had used a cigarette lighter to set fire to an empty bed for no particular reason. When the fire spread quickly and unexpectedly, he got scared (Bibby, 2013). But Dean managed to light a second fire in a room where two elderly women slept before leaving. He said he did not look back to see how the fire was progressing as it was small when he lit it, but once it took hold he tried to make amends by helping residents to escape.

Dean told police that the devil was to blame for his conduct. He said he felt evil and corrupted by evil thoughts that compelled him to act. Dean claimed that he was under spiritual attack and as a result had brought his Bible to read at work. At home, he said he was also having nightmares (Bibby, 2013).

In November 2012, Dean pleaded not guilty to eleven counts of murder and eight of recklessly causing grievous bodily harm. He had asked to plead guilty to manslaughter, but that was rejected by the Crown.

The sentencing

At some point in the lead-up to his trial, Roger Dean decided to change his plea. On what was expected to be the first day of a four-week trial in June 2013, he pleaded guilty to eleven charges of murder and eight counts of recklessly causing grievous bodily harm by lighting two fires at Quakers Hill Nursing Home. Victims' relatives cried and comforted each other as he answered 'guilty' to each charge. It meant they would not face a lengthy and painful trial.

The sentencing hearing, before Supreme Court Justice Megan Latham, heard of Dean's nervousness in the lead-up to the crime after co-workers reported the theft of 238 S8 tablets and the police were notified. CCTV footage showed him entering the treatment room thirty-six times on his last shift before the fires. Staff had then sealed the empty blister packs so police could test them for fingerprints. Late on the night of Dean's final shift, overnight on 17–18 November, two police officers who had arrived to investigate the theft were called to a domestic violence incident, but said they would return soon to question all staff. A colleague noticed Dean's hands shaking as he heard about this (R v Dean, 2013).

Dean French told the sentencing hearing that he had been concerned about his ex-partner's recent strange behaviour, including sleepwalking and becoming forgetful. He was also worried about Roger Dean taking too many different prescription medications. French said Dean would sometimes ring him, apparently unaware that he had already called moments before. On several occasions, after visiting French at his shop, Dean would occasionally return about forty-five minutes later, and have no memory of the previous visit. He also purchased items he did not need, such as crutches. In December 2010 he had bought jewellery from a street vendor and later said he couldn't remember buying it. He ordered legal textbooks by phone, but couldn't recall the conversation.

The court heard that despite his personal issues, Roger Dean was intelligent and well educated. Psychiatrist Michael Diamond found that he had a narcissistic personality that led him to over-focus on his own needs and crown prosecutor Mark Tedeschi QC said this narcissistic history meant that Dean would continue to put his own needs above the rights of others. The only appropriate sentence was therefore life in jail (Wells, 2013).

On 1 August 2013, Justice Latham sentenced Dean to life in jail with no parole, adding that his crimes were in the 'worst case category' and what little remorse he appeared to have shown was qualified by narcissistic attempts to hide his wrongdoing. She acknowledged Dean's difficult upbringing, estrangement from his family and a violent sexual assault at the hands of two men when he was a teenager, but added there was 'no evidence the offender was unable to appreciate . . . the wrongfulness of his actions'.

> The pain and terror experienced by all the victims must have been horrific. For those who were unable to move independently and who faced the prospect of being burned alive, or suffocated by smoke, a worse fate is difficult to imagine. The family members of the victims who lingered on in hospital, only to die days or weeks later, endured the distress of watching their loved ones succumb to burns and respiratory failure. Those who lived no doubt have a compromised quality of life because of their injuries. One of these victims required skin grafts and surgery, a number were intubated because of the effects of smoke inhalation and all of them suffered complications such as infections, myocardial injury, pneumonia and renal failure. (R v Dean, 2013)

Justice Latham said Dean's capacity to control his emotions was compromised by his personality disorder, which meant he put his own needs first when making decisions. 'However, in my view, that relatively limited impairment, particularly when considered against the scale of the offender's reckless indifference, the enormity of the harm which resulted and the objective criminality of the offender's conduct, carries limited weight in reducing the offender's culpability to any material degree,' she found (R v Dean, 2013).

Dean showed no emotion as he was sentenced to spend the rest of his life in jail. Victims' relatives gasped and applauded, while two observers hurled abuse at him.

A 2014 coronial inquest heard that three more people died after the original death toll was established, taking the final count to fourteen. Dean may also have lied about how many fires he lit. An investigator found that in one of the rooms where Dean said he'd lit one fire, it had spread too fast to have had only one source (Bibby, 'Dean might have lit three fires', 2014).

Even in confessing, this man found it hard to tell the truth.

Roger Dean's background

Born in Vietnam, Roger Dean was an infant when he came to Australia with his mother and three siblings as refugees. His father reportedly died while trying to flee at a later date.

Dean realised he was gay from a young age. He was often bullied and socially isolated at school. In his mid-teens he was reportedly sexually abused by two adult men, with one incident involving violence. Dean had an open homosexual relationship when he was eighteen, which led to a rift with his mother. As an adult, he had very little contact with his siblings and a difficult relationship with his mother.

Despite his personal difficulties, Dean graduated in 1996 from the University of Sydney with a bachelor of nursing degree. Between May 1997 and July 2007, he worked as a registered nurse in various positions, including at the St George Hospital Mental Health Unit and St John of God Burwood Hospital's Aged Care Unit. Dean started a Macquarie University law degree in 2004, which he studied part-time while working and had almost finished when he joined the Quakers Hill Nursing Home as a registered nurse in early September 2011. He was one subject away from completing the degree when he went to jail and claimed to have achieved high distinctions and won a university prize for ethics (Wells, 2013).

Dean had been very successful in gaining a place in two prestigious university courses, completing one and nearly completing the other. But Justice Latham noted that maintaining his nursing commitments and university studies resulted in difficult work relationships and disputes with colleagues. 'It is also reasonable to assume that the offender's shift work and study resulted in poor sleeping patterns, which in turn exacerbated the offender's misuse of prescription medications,' she said (R v Dean, 2013).

The 2014 coronial inquest heard that Dean had a history of trouble at his previous workplaces. He was the prime suspect in 2007 when paint was thrown onto the car of St George Mental Health nurse manager Tracey Sheehan. Dean had begun 'stalking' Sheehan after she caught him falsifying medication records. He followed her around with a note pad to record her behaviour, once following her and another nurse to a cafe (Hall, 2014). She then noticed damage to her car. Sheehan said she became suspicious when she twice found identical bolts screwed into one of her tyres. When white paint was poured over her car, she was convinced Dean was responsible. After she reported her suspicions to management, Dean resigned (Crawford, 'Nursing home killer', 2014).

Dean worked part-time in the Aged Care Unit at the St John of God Burwood Hospital from 2000–2011 and also left that position under a cloud. He was once sent home from a morning shift because he was lethargic and could not fulfil his duties. Dean told his boss he had bipolar disorder and had recently changed his antidepressant medication, which had caused side effects. He returned to work after his GP gave him the all-clear, but resigned about three months later after making a complaint about another registered nurse (Hall, 2014).

Dean doctored his CV to avoid revealing the previous work incidents when he applied for the position of night shift nursing manager at Quakers Hill Nursing Home. According to the CV he submitted with his application, he had spent the past four years working at the local Cheesecake Shop (owned by Dean French) and his only referees were French and a supervisor from a nursing job he had had fourteen years earlier (Bibby, 'Nursing home did not check Roger Dean's CV', 2014).

Dean's personal life was as chequered as his employment history. From late 2006 until he went to jail, he lived with Dean French. At one point they broke up, but continued to live together. In March 2008, a friend died by suicide, which distressed Dean and escalated his misuse of prescription drugs. He built up his stockpile of medication by 'doctor shopping', moving to a new doctor when one became reluctant to prescribe any more drugs (R v Dean, 2013).

Dean was diagnosed with a polysubstance abuse disorder, but was in remission when sentenced in 2013. He had started taking benzodiazepines for irritable bowel syndrome, but by 2007 he was taking it as a sedative rather than for the prescribed purpose. At the time of the fires, Dean was taking about fifteen tablets per day, including sleeping tablets in the morning when he finished a night shift. His collection of medications at home included forty-three different prescription drugs, including sleeping tablets, anti-anxiety medication, antidepressants, painkillers, antipsychotic medication, antihistamines, antibiotics, decongestants, penicillin and medications for irritable bowel syndrome, nausea, high blood pressure and asthma.

Dean had also begun to sleepwalk and attempted to fit a latch on his bedroom door so he could be locked in at night. He once ended up outside Peter Arnold's home in the middle of the night, knocking on the door several times. Peter recalls, 'I said, "Roger, you're sleepwalking." He came to my door and asked me a really weird question. It was a really odd sort of thing to do. He only spoke a few lines. He was like a zombie. I said, "Roger, go back to bed."'

Justice Latham found that Dean's actions in lighting the fires were largely due to the intransigence of his personality disorder and its narcissistic features:

> The reckless indifference to human life exhibited by the offender by lighting the fires does not, in my opinion, arise because of diminished capacity to make decisions and carry them out. It arises from his personality disorder and not from an impairment of thinking or capacity to think clearly. The depth of the offender's remorse, such as it was expressed to others and not to the Court, is difficult to gauge, principally because the offender's capacity for insight into his offending is compromised by his personality disorder. That lack of insight and gross preoccupation with his own interests may abate with time and maturity. (R v Dean, 2013)

Despite Dean's eccentricity, Peter Arnold was shocked when told he had lit the fatal fires, but on reflection Peter was not surprised by the impulsive nature of the crime and the lack of consideration given to the consequences. This fitted the pattern of Dean's behaviour leading up to the crime. Anglican minister Geoff Bates, who knew Dean as a church parishioner, was similarly surprised and told the *Sydney Morning Herald* that Dean was loud, needy and disorganised but did not appear to be a bad person. Rev. Bates was surprised by Dean's actions in lighting the fire, having never seen him as a dangerous or harmful person (Slattery, 2014).

In the lead-up to the fire, Dean had begun to disconnect from the church.

Why did he do it?

Roger Dean's motive in lighting the fires was to protect himself from being charged with the medication theft. For some time, he had succeeded in obtaining a range of prescription drugs, to which he had become addicted, by 'doctor shopping'. He had visited many different doctors, who prescribed them without realising others had done the same. As a nurse, Dean was able to create believable stories about his supposed ill-health. At some point, possibly because this was not working as well anymore, he decided to steal drugs from his workplace. He knew police had been notified of the theft and realised that if he was convicted he would be deregistered and unable to work as a nurse for some time. Nor could he realise his dream of becoming a lawyer after he graduated if he had a conviction of this kind. Desperate for a solution, Dean decided that he had to destroy the evidence, regardless of the cost to others.

That evidence included CCTV footage of him entering the treatment room thirty-six times, records of the two S8 audits conducted following the theft, and the empty blister packs that had contained the stolen drugs and could be fingerprinted. The evidence was locked in the office of the Facility Manager, who was responsible for the nursing home's day-to-day operations. The Drug Register, which showed significant irregularities, was in the drug cupboard in the locked treatment room. Dean had keys for the treatment room and cabinet, but not the manager's office. The coroner later suggested that he may have hoped that the fires would destroy the evidence, but, if that didn't happen, they would at least create a distraction enabling him to access the drug cupboard to retrieve and destroy the register. But his plan was doomed to fail.

Dean falsely believed that he was so much smarter than others and could cover his tracks without arousing suspicion. But he didn't think the situation through and became reckless. Dean understood the S8 protocols, but still stole 238 tablets in a very short period of time. Even though he managed to convince fire officers to help him access the treatment room and retrieve the Drug Register, he didn't anticipate the other evidence. He must have been aware of the likelihood of CCTV footage of his trips to the treatment room the previous night, and knew about the daily S8 drug audits. Destroying the Drug Register would not have solved his 'problem' but he clearly thought it would.

Roger Dean's plan was never going to work because he has a personality disorder that distorted his thinking and reduced his capacity to empathise or care about the potential damage and harm his actions could cause others.

Forensic psychiatrist Dr Michael Diamond concluded that Dean had a mixed type personality disorder with a combination of both narcissistic and histrionic traits. However it seems more likely that his behaviour pattern is consistent with his having a primary narcissistic personality disorder (NPD) with some minor histrionic features, such as displays of self-dramatisation and theatricality, exaggerated expression of emotions and attention-seeking behaviour. Dean's primary NPD is apparent in his grandiosity, sense of superiority and entitlement as well as his need for admiration and refusal to accept negative feedback or criticism. His limited concern or empathy for the people in his life, be they family, friends, work colleagues or nursing home residents is also typical of someone with an NPD.

Dean also fits into the compensatory NPD subtype (Millon et al., 2004; see pages 94–95). Those in this category have suffered wounds early in life, such as a traumatic or severely disadvantaged childhood and try to 'compensate' by seeking status, recognition and prestige through succeeding in ways such as gaining qualifications or awards, becoming a celebrity, becoming wealthy or working in a high-status job.

Roger Dean's life was marked by a strong desire to 'achieve something' and be seen as someone special. He desperately wanted people to think he was a high achiever worthy of admiration. In many ways he was. However, his growing addiction to very strong (and mixed) prescription medication and combining them in a dangerous way proved disastrous and exaggerated his tendency to keep making very bad choices. Dean overestimated his medical knowledge and thought he was clever enough to manage all the medication he was taking. He knew that if he was convicted of the medication theft he would lose his registration as a nurse and be unable to work in the legal field. He was clearly desperate.

His personality disorder also made it difficult for him to learn from his mistakes and find more resilient ways to cope, so he continued making bad choices. Ultimately, Dean was motivated more by the desire to preserve his own self-image than by the safety and welfare of others and, consequently, inflicted an unprecedented level of pain, distress, loss and grief on many vulnerable people and their loved ones.

Such cases are often rich in irony and this one is no exception. Dean had tried to make a better life for himself after arriving in Australia as a refugee. Despite a difficult childhood, he had become a registered nurse and was studying law, which could have led to a lucrative and fulfilling legal career with status and future opportunities. Instead, his crime will no doubt become one of the perplexing case studies that those studying law, which he once did, are asked to research and discuss.

ROGER DEAN
DIAGNOSTIC CHART

Diagnosed (in court) with a mixed personality disorder with narcissistic and histrionic traits by forensic psychiatrist Dr Michael Diamond.

Using DSM 5 indicators (APA, 2013), when five or more of these are present, a diagnosis of narcissistic personality disorder (NPD) can be made	Examples of Roger Dean's behaviour that appear to be consistent with each indicator
Has a grandiose sense of self-importance (e.g. exaggerates achievements and talents, expects to be recognized as superior without commensurate achievements).	Tried to present himself to others as a successful registered nurse, but was addicted to drugs and had left two earlier jobs as a result of a variety of incidents related to drug use, incompetence and stalking a superior who had disciplined him. Expected his neighbour to drop everything and go out to lunch with him.
Is preoccupied with fantasies of unlimited success, power, brilliance, beauty or ideal love.	Purchased things he couldn't afford that made him look successful (e.g. a new car), despite owing $80,000. Studied for a law degree so he could enter a prestigious profession.
Believes that he or she is 'special' and unique and can only be understood by, or should associate with, other special or high-status people (or institutions).	

Using DSM 5 indicators (APA, 2013), when five or more of these are present, a diagnosis of narcissistic personality disorder (NPD) can be made	Examples of Roger Dean's behaviour that appear to be consistent with each indicator
Requires excessive admiration.	When talking to other people, such as his neighbour, the conversation was always refocused back on him and his purchases and achievements.
	Purchased things he couldn't afford so that he looked good, such as expensive lunches, a new car and expensive legal textbooks that he could have borrowed from the library.
Has a sense of entitlement (i.e. unreasonable expectations of especially favorable treatment or automatic compliance with his or her expectations).	Found it very difficult to handle being criticised. He took offence after being disciplined in a previous job, and stalked and harassed the senior colleague involved before damaging her car.
Is interpersonally exploitative (i.e. takes advantage of others to achieve his or her own ends).	Forensic psychiatrist Dr Michael Diamond concluded that Dean had the ability to ingratiate himself and to manipulate people to accept his dysfunctional conduct.
	Borrowed and crashed other people's cars.

Using DSM 5 indicators (APA, 2013), when five or more of these are present, a diagnosis of narcissistic personality disorder (NPD) can be made	Examples of Roger Dean's behaviour that appear to be consistent with each indicator
	Stole prescription medication from his employer to feed his addiction once his 'doctor-shopping' was recognised and he was no longer able to get prescriptions.
Lacks empathy: is unwilling to recognize or identify with the feelings and needs of others.	More concerned with his need to protect himself than to prevent loss of life. Told a nursing home resident who wanted to save two others on their way out from the fire that they would be okay, despite knowing they were immobile. Both died.
Is often envious of others or believes that others are envious of him or her.	
Shows arrogant, haughty behaviors or attitudes. * Reprinted with permission from the Diagnostic and Statistical Manual of Mental Disorders, Fifth Edition, (Copyright ©2013). American Psychiatric Association. All Rights Reserved.	Abused a person who parked in the no-standing zone near his ex-partner's shop in an 'over-the-top' way.

CHAPTER 6

KELI LANE

The cast

Keli Lane: Tegan's mother and murderer

Baby girl, TR: Born to Keli Lane in 1995 and adopted out. Father later identified as a boyfriend Lane had had before Duncan Gillies

Tegan Lane: Born to Keli Lane on 12 September 1996; disappeared two days later. No father has been identified

Baby boy, AJ: Born to Keli Lane in 1999 and adopted out. The father was a friend of Lane's brother

Baby girl, BL: The only baby Lane kept was born in 2001

Robert and Sandra Lane: Lane's parents

Morgan Lane: Lane's younger brother

Aaron Tyack: High school boyfriend of Lane and father of her first terminated pregnancy

Duncan Gillies: Lane's partner from 1994–1998. He may have fathered Tegan

Andrew Norris/Morris: Lane claimed he fathered Tegan and that she gave him the baby, but Norris/Morris and Tegan have never been found

John Borovnik: Child protection officer who discovered Tegan was missing, sparking a murder investigation

Virginia Fung: Social worker

Keli Lane's husband: Fathered her fourth full-term child, but later divorced Lane

Patrick Cogan: Lane's partner during her court case

The pregnancies

1992: Keli Lane terminated her first pregnancy when she was still in high school by agreement with her then boyfriend, Aaron Tyack

1994: Lane secretly terminated a second pregnancy; she had told no family or friends about it

1995: Lane had a baby girl, dubbed TR, adopting her out; she told no family or friends

12 September 1996: Lane had Tegan, who disappeared two days later; no family or friends were aware of the pregnancy or birth

1999: Lane had a baby boy, AJ, and adopted him out; she told no family or friends

2001: Lane had a daughter, whom she kept; the father was the man she was living with and later married

The motive

An elite water polo player, Keli Lane did not want the responsibilities that came with having a child and wanted to preserve her 'golden girl' image. Women's water polo was to be included for the first time at the 2000 Olympics, and she wanted to be unencumbered in order to maximise her chances of being selected for the team. In addition, Lane wanted to maintain her carefree lifestyle of socialisation and sexual activity and keep her position at Ravenswood School for Girls, where she had just signed a new employment contract starting in October 1996.

Introduction

If Tegan Lane were alive today, chances are she'd be tanned and fit like her mother, a talented sportswoman who represented Australia as a water polo junior. Tegan would probably be enjoying an outdoor lifestyle on Sydney's northern beaches, maybe studying at university and hanging out with friends like her mother did as a teenager. Like most young adults in this relatively affluent part of Australia's largest city, she would have the world at her feet.

If she were alive today.

Tegan Lane was a tiny, helpless two-day-old when she died on 14 September 1996 – at the hands of her mother. Keli Lane killed her baby simply because she was a source of embarrassment and an inconvenience. The then twenty-one-year-old, who had already terminated two pregnancies and adopted out a baby, did not have a place for Tegan in her life. Her solution was to dispose of her daughter in an unknown location and spin a web of lies to cover her tracks.

This could have been the perfect crime if Keli Lane had learned from her mistakes. But she didn't. If Lane had stopped having unwanted pregnancies, it is highly likely that no-one would ever have noticed her daughter's disappearance. But she continued to fall pregnant and do whatever it took to protect both her lifestyle and Olympic ambitions. In the end, welfare professionals put the pieces together after Lane had a third unwanted baby in 1999. Until then, her life in and around the trendy beachside suburb of Manly revolved around water polo, partying hard, drinking and men. She was once described by someone who knew her as a 'keg on legs' (Saunders, 2013).

In total, Lane had six pregnancies resulting in four live births. Five pregnancies were kept secret from family and friends and the one child she did keep, a girl, was born in 2001. Throughout all the covert pregnancies, Lane's acting was impeccable; not once did she crack. Incredibly, during all these pregnancies no-one asked her directly if she was having a baby. Several friends and water polo teammates assumed Lane had put on weight, but in any case she often wore sporty clothes and loose T-shirts that disguised her changing shape. Nor did anyone notice anything odd about her behaviour when, on the day she rid herself of Tegan, she attended a wedding with her then partner, Duncan Gillies.

Lane's life of partying and sport continued unabated until a child protection worker noticed inconsistencies when she adopted out a boy in 1999. She did not flinch when authorities asked her what had happened to Tegan, maintaining that she had given the baby to her natural father after initially offering several other scenarios. She was also relatively calm when challenged by police with the many inconsistencies in her stories. From that point, however, everything slowly began to unravel and Lane was eventually charged and convicted of the murder of Tegan, whose body has never been found. She continues to protest her innocence and lost a bid to appeal to the High Court in 2014.

At the very least, Keli Lane gave away her two-day-old child without completing the required paperwork and with the intention of having nothing to do with her. The most likely scenario is that she killed and dumped her baby, or left her somewhere to die. Regardless, the ease with which she abandoned her daughter is unsettling. Why did she do it?

The lead-up to the crime

The 1990s were a whirlwind for Keli Lane. She finished school, started university and secured her dream job as a sports coach at a prestigious Sydney private girls' school. As a star water polo player who was desperate to represent Australia when women competed in water polo for the first time at the 2000 Sydney Olympics, she was well suited to working with and coaching students. Lane was also a champion drinker who revelled in her place at the centre of Manly's social scene. However, the supremely confident sports-woman was hiding a number of dark secrets.

In 1992 and 1994, while still a teenager, Lane terminated two pregnancies. The first was with her high school boyfriend Aaron Tyack, who knew about it. It is unclear to whom she fell pregnant a second time, though, as by then she had broken up with Aaron.

Then, in 1995, Lane had a baby mere hours after playing in a losing water polo grand final. When her waters broke, she slipped away from a post-game drinking session at the pub and gave birth to a girl, later dubbed TR by the courts, whom she adopted out. She told authorities that her rugby star boyfriend Duncan Gillies was the father, but also said that they had now separated and he wanted no further involvement with the child. Lane said Gillies was in the UK and planned to return in two weeks. This was untrue and a previous boyfriend, who had no idea at the time, was later identified as the real father (Lane v R, 2013).

Apart from hospital officials and social workers, no-one knew about TR. Lane continued living with her parents near Manly, sleeping over at Gillies's Gladesville home, playing water polo and partying. In 1995, she represented Australia at the junior world water polo championships in Canada, winning a silver medal. At the start of 1996 she enrolled in a fee-paying course at the Australian College of Physical Education, but in mid-1996 she suspended her studies and eventually withdrew from the course ('How Keli Lane's secret life was exposed', 2010). In August she started work as a part-time water polo coach at

Ravenswood School for Girls, where she was popular with the students. But Lane was pregnant again and some students and teammates suspected, particularly when she was in a swimsuit, though no-one raised it with her.

Lane was due to accompany Gillies to his friend's wedding on 14 September. Being pregnant hadn't been part of the plan and she realised she had a major problem to solve. If she attended the wedding, it was likely people would notice that she was heavily pregnant, but she would have to come up with a really good explanation if she were to miss it. Instead, Lane decided that the best solution was to get rid of the baby. In the two weeks before the wedding, Lane went to Ryde Hospital three times and tried to convince medical staff to induce her, by falsely telling them she was 'overdue' and experiencing a lot of pain. All three requests were denied and she was discharged. Then, on 11 September, Lane went to Auburn Hospital and tried to convince the medical staff there to induce her, claiming to be two weeks overdue. They also discharged her but suggested she return the next morning. When she returned, they agreed to induce the birth and, after a ten-hour labour, Tegan was born on 12 September 1996 (Lane v R, 2013).

During and after the birth, Lane had no partner, friends or relatives visit her, and she drew the curtain so she didn't have to talk to other patients. She was referred to social worker Alicia Baltra-Vasquez, to whom she explained that her parents, Robert and Sandra, lived in Perth (though they actually lived in Fairlight, near Manly). Baltra-Vasquez observed the new mother with Tegan and noted that Lane '. . . is happy with her baby girl, breastfeeding her'.

On 14 September, two days after Tegan's birth – and on the day of the wedding – Lane was cleared to leave the hospital. Nobody saw her depart, and staff didn't notice that she had gone until 2 pm, but midwife Ann Marie Hanlon told Lane's trial she could have left as early as 10.30 am (Davies, 'Hospital cleared Keli Lane', 2010). Lane took the baby with her but almost certainly had no baby basket and would have had to carry Tegan in her arms. At around 3 pm she arrived alone at her parents' home in Fairlight, about thirty kilometres away. She dressed for the wedding and waited for Gillies, who was meeting her there. Robert and Sandra Lane noticed nothing unusual in her demeanour. Soon after, Sandra drove the couple to the wedding in Manly, where they stayed until about 11.30 pm.

Lane's life went on as usual. Again.

The murder and aftermath

Auburn was the perfect place for a northern beaches girl to evade notice. About twenty kilometres west of the city, it retains a working-class feel. In 1996 it would have been a world away from seaside Manly and unlikely to be frequented by Keli Lane's family and friends.

When Lane left Auburn Hospital sometime between 10.30 am and lunchtime on 14 September 1996, probably through a fire escape so that no-one could confirm what time she left, locals probably would not have looked twice. Young mothers with new babies leave hospitals all the time. Usually they have a partner with them, but not always. What happened next, however, was highly unusual. This mother, who had breastfed her newborn and, according to hospital staff, appeared to be bonding with her almost certainly drove to a relatively secluded location and either killed her baby or left her to die. In cases where a mother has killed her newborn the most common cause of death is asphyxiation due to suffocation, drowning or strangulation, and the most common implement or device used is a plastic bag. It is likely Lane used one of these methods (Shelton et al., 2011).

Tegan's body probably rests somewhere on the Homebush Sydney Olympics site, or in Lane Cove National Park. Lane would have been familiar with the Homebush area, now known as Sydney Olympic Park, because the Australian College of Physical Education, where she was studying in 1996, moved there from Croydon in 1995. When Tegan was born the Olympic complex, which is near the Parramatta River about six kilometres from Auburn Hospital, was being transformed from a 640-hectare industrial wasteland. It had housed brickworks and a large quarry, an abattoir, an armaments depot and eight of Sydney's rubbish dumps. In the mid-1990s it was mostly expanses of vacant land, extensive bushland and mangrove swamps, several bodies of water and deserted roads that were even quieter on weekends, making the area ideal to dump something unwanted on an early spring Saturday afternoon. It would have taken Lane about ten minutes to drive from Auburn to Homebush. The hospital is in a residential area, so she could easily have parked her car a few streets away and left it there for the two days she spent in hospital. Lane Cove National Park is another possible location, situated between the hospital and Lane's family home and offering plenty of secluded spots along the Lane Cove River.

Questions were not raised about Tegan until Lane had yet another baby in 1999, a boy dubbed AJ. Again, she told no-one she was pregnant and had no visitors to the hospital. Soon after, Lane contacted the Anglicare Adoption Agency, a different agency from the one she had used with her first adoption, and told social worker Virginia Fung that AJ was her first live birth, when in fact he was her third. She said she had had antenatal care at a Brisbane hospital after living in London with Gillies. She also provided false contact details (Lane v R, 2013). Fung was suspicious when her investigations into Lane's adoption history didn't add up, so she initially placed the child, who was eventually adopted by a couple, in temporary foster care.

Department of Community Services child protection officer John Borovnik, who worked on the adoption, also noticed inconsistencies in Lane's story. When he first contacted her, she denied giving birth to Tegan and swore an affidavit identifying AJ's father, later referred to as 'AW', as a man she had met while both were living in London. It later emerged that AW did not exist and the father was really a friend of her brother's with whom she had a brief affair. A few days after Borovnik called her, Lane faxed him, asking him not to contact anyone without telling her. Soon after, he reported the matter to local police, who referred it to Manly detectives.

As someone who had himself survived an abusive childhood, Borovnik later explained that he had wanted to ensure that all was in order with Lane's adoption paperwork. Puzzled by the lack of answers, he had dug deeper. 'The nurse told me that the woman had said this was her first pregnancy,' he told journalist and author Sue Williams in 2013.

> But they said it was strange: the doctors reported that it really didn't look like her first baby. There was something about it that still didn't feel right. There were a lot of questions I had, and there didn't seem to be any rhyme or reason for this woman's behaviour. It just didn't stack up.
>
> I made some inquiries and discovered there was something missing. To my horror, I discovered it was a child, a child by the name of Tegan. After that, it was all about finding justice for Tegan. My work is all about protecting children and it was terrible to think this child had been born and then no-one had even noticed that she'd disappeared. I wanted justice for Tegan, whatever the

outcome of the case itself. I wanted her to be recognised and acknowledged as every child in Australia should be. (Williams, 2013)

After an adoption order was made for AJ in the New South Wales Supreme Court, police began investigating Tegan's disappearance. After a slow start, they interviewed Lane in February 2001, October 2002 and again in May 2003. The investigation was painstaking as officers searched for Tegan and her supposed biological father based on the mountains of false information that Lane had provided. Her story was incredible, contradictory and, as it turned out, full of lies. Lane told Virginia Fung that Tegan was living with a Perth family, then told detectives she had given Tegan to her biological father, Andrew Morris. She later said his name was Andrew Norris. To try to find Tegan and Andrew Morris/Norris, police examined records of the Australian Electoral Commission, Australian Taxation Office, police, the Road Traffic Authority, New South Wales Births, Deaths and Marriages, the Department of Immigration and telephone and electricity providers in the Balmain/Rozelle area. The exhaustive and expensive Australia-wide search, complicated by Lane's deceit, found no trace of either (Lane v R, 2013).

An inquest began in 2005. In February 2006, Chief Coroner John Abernethy concluded that he was satisfied Tegan was dead, although he acknowledged that there was a small chance she was alive. Due to the time that had elapsed since the disappearance, the chances of finding a body, especially if it lay under one of the sports stadiums at Homebush, were almost nil. The case was handed to the Homicide Squad cold case team.

When she was asked at the inquest what had happened to Tegan when she left the hospital with her on the afternoon of 14 September 1996, Lane refused to answer. Her lawyer Peter

Hamill SC told the court he had instructed his client not to give evidence as it might be used against her later.

In August 2008, police dug under Duncan Gillies's old Gladesville house looking for Tegan's remains. They even used cadaver dogs, but found nothing. By then, it was way too late (Welch, 2008).

In 2009, Lane was finally charged with murdering Tegan. She continued to maintain her innocence and pleaded not guilty.

The trial

Keli Lane's trial began in August 2010. She was charged with one count of murder and three of perjury over lies she had told authorities. Prosecutors had to prove that Lane intended to kill Tegan, as the evidence was circumstantial and they had not located a body. The Crown argued that Lane intentionally killed Tegan sometime between leaving Auburn Hospital and arriving at her parents' home on 14 September 1996, and that her conduct followed a pattern of keeping her pregnancies secret and finding permanent solutions for children she did not want.

Prosecutors claimed that Lane had a strong motive, including her desire to maintain her sporting life, social commitments, job and Olympic ambitions. Prior and subsequent pregnancies had resulted in two abortions and two adoptions. But Lane's defence argued that no-one knew whether Tegan was dead and, if she was, no-one knew how she died. There was no scientific evidence and her possible death could have been an accident that Lane had tried to cover up.

It was alleged that when Tegan was born on 12 September 1996, Lane, who did not give evidence in court, decided to kill her so she could continue her life unencumbered. Crown prosecutor Mark Tedeschi QC noted that Lane had an extremely active social and sex life and a child would seriously cramp Lane's style and hinder the pursuit of her sporting goals. He said

Lane also worried about how her family would react to her being pregnant. (Davies, 'What happened to Tegan Lane?', 2010). He also pointed out that Lane had signed a teaching employment contract due to start on 9 October 1996. This contract, Tedeschi said, showed that Lane never intended to keep her baby (Davies, 'Keli Lane climbed down fire escape', 2010).

In his final address, Mr Tedeschi questioned why Keli Lane would offer eight different versions of what happened to Tegan and add the baby to her Medicare membership at Auburn Hospital if she was about to hand her to someone else. He asked why it took four hours to make the thirty-odd kilometre trip from Auburn Hospital to Fairlight and why, if Tegan's natural father had taken her, he did not lodge birth registration forms.

On 13 December 2010, the jury returned unanimous guilty verdicts on each of the false swearing charges. In the early afternoon, the jury foreman announced that they had also found Keli Lane guilty of murder by a majority of eleven to one. More than fourteen years after Tegan disappeared, her mother had been convicted of killing her. On 15 April 2011, Justice Anthony Whealy jailed Lane for eighteen years with a non-parole period of thirteen years and five months. On the false swearing convictions, he imposed another twenty-one months that was subsumed by the murder sentence.

But Keli Lane continued to protest her innocence. In a 2011 interview with Channel 7's *Sunday Night* program, she insisted that she gave Tegan to her biological father Andrew Norris (or Morris), adding that someone watching or reading about the case might come forward with information about them – possibly Tegan herself. Lane excused her countless lies by saying she wanted to keep her pregnancies 'private'. *Sunday Night* offered a $500,000 reward for information about Tegan's whereabouts, which remains unclaimed.

In July 2013, Lane appealed the murder conviction in the New South Wales Court of Criminal Appeal. Her barrister Winston Terracini SC argued a number of grounds, including that the murder trial jury should have been able to consider the lesser charge of manslaughter. He also said the Crown could not rule out that Tegan may have died from gross negligence, such as being dropped or put in a bag. Lane also continued to insist that she had given Tegan to her natural father. All eight grounds were rejected on 13 December.

In 2014, Lane lost an attempt to appeal to the High Court.

Keli Lane's background

When Keli Lane was born in March 1975, her father Robert reportedly brought drinks for everyone in the Steyne Hotel and filled the hospital ward with flowers – extravagant gestures for a first-time father (Duff, 2010). Such a celebrated entry into the world set the scene for a privileged upbringing that saw the talented young sportswoman get her way in many aspects of her life. Lane was supported unconditionally by her well-meaning parents, Robert and Sandra, and had a number of close friends and several boyfriends, who by all accounts treated her well.

Growing up in Sydney with her parents and a younger brother, Morgan, Lane was a tomboy and a natural sportswoman like her father, a former champion surfer and rugby player. Robert Lane finished third to Nat Young and Mick Dooley in the first Australian surfing championships at Bondi Beach in 1963. He was a talented rugby player for Manly in the late 1960s and 1970s, coaching the team over two periods in the 1980s.

Robert became a local policeman who rose to the rank of inspector, while Sandra worked in hospital administration. In 2010, *Sydney Morning Herald* journalist Eamonn Duff wrote that by the early 1990s, Robert and Sandra Lane were an important part of Manly's social scene. They lived in nearby Fairlight and regularly attended local functions, telling acquaintances how proud they were of their children, who both had promising futures (Duff, 2010).

In 1987, Keli Lane entered Year 7 at Manly Vale High School, now known as the Mackellar Girls Campus of Northern Beaches Secondary College. She didn't stand out academically but was a determined, popular and talented swimmer and water polo player. As a member of the Balmain Water Polo Club in the mid-1990s, Lane dreamed of making Australia's Olympic team. Bruce Falson, who coached the Australian junior women's water polo team when Lane competed at the 1995 world championships in Quebec, described her as a formidable competitor. 'She was very tough,' he told journalist Jane Cadzow. 'She was probably not as gifted as some of the other players as far as some of the skills go, but she was really, really tough' (Cadzow, 2005).

Once Lane hit her teenage years, life was a whirlwind of training, partying and boyfriends. In 1993, she enrolled in a Bachelor of Arts degree at Newcastle University's Ourimbah campus and continued to play water polo while there. She dropped out of the course before completing it, but received university sporting awards for water polo in 1993 and 1994.

Lane was never short of male company. In 1991, while still at school, she started dating Aaron Tyack, who has since described her as being 'like the golden girl down there [in Manly]. Blonde hair and tanned. I thought she was beautiful' (Cadzow, 2005). Towards the end of 1992, Lane became pregnant and, in consultation with Tyack, agreed to have a termination. Although she lived with her parents, they did not know about the pregnancy. In November 1993, she became pregnant again. She told no-one and terminated the pregnancy in March 1994, around the time she broke up with Aaron, a surf lifesaver who hoped to be a tradesman.

In May 1994, Lane dated another man, identified in court as PR. That relationship only lasted six to eight weeks, but she became pregnant again and had a termination. Also in 1994, Lane started seeing rugby union and league player Duncan Gillies. The popular and sociable couple dated until 1998 and she often stayed at Gillies's Gladesville home. Those close to her, including Gillies, knew Lane was on the contraceptive pill – the possibility of her becoming pregnant was far from their minds. When she played a 1995 water polo final, they had no idea she would give birth just hours later. Nor did they have any idea about the litany of lies Lane told hospital officials each time she had a baby. Outwardly, she was a regular girl with exceptional sporting talent.

Gillies later told Tegan's inquest that he'd had no idea his partner was pregnant: 'I had no comprehension whatsoever that she had two babies while I was sleeping with her during the four years we were going out. I did see Keli naked . . . but at no time did I assume she could have been pregnant' (Chin, 2011). Sandra Lane told the inquest she never noticed that her daughter, who lived at home most of the time, was pregnant. 'She lived in track-suits most of the time because she was involved in sport and that's what she wore,' she said, describing her daughter as 'a beautiful, loving girl' (Chin, 2011).

In August 1996, Lane started working part time at Ravens-wood School for Girls as a water polo coach, and eventually rose to become the primary physical education program coor-dinator. After giving birth to Tegan the following month, she continued working as if nothing had happened. Her relationship with Gillies ended in March 1998, after he met his future wife. Meanwhile, Lane continued her quest to make the Olympics, which ultimately failed.

A few months later she began a relationship with a man known to the court as AH. She was still living with her parents in

Fairlight, but became pregnant and did not tell AH, her parents or friends. Lane went to Queensland to seek a termination, but at six and a half months was told she was too far advanced. In 1999, she had a boy, AJ, at Ryde Hospital. Again she lied to officials about his parentage and her personal situation. DNA tests later confirmed that AH, who had no idea about the pregnancy, was the father. Lane started adoption proceedings, but continually evaded social worker Virginia Fung. She claimed Gillies was AJ's father and had left her – yet another untruth. In July, Fung contacted the Department of Community Services and spoke to John Borovnik, who had been assigned as AJ's caseworker, to obtain a care order. He found Lane's medical records and discovered the earlier births. The investigation began soon after.

Letters written by Lane when authorities queried her past show that she was at first evasive then tried to excuse her lies. She continued to lie and blame others, changing her story when she looked like being caught out. On 25 October 1999 Lane sent Virginia Fung a fax, which was reproduced in Rachael Jane Chin's book, *Nice Girl: Whatever happened to baby Tegan Lane*, and said in part:

> So where do I start? I'm not sure? My life for the last six years has been a nightmare . . . Many people, including my family, have disowned me and looking at the situation I guess it's not hard to figure out why. There were three children. Obviously I can't lie anymore as the paperwork is there. The middle child lives with a family in Perth although I have not had contact with them for a long time. They befriended me just before I had her and supported us. I am not able to give you many details as I am not sure of them myself. If my story isn't unusual enough as it already is! I know you probably can't believe

it but I know somehow that you know I am now being
honest with you . . . (Chin, 2011)

Lane also claimed, 'People dropped off me when they realised
that I was going to relinquish the babies.' This was another lie.
Far from disowning her, her family didn't even know about the
pregnancies.

When Detective Richard Gaut took over the police investiga-
tion in October 2002, Lane told him Tegan's father was Andrew
Norris, after earlier telling another detective the surname was
Morris. She said Andrew, his mother and his girlfriend Melanie
came to Auburn Hospital when she was discharged and picked
Tegan up from there, after which she caught a taxi home to
Gladesville alone. Lane claimed her friend Lisa Andreatta, from
Brisbane, was a friend of Andrew's and knew about the situ-
ation. Lane had met Lisa in 1996 at the Australian College of
Physical Education, but never told Lisa she was having a rela-
tionship with an Andrew Morris or Norris. Nor had Lisa lived
in Brisbane.

When some of her lies about Tegan were exposed, Lane
blamed them on a fear of her parents' reaction to the pregnancies.
In January 2004, she claimed that if her parents had found out
about Andrew and Tegan they wouldn't understand and there
was 'no way' they would let her keep the one child she *hadn't*
given up, who was born in 2001. But Robert Lane attended the
2005 inquest and some of the court hearings, often linking arms
with his daughter or holding her hand. When she was committed
to stand trial, he pledged to forfeit $30,000 if Lane breached her
bail conditions and helped fund a QC for her defence. He also
said he believed Tegan was alive. Asked during the inquest how
he would have reacted if he'd learned his daughter was pregnant,
he said he would have supported her. Her mother concurred.

When she was convicted of murdering Tegan, Keli Lane was successfully raising the child she kept. The father, whose parents were friends with Lane's parents, had come to stay with the Lanes in 2000. He and Keli moved out together and became a couple, having a daughter in 2001 and later marrying. But the inquest took its toll and they separated in 2007; the burden of her past – of which he had almost certainly been unaware when they married – was too much to bear.

Why did this privileged and well-educated woman have so many unwanted pregnancies? Most likely Lane forgot to take the contraceptive pill. Rather than prevent herself from getting pregnant in the first place, she perhaps reasoned that she was always clever enough to get herself out of a 'mess', so focused less on preventing possible consequences and more on problem-solving when things went wrong. Heavy drinking can also diminish the contraceptive pill's effectiveness. If she threw up, for example, it would not have been properly absorbed, even if taken several hours before the heavy drinking and vomiting. At Lane's trial, prosecutor Mark Tedeschi QC said she was often ill after a night's drinking.

And why didn't others realise that she was pregnant? Tegan was only one of three full-term babies Lane carried without anyone else knowing, including Duncan Gillies, her partner while she carried two of them. A range of accounts have been given by those who knew her to explain how this could have happened. Gillies often saw contraceptive pills in Lane's handbag and assumed she took them reliably; it never occurred to him that she might be pregnant. She undressed in the dark when with him and also when she had a friend stay in her room at her parents' house. When she had sex with Gillies, they did so with him lying behind her, and she asked him not to touch her tummy as she was embarrassed about putting on weight.

Lane's weight had always fluctuated. She is big-boned with very broad shoulders due to all the sport she played, making it easier to hide a baby bump. She also told police when they were interviewing her that she was a big girl who carried a pregnancy 'very wide' ('How Keli Lane's secret life was exposed', 2010). While they suspected she was pregnant with Tegan, her friends and teammates believed it would be insulting to ask. Some of the men in their social group would spread rumours about girls being pregnant if they put on even a little weight. Those who had been mocked like this didn't want to put Lane in the same position by talking about her weight.

Lane's mother, Sandra, sometimes gave her money to buy the pill, so never considered that she might be pregnant. Her daughter also dressed in oversized T-shirts, shorts and track-suits, which proved an effective cover for her growing belly. Lane's water polo coach assumed that her parents wouldn't allow her to compete and train if she was pregnant, as did her teammates. When she was pregnant, Lane entered the pool after quickly discarding a big beach towel she wrapped around herself. She also avoided a social beach trip with teammates because it would be more difficult to slip out of a towel into the water (Chin, 2011).

Despite all the deception, Lane was still able to attract men, even after being charged with murder. After her marriage broke up, she started dating teacher Patrick Cogan, who attended her trial. He and others she knew found it hard to believe that she was a killer. A former Ravenswood student and journalist, Alissa Warren, revealed her dismay in the *Daily Telegraph*. Warren wrote that Lane had treated students with respect and was much admired by her students. She said her teacher was straight-talking and did not suffer fools; students had to earn her trust. Lane had also taught them about manners, respect and even sex education. For Warren, discovering what Lane had done was surprisingly devastating (Warren, 2011).

Why did she do it?

How does a talented and popular young woman who taught sex education to teenagers find herself pregnant five times with unwanted babies? And why did Keli Lane, who adopted out her third and fifth children, kill the fourth? Why didn't she adopt out Tegan too?

As well as falling victim to her mother's callousness, Tegan may also have been a victim of timing. When Lane adopted out an earlier baby and a later one who was born after Tegan, she had time to process their adoptions. Tegan's birth was due around the same time that Lane was committed to attending a wedding with Duncan Gillies. Did she murder her daughter simply so she could attend the wedding and avoid arousing suspicion by her absence? Possibly. But other factors were also at play. Ultimately, a number of elements contributed to Keli Lane continually falling pregnant and to the way in which she dealt with each pregnancy.

A court report by psychiatrist Dr Michael Diamond, who did not meet with or speak directly to Lane and based his report on case material, said she exhibited signs of a personality disorder. He described Lane's ability to 'shut down emotionally and to experience emotional numbing or detachment' as striking: 'She is capable of carrying out audacious and extremely difficult actions in order to solve the problems that are in front of her,' he said. 'It is in a similar state of mind that I believe she determined the fate of Tegan Lane' (Arlington, 2011).

Keli Lane's pattern of behaviour is consistent with her having narcissistic personality disorder (NPD), which includes a grandiose self-image, a need for admiration, a sense of entitlement and a lack of empathy. She fits into the elitist subtype of NPD

Millon et al., 2004; see pages 94–95 as she was obsessed with culti-
vating an inflated self-image and felt privileged and empowered
by her 'special status', which derived from a combination of
her father's sporting background, being part of Manly's 'elite'
sporting culture and her competitive successes. She was a 'golden
girl' who lived at home well into her twenties and was particularly doted on by her father, who saw his sporty daughter as a
'chip off the old block'.

People with personality disorders lack insight and tend
not to learn from their mistakes; they keep repeating the same
maladaptive behaviour patterns. They lack resilience and
would rather cover up a mistake than admit it and deal with
it, which is consistent with how Lane handled her pregnancies.
She also dropped out of her arts degree at Newcastle University and didn't complete her course at the Australian College of
Physical Education. She suspended her studies between July and
December 1996, and then withdrew from the course. Apart from
her sporting endeavours, she seems to have just walked away
from many other challenging problems in her life or taken what
seemed to her to be the easy way out.

The fact that Lane had five unwanted pregnancies is extra-
ordinary, but fits with a diagnosis of NPD. She doesn't appear to
have tried to work out what she needed to change to avoid getting
pregnant in the first place. Given she tried to have a late-term
abortion, she doesn't appear to have learned from her previous
pregnancies to recognise the early signs of pregnancy either. The
most important thing to her was maintaining her public image
and being a 'winner'.

Essentially, Lane murdered Tegan to avoid feeling embarrassed and ashamed, to protect her image as a successful and
popular elite athlete and to be able to continue her new job unencumbered. She kept the last child she gave birth to, but by then

she was older, possibly more mature and no longer hankering for Olympic glory. Lane had a good relationship with the baby's father. However, due to her past actions that relationship broke up. Her attempts to build a legitimate life for herself ended in disaster due to her earlier self-absorption and tunnel vision.

Whatever her motivation, Keli Lane's actions constitute 'neonaticide', which is generally defined as intentionally killing one's biological child within twenty-four hours of birth (Resnick, 1970). Although Tegan was two days old when she died, Cleveland forensic psychiatrist Professor Phillip Resnick, who identified neonaticide in the 1970s, suggested her case 'would fit the characteristics of neonaticide rather than the killing of an older child' (Elder, 2010). Nearly all neonaticides are carried out by the child's mother (Hatters Friedman and Resnick, 2007). In a study of fifty-five women perpetrators, researchers found that 96 per cent had managed to hide their pregnancy from family and friends, despite most experiencing an enlarged abdomen and breasts and a changed walking style (Shelton et al., 2011).

The overwhelming majority also exhibited a high degree of physical resilience prior to, during and after the birth of their child. For example, many participated in physical and athletic events, even during labour, such as basketball, volleyball or dancing. A Finnish study found that of thirty-two women who committed neonaticide, 91 per cent had concealed or denied their pregnancy (Putkonen et al., 2007). Two-thirds had had prior pregnancies and the most commonly reported motive was that the baby was unwanted. The researchers also estimated that 71 per cent of them had a personality disorder of some kind.

Keli Lane, who fits these criteria well, almost certainly killed Tegan to preserve her lifestyle, image and Olympic hopes. A lack of empathy and a sense of entitlement, characteristic of those with an NPD, allowed her to murder her own daughter where most others would have baulked. Many parents are unsure about whether they want a child, or become frustrated when a child turns out to be difficult. But rarely if ever do they consider seriously harming them. Rather than feeling guilty about killing her child, Lane was probably relieved that she had rid herself of yet another 'problem'. Her number-one concern was always herself and the image she portrayed to others.

In the ultimate irony, by the time Lane's lies came back to haunt her she was by all accounts a good mother to the one child she kept. She was happily married to the father, but their relationship also broke down when her deception was finally exposed. In the end, Keli Lane lost everything that really mattered and will be in jail while the one daughter she actually wanted grows up without her.

KELI LANE
DIAGNOSTIC CHART

Using DSM 5 indicators (APA, 2013), when five or more of these are present, a diagnosis of narcissistic personality disorder (NPD) can be made	Examples of Keli Lane's behaviour that appear to be consistent with each indicator
Has a grandiose sense of self-importance (e.g. exaggerates achievements and talents, expects to be recognized as superior without commensurate achievements).	Teammates described her as annoyingly arrogant, despite not being nearly as successful in water polo as she wanted to be and not completing her Newcastle University arts degree nor her course at the Australian College of Physical Education. Believed that her right to a carefree lifestyle was more important than Tegan's life. Not prepared to ask for help when she needed it.
Is preoccupied with fantasies of unlimited success, power, brilliance, beauty or ideal love.	Was obsessed with her dream of making the Australian Olympic water polo team.
Believes that he or she is 'special' and unique and can only be understood by, or should associate with, other special or high-status people (or institutions).	Associated mostly with high-profile sporting people and was part of a Manly social clique.
Requires excessive admiration.	Revelled in being socially popular and the life of the party.

Using DSM 5 indicators (APA, 2013), when five or more of these are present, a diagnosis of narcissistic personality disorder (NPD) can be made	Examples of Keli Lane's behaviour that appear to be consistent with each indicator
	Could not stand the thought of her partner, friends or family finding out about her many pregnancies; didn't want to be embarrassed or thought of as promiscuous.
Has a sense of entitlement (i.e. unreasonable expectations of especially favorable treatment or automatic compliance with his or her expectations).	Assumed that people would do as she asked (e.g. when she pressured medical staff at Ryde and Auburn hospitals to induce Tegan's birth in order to attend a wedding). Expected people to believe her false assertion that on the day of the wedding she had handed Tegan over to her biological father, the so-called Andrew Morris/Norris.
Is interpersonally exploitative (i.e. takes advantage of others to achieve his or her own ends).	Continually lied to officials about her life situation after her first three live births and expected to be believed. Falsely named the mother of her ex-boyfriend Duncan Gillies as her midwife to Auburn Hospital staff. Falsely named Duncan Gillies as the father of some of her children to prevent officials from digging more deeply into her past. Did not inform two of the biological fathers that she had

Using DSM 5 indicators (APA, 2013), when five or more of these are present, a diagnosis of narcissistic personality disorder (NPD) can be made	Examples of Keli Lane's behaviour that appear to be consistent with each indicator
	given birth to and then adopted out their child. Tried to manipulate her friend Lisa Andreatta into saying she had met 'Andrew Norris' when Lisa hadn't and later said so in court. Did not speak up while an extensive (and expensive) Australia-wide search was undertaken to try to find the non-existent Andrew Norris/ Morris.
Lacks empathy: is unwilling to recognize or identify with the feelings and needs of others.	Was prepared to kill Tegan so she could attend a friend's wedding, despite having already breastfed her at least once.
Is often envious of others or believes that others are envious of him or her.	
Shows arrogant, haughty behaviors or attitudes. *Reprinted with permission from the Diagnostic and Statistical Manual of Mental Disorders, Fifth Edition, (Copyright ©2013). American Psychiatric Association. All Rights Reserved.	Described by several teammates as arrogant. Stated that her friends should have known each time she was pregnant and should have reached out to her.

CONCLUSION

What we can learn from the murders committed by Peter Caruso, Gerard Baden-Clay, Roger Dean and Keli Lane

Dangerous people don't often advertise their malicious or deceptive intentions when you meet them. Gerard Baden-Clay and Peter Caruso, for example, lived outwardly respectable lives and convinced most of their acquaintances that they were upstanding citizens. But like many others with a narcissistic personality disorder (NPD), they hid their grandiose lies and abusive behaviours beneath a veneer of respectability that suited their ulterior motives. As well as being potentially dangerous, many people with an NPD don't feel responsible for their cruel and selfish behaviour. They shift the blame onto others. They may also try to isolate their partner from those who might offer a different view, such as close friends and family.

When dealing with someone who shows signs of an NPD, look for the red flags. Be cautious about starting a new friendship, business partnership or intimate relationship with someone who displays the characteristics of an NPD. Be especially cautious if it is someone who is known to have previously engaged in behaviour that could be viewed as 'narcissistic rage'.

If someone in your life appears to have an NPD and is trying to control you by belittling or humiliating you, don't let them. Trust your judgment about yourself and ignore what they say to try to bring you down. Remind yourself that they are the one with the problem and not you. Where possible, discontinue or limit contact with someone who behaves towards you in these destructive ways.

Be cautious about lending money to someone who appears to have an NPD, as it is unlikely to be repaid. If you work with someone like this and they try to manipulate you or their behaviour begins to concern you in other ways, as Roger Dean's did when he vandalised a colleague's car after a negative appraisal, consider finding another position – people with an NPD rarely change. Look out for their attempts to present themselves as something they are not, undermine you, blame you for things you are not responsible for or take credit for work or ideas that are not theirs. Be on the alert for the dangers associated with grandiose and unrealistic proposals and 'grand plans' that haven't been properly researched. If you are interviewing people for jobs, don't automatically assume that a style of presentation that incorporates external social confidence, high levels of optimism and a strong belief in their ability to create positive change is always a sign of ambition and good interpersonal skills. Dig more deeply.

Rosa Caruso and Allison Baden-Clay lost their lives to partners who were always going to do what it took to preserve their 'superiority' and 'image'. Peter Caruso and Gerard Baden-Clay believed it was their right to belittle their wives, control them and destroy their self-esteem to the point where they became despondent and dependent. Such partnerships are one-sided, deflating and potentially dangerous. A person with an NPD will not readily change and things will probably get worse.

Research has demonstrated that the most dangerous time in an abusive relationship is when a woman decides to leave or actually leaves. When they are in a relationship with someone who has an NPD, the risk is further magnified. Rosa Caruso belonged to the most vulnerable group of all – migrant women who often have fewer close confidants and less general community support. Allison Baden-Clay also struggled with her husband's ongoing infidelity and had probably given him an ultimatum when she was killed.

The murders of Rosa Caruso and Allison Baden-Clay high-light the dangers faced by all women in abusive relationships, particularly if the man has an NPD. Some people with an NPD also harm others outside their family. Gerard-Baden Clay borrowed large amounts of money from friends that probably will never be recovered, so it isn't just partners who need to be wary. If someone with an NPD borrows money, they will feel no guilt if they cannot pay it back. If they borrow and crash your car, they won't care about the inconvenience it causes you, as those who allowed Roger Dean and Gerard Baden-Clay to borrow their cars discovered.

Roger Dean and Keli Lane did not kill their partners, but one was prepared to let elderly nursing home residents die and the other to kill a baby because it suited their own needs.

If you think a person has this personality disorder, consider talking to a psychologist to discuss the possibility and learn about positive and effective responses to the situation.

PART III

BORDERLINE
PERSONALITY
DISORDER

INTRODUCTION

Borderline personality disorder (BPD): Never ever leave me

A borderline personality disorder (BPD) is a pervasive pattern of unstable interpersonal relationships, self-image and emotions combined with impulsive behaviours. It begins by early adulthood and presents in a variety of contexts, with its severity strongly connected to negative experiences in childhood. It is called 'borderline' because the key characteristics of the disorder lie somewhere between the psychoses (e.g. schizophrenia, in which sufferers are often unable to connect with reality) and the neuroses (e.g. anxiety and depression).

The behaviour of Glenn Close's character Alex Forrest in the 1987 movie *Fatal Attraction* is typical of those with a BPD. After a brief sexual encounter with Michael Douglas's character Dan Gallagher, Alex assumes they will continue their relationship. When he declines to do so, she sees it as rejection and starts stalking him, calling at all hours of the day and night and becoming increasingly violent. In the end, Alex attacks Dan's family, scares their daughter, kills and cooks the family's pet rabbit and tries to kill his wife, Beth. Eventually Beth manages to kill Alex. The term 'bunny boiler' has become a slang expression for the type of person who engages in this kind of vengeful behaviour.

Marilyn Monroe was diagnosed with a borderline personality disorder by her treating psychiatrist Dr Ralph Greenson, and consultant psychologist Dr Milton Wexler (Taraborrelli, 2009); her background was typical of those with the disorder. Her mother and maternal grandmother suffered from mental illness and had many hospital admissions. Marilyn's mother was periodically forced to place her in an orphanage and a variety of foster homes when she was very young. When her mother was well enough to rent a house for them, she sublet two rooms to male lodgers. Marilyn, who had already been sexually abused by a man in one of the foster homes, was then abused by one of the lodgers in her own home (Leaming, 2006; Monroe et al., 2007). Although she became a movie icon, her life was blighted by three failed marriages, affairs with powerful men who eventually rejected her (such as Robert Kennedy), excessive drug and alcohol use, several suicide attempts, extensive psychiatric treatment and job losses due to erratic behaviour. Eventually, at thirty-six, she took her own life by swallowing forty Nembutal tablets (though conspiracy theories persist, with some believing she either died from an accidental overdose or was murdered).

Katherine Knight, who brutally killed her partner John Price, has an extreme form of BPD. She murdered 'Pricey' when he wanted to end their relationship and asked her to leave his house, where she had been living with him part time for several years. After killing him she skinned his corpse, cooked his body parts with vegetables and set up an elaborate tableau, as if she was serving him up for dinner, for his adult children to discover when they visited.

Recognising someone with a BPD

Diagnosing a personality disorder is difficult and requires some professional knowledge. However, the criteria are helpful in determining a general outline. The DSM 5 describes a border-line personality disorder as 'a pervasive pattern of instability of interpersonal relationships, self-image, and affects, and marked impulsivity, beginning by early adulthood and present in a variety of contexts', as indicated by five (or more) of the following:

1. Frantic efforts to avoid real or imagined abandonment. (**Note**: Do not include suicidal or self-mutilating behavior covered in Criterion 5.)
2. A pattern of unstable and intense interpersonal relationships characterized by alternating between extremes of idealization and devaluation.
3. Identity disturbance: markedly and persistently unstable self-image or sense of self.
4. Impulsivity in at least two areas that are potentially self-damaging (e.g. spending, sex, substance abuse, reckless driving, binge eating). (**Note**: Do not include suicidal or self-mutilating behavior covered in Criterion 5.)
5. Recurrent suicidal behavior, gestures, or threats, or self-mutilating behavior.
6. Affective instability due to a marked reactivity of mood (e.g. intense episodic dysphoria, irritability, or anxiety usually lasting a few hours and only rarely more than a few days).
7. Chronic feelings of emptiness.
8. Inappropriate, intense anger or difficulty controlling anger (e.g. frequent displays of temper, constant anger, recurrent physical fights).

9.   Transient, stress-related paranoid ideation or severe dissociative symptoms.

Prevalence

The prevalence of BPD in the general population is estimated to range between 1.6 and 5.9 per cent (Torgersen, 2009; Grant et al., 2008). According to the DSM 5, it is diagnosed predominantly in females (about 75 per cent). It has been estimated that between 25 and 50 per cent of all prisoners in jail have a BPD and that twice as many female prisoners as male prisoners meet the criteria for a BPD diagnosis (Black et al., 2007, Sansone and Sansone, 2009).

Comorbidity (other disorders that often co-occur with BPD)

In some people, BPD co-occurs with anxiety, depression, bipolar disorder or antisocial personality disorder and, sometimes, post-traumatic stress disorder (PTSD).

Typical behaviours of someone with a BPD

As with other personality disorders, BPD can range from mild to extreme. Two people with a BPD may also behave differently in some ways, depending on which criteria they meet and other factors in their childhood and current life. But there are a range of typical behaviours someone with a BPD may display.

They generally cannot tolerate being alone and try to have other people around them most of the time, especially a romantic partner. This can lead to poor relationship choices and decisions, but they would rather be in a bad relationship than be alone. Initially they see a new partner in an idealised way as wonderful, 'the best' and 'perfect'. They tend to view others as either 'good' or 'bad', so when the relationship falters, even slightly, their perception dramatically switches to disillusionment with their partner, devaluing them and feeling let down or abandoned by them. This process can happen not only within their romantic relationships, but also in their relationships with family, friends or workplace colleagues. This sudden switch from 'overvaluing' (e.g. 'the best co-worker I have ever had') to 'devaluing' (e.g. 'I hope she resigns soon – I hate working with her') is confusing for all involved.

Those with a BPD may continually seek reassurance that they are loved, wanted, respected and valued, and tend to be hypersensitive to behaviours or comments that they see as criticism or rejection. They may stalk someone they fear is rejecting or abandoning them and can become angry, panicky, tearful or hysterical when someone who is close to them or on whom they rely does something, however minor, that triggers their deep feelings of insecurity and fear of rejection or abandonment. They will often feel jealousy or fear even if the other person is unavoidably running late, was forced to cancel a meeting or simply behaved positively towards someone else. These angry and fearful behaviours are more likely to be directed at a partner or relative but can occur in a friendship or at work.

Mood swings and outbursts of uncontrolled anger or rage are also common. These may involve verbal outbursts and attacks, temper tantrums, and physical attacks or fights. The catalyst is often behaviour by a partner that is perceived, often incorrectly, as rejection or abandonment. Katherine Knight often flew into a rage and physically attacked her current live-in partner – once with a hot iron – because he came home late. She also once slashed the throat of her partner's puppy after an altercation with him.

Someone with a BPD has an unstable view of themselves that can jump between extremes. They may see themselves as a loving partner one day and an angry but righteous punisher the next. They are also prone to histrionic and repeated threats to suicide or self-harm, such as cutting or burning. About 70 per cent of people with BPD will attempt suicide at least once, and many will try multiple times. They make an average 3.4 suicide attempts throughout their lifetime and up to 10 per cent of those with a BPD will succeed, making them more likely to suicide than those with any other personality disorder (Black et al., 2004; Soloff et al., 2002).

Those with a BPD often give in to their impulses and indulge in risky behaviours, such as excessive alcohol and/or drug use, binge eating, overspending, gambling, fighting, reckless driving, sexual promiscuity or high-risk sexual behaviour. They may also experience temporary episodes of paranoid thinking and become convinced that someone is trying to harm them or their loved ones. Under extreme stress, some experience episodes of 'disassociation', in which they feel what is happening is not 'real'. They may have a sense of being detached from themselves or an unreal or distorted perception of people and things. Some have no memory of specific time periods, events or people. However they are not 'psychotic', which involves being unable to differentiate between what is real and what isn't.

Someone with a BPD is aware of what is happening around them and knows right from wrong, but they often have difficulty coping with these realities and react in an extreme way when things go wrong or appear to.

What causes a BPD?

Most research indicates that a BPD is caused by a combination of life events and genetic predispositions. Compared to the general population, the disorder is about five times more common in people with a first-degree family member – a parent, sibling or child with whom they share 50 per cent of their genetic make-up – who has a BPD, antisocial personality disorder or one of the depressive or bipolar disorders. So it isn't surprising that the heritability of borderline personality disorder is an estimated .67 (Torgersen et al., 2012). This means research studies have found that 67 per cent of the differences between those who had a BPD and those who didn't were due to genetic differences between them. A number of different genes have also been shown to play a role in developing some components of a BPD, such as irritability, emotionality and impulsivity, but no specific gene has yet been shown to directly influence the disorder itself.

A great many people who develop a BPD have experienced unstable childhoods characterised by, for example, inconsistent parenting, parental abandonment or placement in many different foster homes and orphanages. BPD is also very strongly associated with a history of childhood sexual and/or physical abuse, especially when it occurred at a relatively young age. Compared to those with other personality disorders, those with a BPD are more likely to have experienced the highest rate of traumatic exposure to abuse, particularly sexual abuse, when they were very young (Yen et al, 2002). The longer a child lives in an environment in which they are harmed, fear being harmed or see others being harmed, the more severe their trauma is likely to be. The younger they were at the time and the more severe or extensive the abuse, the more severe the BPD usually is.

As they get older, abused children often continue to re-experience images, feelings and thoughts associated with the traumatic situations they endured. Their bodies may regularly feel 'fearful' even when there is no hint of danger, and they may not link these feelings to their earlier experiences of abuse. This can make them jumpy, irritable, teary or apprehensive in situations other people would perceive as non-threatening.

Studies have found evidence of disrupted brain development and neurological deficits in the brains of many children who have been abused when they were young (e.g. Soloman and Heide,

2005). When researchers used sophisticated brain-imaging techniques to compare the brains of people who had been abused as children with those who had not, they found that those who had been abused had:

- Much smaller volumes of grey matter and other abnormalities (e.g. thinning) in certain brain areas such as the hippocampus, which plays an important role in our emotions and memory in three key areas, and the prefrontal cortex, which regulates behaviour and social control and controls abstract thinking and thought analysis (Teicher et al, 2003; Herringa et al., 2013; Lim et al., 2014).
- Weaker connections between the prefrontal cortex and the hippocampus, which lead to dysfunction in the brain's 'fear circuitry'. This results in hyperarousal (always feeling scared or anxious, often in response to something as small as a loud noise or a touch of the arm), hypervigilance for potential danger and a focus on survival and responding to threats (Herringa et al., 2013).
- Damage to their amygdala, the key area of the brain which processes emotions, causing it to go into 'overdrive' and signal danger even when there is no obvious threat.
- Altered ability of their brain to access and use serotonin, an important neurotransmitter chemical that 'speaks' to other parts of the brain to help produce feelings of wellbeing, positive mood and emotional stability (e.g. Miller et al., 2009). A study by Koch et al. (2007) also identified this type of serotonergic dysfunction in patients with BPD.
- More stress hormones, especially cortisol. High cortisol levels reduce the ability of the prefrontal cortex to function properly, reducing a child's capacity for rational problem solving when under pressure or fearful (McGowan et al., 2009).

Young lives lost. The Farquharson boys, Jai (ten, left), Bailey (two, middle) and Tyler (seven, right), died when their father, Robert, intentionally drove his car into a dam outside Winchelsea on Father's Day 2005 and left them to drown.

Emergency services took several hours to locate and haul Robert Farquharson's white 1989 VN Commodore from the dam. His boys had no hope of surviving after he deliberately left them trapped inside.

AAP Image/Joe Castro

Robert Farquharson's older sister, Kerri Huntington, takes charge and ushers him across the road like a child during his hearing at the Supreme Court of Victoria on 30 December, 2005.

Kelly Barnes/Newspix

A murderer pretends. Robert Farquharson and Cindy Gambino at the funeral for their three sons, with Farquharson pretending to feel grief over their loss. At that stage he hadn't yet been charged with their murders.

LEFT: Crocodile tears. John Myles Sharpe appeared on TV in May 2004, pleading for the safe return of his wife Anna Kemp and daughter Gracie, 19 months, knowing that he had brutally killed them and dumped their bodies at a local refuse station.

BELOW LEFT: Tragic loss. Anna Kemp, seen here holding her daughter Gracie as a baby, was five months pregnant with a boy when her husband shot and killed her with a spear gun. He then used it to kill Gracie four days later.

BELOW RIGHT: Grim discovery. More than three months after they went missing in March 2004 and following an extensive search by dedicated police, the remains of Anna Kemp and Gracie Sharpe were found at a waste management centre near Mornington.

AAP Image / Julian Smith

Michael Potter / Newspix

ABOVE: Santo Caruso, left, walks out of Victoria's Supreme Court with his father Peter in July 2008. The Templestowe retiree was granted bail after being charged with killing his wife, Rosa. Santo soon realised his father was lying although Peter claimed he was innocent.

RIGHT: Rosa Caruso's grave at Templestowe Cemetery, where she rests next to her parents, Giuseppe and Costantina Pallante. Rosa's son, Santo, says as long as he is alive, his father will not join his wife in the double grave.

Missing. A detective holds a picture of Allison Baden-Clay at a press conference about her disappearance in April 2012. Allison went missing overnight on 19 April; her body was found on 30 April after an extensive search.

Gerard Baden-Clay, pictured with his sister Olivia Baden-Walton, made a brief comment to a Channel Nine reporter outside his home. He insisted that he was helping police, but never actively helped in the search.

RIGHT: Hundreds packed St Paul's Anglican Church in Ipswich for the funeral of Allison Baden-Clay, whose body had been found under a bridge at Kholo Creek.

Celebrating the Life
of
ALLISON BADEN-CLAY

Friday 11th May, 2012

ST PAUL'S ANGLICAN CHURCH
IPSWICH

CELEBRANT: REVEREND BEVERLEY BELL

BELOW: Gerard Baden-Clay at his wife's funeral with their three daughters. Police bugged the flowers on her coffin in case he confessed to killing her while saying goodbye.

Roger Dean receives oxygen outside the Quakers Hill Nursing Home after he started a fire which killed eleven residents in September 2011. Another three people died from complications after he was charged.

Roger Dean told police that he loved the nursing home residents, but was overcome by 'evil' that made him light the fires. Dean acted to cover up his theft of prescription medication.

RIGHT: Keli Lane, left, with friend and former water-polo teammate Taryn Woods at Taryn's twenty-first birthday party in August 1996. Lane gave birth to Tegan in September 1996.

AAP Image/Supplied

Cameron Richardson/Newspix

LEFT: Keli Lane outside the NSW Supreme Court in 2010. Charged with murdering her two-day-old daughter, Tegan, she claims she gave the baby to her biological father.

Stephen Cooper/Newspix

Still protesting her innocence, Lane was found guilty in December 2010, after a four-month trial, of the murder of her baby daughter.

LEFT: Katherine Knight, convicted of murdering, beheading and skinning her partner John 'Pricey' Price in 2000, pictured in 1997. The killing was so gruesome, experienced police had to take stress leave.

RIGHT: Pictured in the 1990s, Katherine Knight had a troubled childhood and many violent relationships. However many family members and some others who knew her described her as caring and generous.

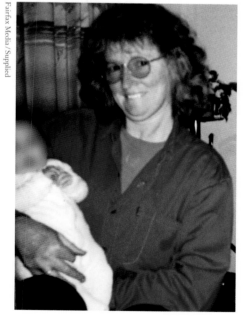

ABOVE: CCTV footage showed Simon Gittany grabbing his fiancée Lisa Harnum as she tried to leave their luxury Sydney apartment, and then dragging her back inside. Sixty-nine seconds later, he threw her over the balcony to her death.

LEFT: Simon Gittany outside the New South Wales Supreme Court during his 2013 murder trial with his then new partner Rachelle Louise, who protested his innocence. Gittany was found guilty.

RIGHT: The fifteenth floor balcony from which Lisa Harnum fell to her death. A witness saw Gittany 'unload' an object over the balcony, but Gittany claimed that Lisa climbed over and either jumped or fell.

LEFT: Adelaide pensioner Vonne McGlynn, eighty-two, was brutally murdered in 2008 by Angelika Gavare, who planned to sell her home and contents and pocket the proceeds.

RIGHT: Angelika Gavare, seemingly relaxed during a 2009 police interview. After her story began to fall apart, she blamed her ex-partner Giuseppe Daniele for Vonne's death.

BELOW: Father of four and recidivist rapist Adrian Ernest Bayley claimed he raped and killed Jill Meagher in a laneway off Hope Street in Brunswick in September 2012 because she 'flipped him off'. He later told police: 'They should have the death penalty for people like me anyway.'

ABOVE: Irish-born Jill Meagher, twenty-nine, was a popular Melbourne ABC radio employee when her life was cut short. A week later, 30,000 people marched down Sydney Road, Brunswick, to remember Jill and condemn violence against women.

Jill Meagher's husband Tom and other loved ones release doves at Fawkner Cemetery after her Melbourne memorial service in October 2012.

In summary, children who have been abused are likely to show such signs of significant delayed brain development and neurological deficits. As a result, they are also more likely to develop into adults who are generally fearful and anxious, are hypervigilant (e.g. they overreact to perceived potential threats to their own safety or the safety of those they care for), and experience higher stress levels and lower levels of wellbeing. Many also behave more aggressively, have difficulties concentrating and learning at school, tend to distrust other people, are often emotionally immature and have troubled relationships (Scannapieco and Connell-Carrick, 2005; Soloman and Heide, 2005).

Many people with a BPD have reduced capacity for emotional empathy. One study found that people with a BPD appear to have a different empathy process that makes them seem to be more attentive than most to the social and emotional behaviour of others, but the way they *interpret* what they see or hear means that they respond in a dysfunctional way (Dinsdale and Crespi, 2013). They over-focus on 'signs' of threat or rejection rather than looking for information about the feelings of the other person.

Treatment

The current available evidence suggests that certain medications have some impact on the core symptoms of BPD, such as mood swings (Lieb et al., 2010). These include mood-stabilisers such as topiramate, valproate semisodium and lamotrigine, and antipsychotic medications such as olanzapine and haloperidol. There is also some support for the use of omega-3 fatty acid supplements. It appears that SSRI (selective serotonin reuptake inhibitors) medication has little effect, except when the person with a BPD also has a co-occurring major depressive disorder. No medications have been shown to directly impact the severity of the disorder itself.

Among the psychological approaches most likely to improve the behaviour of someone with a BPD is interpersonal psychotherapy, which teaches new and effective skills and strategies for managing and enhancing relationships with key people in their lives (Stoffers et al., 2012). Cognitive behaviour therapy is a short-term, goal-oriented treatment that can also help some people with a BPD. It focuses on reality testing, changing your thinking to change how you behave and problem-solving. Dialectical behavioural therapy has also been shown to help some people with a BPD to learn skills for coping with their thoughts and strong emotions, to resist urges and to change the ways in which they typically react and respond to interpersonal situations. It often includes some work in 'mindfulness' for self-calming. For those with a BPD who were sexually abused as children, appropriate trauma counselling at a specialised centre can also help.

CHAPTER 7

KATHERINE KNIGHT

The cast
Katherine Knight: Born October, 1955. The killer and partner of John 'Pricey' Price
Katherine Knight's children:
    Melanie* (born in 1976 to David Kellett)
    Naomi* (born in 1980 to David Kellett)
    Monique* (born in 1988 to David Saunders)
    Evan* (born in 1991 to John Chillingworth)
    *Not their real names
Barbara Roughan (nee Thorley): Katherine Knight's mother
Jack Roughan: Barbara's first husband, with whom she had four sons.
    He had custody of them after the pair separated but died in 1957
Ken Knight: Katherine Knight's father, with whom Barbara moved
    in after leaving Jack Roughan
Katherine Knight's half-brothers:
    Patrick John Roughan (born 1945) lived with his father after
    his parents separated but moved in with his mother and her
    partner Ken when his father died

Martin Roughan lived with his father after his parents separated but moved in with his mother and her partner Ken when his father died

Neville Roughan was raised by an aunt in Sydney after his parents separated, but lived with his mother and her partner Ken for a short period of time

Barry Roughan (born c. 1953) was raised by an aunt in Sydney after his parents separated

Katherine Knight's full siblings:

Kenneth Charles Knight, known as Charlie (born c. 1954)

Joy Knight: Katherine Knight's twin sister (born October 1955)

Shane Knight (born 1961)

Katherine Knight's partners:

David Kellett was Knight's first husband and the father of Melanie and Naomi; they married in 1974 and separated in 1984

David Saunders fathered Monique and was in a relationship with Knight from 1987–1988

John Chillingworth fathered Evan and was in a relationship with Knight from 1990–1993

John 'Pricey' Price was Knight's partner from 1994 until she killed him in 2000.

Colleen Price: Pricey's ex-wife and the mother of their three children

The motive

Katherine Knight hoped to exact revenge on John 'Pricey' Price for wanting to leave her. She tried to set up a scenario that would make people believe she was mentally ill in order to avoid a murder charge.

Introduction

When her neighbour's tradesman son was working on the house next to Katherine Knight's in the small New South Wales town of Aberdeen, the much older woman decided she'd use her feminine charm on him. The well-built handyman was only half her age, but this did not deter Knight, who had long used sex as a tool to attract and control the men in her life. Never mind the fact that this was her neighbour's son.

Donning short shorts and a bikini top, Knight went over to her neighbour's house, sidled up to the young man, lifted an arm around the back of her neck and crooned, 'Hello, how are you?' Former neighbour Geraldine Edwards recalls that her bemused son couldn't escape fast enough, mumbling excuses and racing inside to see if lunch was ready. 'She was a real siren,' Geraldine recalls. 'She thought she was the woman of the moment.'

By all accounts Knight had a traumatic childhood, which undoubtedly contributed to the seductive but also abusive and combative way she interacted with men. Her father Ken was a violent alcoholic and her mother Barbara was emotionally volatile. The household was more like a TV soap opera than a family home. Ken would demand sex from Barbara, openly and loudly, even when their children were around and often knocked her to the ground if she didn't comply. Knight was frequently beaten by both of her parents, usually with a dog lead or an appliance cord. She claims her father physically assaulted her when she was in grade six and that he was charged with assaulting her many years later. Knight was probably sexually abused from the age of six or seven by a much older half-brother, and relatives say another brother sometimes joined in (Lalor, 2002).

As a result Katherine Knight was troubled, frightened, angry, needy and violent from a young age. But nothing excuses what she did to her de facto partner John Price, a likeable bloke known to all as Pricey. When Pricey decided he'd had enough of her violent behaviour towards him and moved to end their relationship, she planned the ultimate revenge. Overnight on 29 February 2000, after having sex with forty-four-year-old Pricey in his home and allowing him to drift into a satisfied sleep, the former abattoir worker stabbed him at least thirty-seven times, let him bleed to death and then skinned him and cooked parts of his body, including his head. She hung his pelt on a meat hook on the architrave of the door of the lounge room, put Pricey's head in a large pot in the kitchen and stewed it with potatoes, zucchini, pumpkin, carrot and squash. When police arrived his skinless body was on the floor of the lounge room. Two dishes of stew containing vegetables mixed with chunks of his oven-baked buttocks had been placed on the kitchen table as if waiting for guests to come to dinner. Vindictive notes had been left for his children to find.

The killing was so horrific that several seasoned police officers who attended the crime scene had to take stress leave. Yet Knight's reason for her shocking brutality was quite simple: she wanted to exact revenge on Pricey for wanting to leave her. She was also cunning enough to do it in a way that would make people think she was mentally ill and allow her to avoid a murder conviction. But it didn't work, because mental health experts concluded that she knew what she was doing.

Such crimes are rare in women, but not unheard of. Knight's actions seem even more incomprehensible when you consider they were perpetrated by someone who was a mother, partner and sister, relationships which should have helped her to develop some empathy for others. Katherine Knight was frightened, violent, manipulative and ultimately murderous. But she was not mentally ill, so why would she do something so truly awful?

The lead-up to the crime

Katherine Knight and John 'Pricey' Price met in late 1993, while she was still technically with her previous partner, John Chillingworth. Knight had four children from earlier relationships and Pricey had three from his former marriage. She moved into his home in Aberdeen part time a year or two later, but maintained her own place. At one point they broke up and she went to Queensland for six months before they reconciled.

The relationship was stormy and Knight often acted violently or out of spite. In one case she made a secret video, complete with running commentary, of a first-aid kit and other items Pricey had taken from work. She waited until he did something she didn't like and then sent the video to his employer. Despite Pricey having retrieved many of the items from the company's rubbish-disposal sites, he was sacked from his $100,000 p.a. job. The fights and disagreements continued and about six months before he died, Knight sliced her partner on the chest with a knife. She also tried to pay a nephew to steal and destroy Pricey's uninsured car and to throw acid in his face. The nephew refused (R v Knight, 2001).

Knight made a number of threats to kill or injure Pricey directly to him as well as to their friends and family. She also pressured him to give her a share in his house. He refused, arguing that the home and contents would go to his children. She suggested that he give her $10,000 instead, but he wasn't persuaded.

In the months leading up to his death, Pricey was clearly worried about his safety and wanted to leave the relationship. But he feared repercussions against his children. He continued to put up with the erratic and violent Knight, who made no secret of having murder on her mind. At one point she told her daughter Naomi, 'If I kill Pricey, I'll kill myself after it.' About five months before the crime Knight told her brother Kenneth

'Charlie' Knight: 'I am going to kill Pricey and I am going to get away with it. I'll get away with it 'cause I'll make out I'm mad.' Knight also told Pricey in front of a friend, Trevor Lewis, 'You'll never get me out of this house, I'll do you in first' (R v Knight, 2001).

It all came to a head at the end of February in 2000. On 27 February, Pricey and Knight fought and she scratched his eye and pulled a knife on him. He retaliated, leaving her with several bruises.

On Monday, 28 February, Pricey woke at 2.30 am to find Knight at the end of the bed with her hands behind her back. He believed she was holding a knife and later told others he thought he was 'a goner' before leaping out of bed and escaping. His boss, Geoff Bowditch, offered to put him up but Pricey refused because he thought that his children could become targets. Later that night, police attended Pricey's home while Knight was present to tell him she had applied for an Apprehended Violence Order (AVO) against him following their altercation.

Pricey confided to Lewis that he believed Knight would end up killing him. On Tuesday, 29 February, Pricey went to a chamber magistrate at Scone Court House to seek his own AVO against Knight, saying he wanted to end his relationship and prevent her from entering his house. He told police about the recent altercation, the stabbing incident six months earlier and Knight's threat to cut his penis off. Meanwhile, she was seeing a solicitor and showing her doctor and other people bruises from the altercation in an attempt to paint herself as a victim. But she did not seek treatment and only attended the doctor to have her bruises recorded. Her trial judge later concluded that this was 'part of creating a suitable setting into which the killing of Mr Price could be placed' (R v Knight, 2001).

At 4 pm on 29 February, Knight retrieved her video camera from her twin sister Joy's house and used it to record a curious statement: 'I love all my children and I hope to see them again.' (R v Knight, 2001)

Before he left work that day, Pricey told colleagues at the earth-moving business where he was now employed that if he did not turn up the next day it was probably because Knight had murdered him. At 8 pm, he took two beer stubbies to his neighbour Anthony Keegan's house and stayed to have a drink with him until 9.30 pm. He was in bed by 10 pm. Meanwhile, Knight took her daughter Naomi and others out for dinner, saying she wanted it to be special. She then left her two younger children with Naomi and headed to Pricey's house.

The murder

Knight arrived at Pricey's at about 11 pm on 29 February. She briefly watched TV and had a shower, before putting on a black nightdress and seducing him. They had sex and he went to sleep. As Pricey lay in bed, Knight began to stab him in a frenzy. He managed to stagger down the hallway, blood spurting, and tried to escape out the front door. As Knight continued to stab him in the back, he opened the door but either came back in or was dragged in. He then fell in the hallway near the open doorway leading into the lounge room and bled to death.

The house was covered in blood – one pool measured one by two metres. But stabbing Pricey at least thirty-seven times was not enough for Katherine Knight. She dragged his body into the lounge room and used a sharp butcher's knife to skin and behead her partner. Such was her expertise as a former abattoir worker, Knight managed to remove the skin, including that of the head, face, nose, ears, neck, torso, genital organs and legs, to form one pelt. One small segment was left in place – the skin on the left upper chest where she had earlier stabbed him. Knight then hung the pelt on a meat hook on the architrave of the lounge room door.

After removing the head, Knight arranged what was left of the body with the left arm draped over an empty soft drink bottle and the legs crossed. Moving into the kitchen, she peeled and prepared vegetables and cooked Pricey's head in a large pot with some of them. She baked pieces of flesh from his buttocks in the oven with the other vegetables.

As sentencing judge Justice Barry O'Keefe later noted, 'The gruesome steaks were then arranged on plates together with the vegetables which she had baked and left as meals for the son and daughter of the deceased, accompanied by vindictive notes. A third piece was thrown on the back lawn, whether for consumption by dogs or for some other purpose is not revealed in the evidence' (R v Knight, 2001).

At some point during the night, Knight drove to an automatic teller machine in Muswellbrook, a round trip of about thirty minutes and withdrew $1000 from Pricey's bank account. She returned to the house and took some medication, including two of her prescribed 'nerve tablets' – Luvox and the antihistamine Phenergan, to make it look like she'd overdosed, but not enough to be dangerous, and was woken when police arrived at 8.14 am, alerted by worried colleagues when Pricey did not turn up for work.

When she was arraigned on 2 February 2001, Katherine Knight pleaded not guilty to murder. But when she was formally charged on 18 October, she changed her plea to guilty after being psychiatrically assessed and found to be capable of understanding the legal effects and consequences of pleading not guilty.

In other words, she was not mentally ill.

The sentencing

Katherine Knight's 2001 sentencing for the murder of John Charles Thomas Price heard some of most horrific details ever put before an Australian court. The court was told that Knight, who used to work in an abattoir, skinned, beheaded and cooked parts of Pricey to make it appear that she was mentally unhinged and not responsible for her actions. Health professionals found that she had a personality disorder, not a mental illness.

New South Wales Supreme Court Justice Barry O'Keefe said Knight showed 'no mercy whatsoever' to her victim:

> The last minutes of his life must have been a time of abject terror for him, as they were a time of utter enjoyment for her. At no time during the hearing or prior thereto did the prisoner express any regret for what she had done or any remorse for having done it; not even through the surrogacy of counsel. Her attitude in that regard is consistent with her general approach to the many acts of violence which she had engaged in against her various partners, namely *they deserved it*. (R v Knight, 2001)

Justice O'Keefe described the crime as 'horrendous' and 'in the most serious category':

> The level of culpability of the prisoner is, as I have determined, extreme. The murder was premeditated. The prisoner not only decided to murder Mr Price, but planned the timing and what she was going to do in a manner which left open to her, as she thought, a way of escaping punishment, namely that she would [be] considered as mad. Furthermore, the prisoner . . . has no real prospects of rehabilitation and would be highly dangerous to the community were she to be allowed out of prison.

In an attempt to mitigate the gravity of what she had done, Knight's lawyers claimed she had tried to take her own life afterwards. But she had no alcohol in her blood and normal levels of the prescribed drugs she had taken. Her counsel argued that Knight claimed she could not remember committing the crime. However, she did remember quite vividly events which appeared to have immediately preceded it, as well as the doses of the tablets she had taken.

'This is not a credible pattern for a true amnesia, according to the psychiatric evidence which I accept,' Justice O'Keefe found, adding that he did not believe Knight's story.

> Moreover, during the time of which she claims to have no recollection, she performed a number of tasks that required a steady hand, the application of skill and an understanding of driving a motor vehicle and of operating an automatic teller machine. She also showered, changed her clothes and walked from her house back to Mr Price's house. I am satisfied beyond reasonable doubt that she has much more recollection than she has claimed and that her claimed extent of amnesia is convenient for her, both emotionally and litigiously.

The court heard from several psychiatrists, including Dr Robert Delaforce, who interviewed Knight for nine hours, an experience that Knight later said she enjoyed. He and another psychiatrist diagnosed a borderline personality disorder (BPD) and post-traumatic stress disorder. Among other things, Dr Delaforce discovered Knight's interest in violent and macabre videos, such as *Resurrection*, which depicted gruesome murders, decapitation, a skinned body and the hanging of a body on a meat hook. 'Dr Delaforce was of the view that there were many indications that in killing Mr Price the prisoner was carrying out planned behaviour and that this was consistent with her ongoing violent fantasies and vindictive characteristics,' Justice O'Keefe found.

He was of the view that she suffered from a borderline personality disorder, but that 'probably her killing of Mr Price and the mutilation of his body were premeditated acts of revenge and perverted pleasure derived from her grossly violent fantasies'. I have no doubt that he is correct.

Dr Delaforce also believed that Knight's BPD had no significant or immediate connection with her crime:

What she did on the night was part of her personality, her nature, herself, but it is not a feature of borderline personality disorder. It is not even significantly connected. She knew the nature and quality of the acts that she was doing and she was aware at that time that those acts were wrong. It is very important to realise that the pleasure in getting rid of him and getting away with it by making out that she is mad, that in a sense is a payback, but it is the way she gets rid of him that shows the absolute depravity of what she was doing. But that does not in itself mean madness, that type of interest; not to a psychiatrist, but to a layperson it would.

Forensic psychiatrist Dr Rod Milton also testified that Knight was not mentally ill:

The personality problems demonstrated in the history of Ms Knight's life are not in my view psychiatric disease – they are her nature. These personality problems did not stop her from knowing what she was doing or whether it was right or wrong. Nor did they stop her from exercising control over her actions when she chose.

On 8 November 2001, Justice O'Keefe sentenced Katherine Mary Knight, who had just turned forty-six, to life in prison without parole – the first Australian woman to receive such a sentence. Knight appealed, arguing that the sentence was excessive. But on 11 September 2006, Supreme Court of New South Wales Court of Criminal Appeal Justices Peter McClellan, Michael Adams and Megan Latham dismissed it. 'This was an appalling crime almost beyond contemplation in a civilised society,' Justice McLellan found.

> The crime was the product of a violent personality intent upon claiming the life of her de facto in a relationship which was plainly failing. She expressed no remorse or contrition. The psychiatric evidence indicates that her personality is unlikely to change in the future and, if released, she would be likely to inflict serious injury, perhaps death on others. The deceased's family may be at particular risk. (Knight v R, 2006)

Katherine Knight's background

One of eight children – six boys and twin girls – Katherine Knight had a childhood that was far from ideal. Her mother, Barbara Roughan (nee Thorley), also had a tough upbringing. Barbara's father left when she was young and she may have been sexually abused by relatives. She became a troubled young woman, as her daughter Katherine would be, and at one point was placed in a home for wayward girls.

Barbara moved to Moree with Katherine's father, Ken Knight, after having an affair with him while still married to her first husband, Jack Roughan, with whom she had four sons. Under family law in the 1950s, custody was routinely given to the father. The two oldest boys, Patrick and Martin, stayed with Jack and continued to live in Aberdeen. The younger two, Neville and Barry, were both under eighteen months old, making it very difficult for their father to take care of them while working full time, so both were sent to live with an aunt in Sydney (Lee, 2002).

Jack Roughan, who had been a drunk and neglectful husband, died in 1957. Patrick and Martin then moved in with Barbara, Ken and their three young children, Kenneth Charles (known as Charlie), Joy and Katherine, while Neville and Barry stayed in Sydney. Shane was born in 1961, completing the family, which was already known for being quite dysfunctional (Lalor, 2002).

Fraternal (non-identical) twins Joy Gwendoline and Katherine Mary had been born on 24 October 1955, in Tenterfield, New South Wales. Arriving thirty minutes earlier, Joy was the more outgoing. She was a tomboy and more of a leader, while Katherine was quieter and more girly. Katherine also struggled academically and repeated grade five. The twins' early years were spent in Wallangarra in Queensland and Gunnedah and Moree in New South Wales, partly to escape the scandal of Barbara and Ken's affair.

In 1969, the family returned to Aberdeen, where the extended Knight family was firmly entrenched. Ken worked at the local meatworks and was a respected employee. But he was also an alcoholic who regularly beat his children and frequently attacked and raped his wife Barbara. In his book *Blood Stain*, Peter Lalor wrote that Katherine Knight's childhood memories included her father demanding sex from her mother, publicly and violently. Ken apparently knocked his wife out in his pursuit of sex, leaving bruises on her face. 'One visitor remembers him chasing his wife up and down the corridor in the last year of her life yelling, "Give us a root, come on, fuck ya, give us a root,"' (Lalor, 2002).

Knight later told a psychiatrist she had been repeatedly sexually abused when she was about six, possibly older. Knight reportedly claimed than an older brother would spit on his fingers and rub her vagina, but had trouble remembering the exact details. Some psychiatrists accepted this but with room for minor doubts. One of Knight's daughters also told police that her mother had told her she was sexually abused by an older half-brother from the ages of five to nine, and that Charlie had joined in but was younger and had been convinced to join 'the game' (Lalor, 2002). Knight later named her older half-brother Patrick John Roughan as the perpetrator when he was charged in 2006 with sexually abusing a young girl but later found not guilty. A statement was produced in court in which Katherine Knight wrote her life would probably have been different if Patrick hadn't abused her ('Ex-Minister pleads innocent to sex crime', 2007).

According to Lalor, Knight, who wet the bed until the abuse stopped when she was eleven, was afraid of the dark and kept a doll to protect her:

> She said she has a memory of Ken trying to get into her bed after her mother refused to have sex with him, but she never claimed he sexually abused her. However her fear of rape, which clearly evolved from these early traumas, seemed to develop into a paranoia that manifested itself on many occasions. Katherine was forever making allegations that men had or wanted to abuse her children. None of these allegations was ever substantiated, but the fears were terribly real in her own mind, no matter how trivial or malicious they looked to anybody else. Katherine viewed all men as possible sex offenders where her daughters were concerned.

Barbara didn't show her children much affection as she was too busy fighting off Ken's sexual advances and raising her brood. Beltings were also common (Lalor, 2002). In *Beyond Bad, The Life and Crimes of Katherine Knight, Australia's Hannibal* (2002) Sandra Lee wrote that Barbara had a fiery temper like her daughter:

242

Barbara Knight could be a bit of a hothead, and was known to swear. She was a tough disciplinarian and neighbours remember her for her short-fused temper and obscene language which she rarely censored. Like most couples, Barbara and Ken had their moments but they stayed together through the good times and bad. (Lee, 2002)

When Katherine Knight was on her best behaviour, she was pleasant to be around. But if something went wrong she would explode with rage. At Muswellbrook High School she was a loner who could behave when she wanted to, but also got into fights. When boys teased her on the bus about her looks, she would hand her glasses to Joy and lay into them. She was scared of no-one. Katherine and Joy didn't necessarily instigate school-yard spats but were known for fighting others and each other. Katherine was often in trouble with teachers and refused to do what she was told. Some say she lorded it over younger students, but her younger brother, Shane, disputed this and said she was 'always a good kid' (Lee, 2002).

Others remember her differently. A friend told Lee that Knight once pulled a knife in town when teenage boys were skylarking:

We didn't know she had this long-bladed knife . . . and that day she pulled out the knife and said, 'Come on, if you want to have a go at us, come on.' . . . We all just looked at each other and still couldn't believe it the next day. Well, you don't expect someone of that age to have knives, and particularly back then because things were quite calm and harmless . . . not like it is today. But that's how she was . . .

After leaving school at fifteen, Knight worked as a cutter in a clothing factory before securing her dream job a year later, cutting offal at the local abattoir. She became a boner and was given a set of butcher knives that she treasured.

From a young age, Knight's relationships with men were unstable and violent – mostly on her part. At just eighteen, she married truck driver David Kellett in 1974. They had two children – Melanie in 1976, and Naomi in 1980 – before the marriage broke up in 1984. Knight later claimed Kellett physically abused her and was unfaithful, causing her to have a nervous breakdown. During her sentencing he denied ever hurting her and said it was Knight who was unpredictably violent: 'I never raised a finger against her, not even in self-defence. I would just walk away' (R v Knight, 2001).

Before the wedding, Barbara had warned Kellett that if he played up her daughter would kill him. It didn't take long for him to see that side of her. Kellett's sentencing hearing evidence revealed that on their wedding night, Knight choked him by grabbing his throat due to the 'comparative inadequacy' of his sexual performance – her parents had done it five times on their wedding night and she liked to compare herself to them. Later in their marriage, Knight attacked him with an iron and then set fire to all his clothes. One morning he woke to find her sitting on his chest in bed holding a meat knife to his throat saying, 'You see how easy it is?' and asking, 'Is it true that truck drivers have different women in every town?' He denied any infidelity.

Knight asked her husband to mount her two slicing knives so she could keep them above her bed. When Melanie was a baby, he decided he'd had enough and left for another woman. The next day Knight was seen with a pram in Aberdeen's main street, throwing it violently from side to side. She was diagnosed with postnatal depression and spent several weeks in hospital. After being released, she placed two-month-old Melanie on a railway line shortly before the train was due, but luckily an old man rescued the baby. Knight then stole an axe, went to the main street and threatened to kill anyone she encountered. She was arrested and again taken to hospital but managed to discharge herself the next day. A few days later, Knight slashed the face of a teenage neighbour, Margaret Perry, in an attempt to get Margaret's mother Molly to drive them to where David was living with his new girl-friend. This resulted in another psychiatric admission (Lee, 2002).

Knight and David Kellett reconciled and had another daughter, Naomi, in 1980, but they broke up again after she had a 'payback' affair. Her erratic and violent behaviour continued and at one point she hit David on the head with a sharpening steel, inflicting an injury requiring hospital treatment. He didn't press charges because he was worried about what his wife would do to their children. In the end Knight suddenly left their home, clearing the house of almost everything.

In 1986, the year Barbara died at the age of fifty-nine, Knight met former racing car driver and miner David Saunders. Their daughter Monique was born in 1988. Knight complained that Saunders mistreated her and was violent, once kicking her in the stomach when he thought she was pregnant. To retaliate she went into the backyard and slit the throat of his eight-week-old dingo puppy killing it. She also damaged his car and took an overdose of sleeping tablets, after which she was admitted to a psychiatric hospital. In a later court statement, David Saunders said he never cheated on Knight, although she constantly claimed he did. He denied the kicking incident and said that despite their relation-ship being 'basically good', she took out domestic violence orders against him when he was the one being assaulted. Knight once stabbed him in the right side of the stomach with a pair of scissors and another time cut all his clothing into small pieces, leaving him with only the clothes he was then wearing. He eventually fled to Newcastle (R v Knight, 2001).

In 1989, Knight paid off her modest house – which she decorated with symbols of death such as cow hides, water buffalo horns, deer antlers and cow and sheep skulls – following a $15,000 workers compensation payout (Lee, 2002). In 1990, she met fellow slaughterhouse worker John Chillingworth and they had a son, Evan. In 1991, she claimed her partner assaulted her but her sentencing hearing heard that no available records supported those claims. In a court statement, John denied being violent towards her except when he retaliated after she snatched his glasses from his face and broke them. He said that, among other vindictive acts, Knight smashed his false teeth, claiming he had smacked one of her daughters (R v Knight, 2001).

In Lee's book, John Chillingworth offered some insight into Knight's way of thinking. He said she never wanted to be alone and would tell him that if something happened to him she'd have another bloke 'within a day or two':

> You never knew what you had with Kathy. She had a saying, she'd say, 'I love ya, I love ya, if I hate ya, I hate ya.' And if Kathy Knight hated ya, there was no limit to what she could do or would do to ya, in some way. It may not be personal. It might be the car or the house, your cat or your dog, or whatever. But if she loved ya, you'd have sex ten times a day, it comes back to that sexual thing. The violence a guy'd dish out Kathy, she'd give him back tenfold, oh yeah . . . I had no doubt she was going to maim somebody. I expected to read in the paper one day that she de-knackered someone.

Knight punched and hit her then partner, but when he hit her back, she took out an AVO against him. They split up for a week, then got back together, but John still had to go to court as she didn't withdraw the charge. After he was fined $619 for assault and placed on a two-year bond, they went home and had sex. By the time John Chillingworth moved to Queensland in December 1993, Knight was already having an affair with Pricey, whom she met on 8 October 1993.

At first Pricey and Knight got along well. They loved to go dancing together and had a very healthy sex life. Knight sewed for him and rose at 5 am to make his breakfast and lunch to take to work. She was in love. But then the arguments and violence began. They continued to fight and he threatened to end the relationship a number of times. When Pricey kicked Knight out of his home in 1998, after she had him sacked by sending his employer the misleading video, she threw all the meat from his freezer into the backyard. But Pricey, who secured another job at a local earth-moving company, eventually took her back. He did well at his new job and was soon promoted.

Geraldine Edwards, who owned a general store next door to Knight's house, was scared of her neighbour and says there was 'something about her'. 'She frightened me but I couldn't put it into words about how she made me feel. It was just something about her.' Most of the time, Knight was friendly towards Geraldine, but she did lose her temper in front of customers in Geraldine's shop. 'Once she was aggressive and angry and going off her face . . . because someone who came to visit me parked outside the front of her house,' Geraldine recalls. 'I said, "Katherine, I'm so sorry, I had no idea that was going to be an issue" . . . and straight away she said, "Oh, okay." Everyone just stood there opened-mouthed. It's not like normal people.'

Another time, one of Knight's daughters was with several young men in Knight's house next door to Geraldine. As Geraldine's son worked on Geraldine's bathroom tiling, the three men in Knight's house started yelling and threatening Geraldine's son through the bathroom window, so Geraldine rang Knight at Pricey's house. Knight said she'd sort it out and came over to confront them. Recalls Geraldine:

> She came out the back door and said 'what the fuck is going on here?' You have never seen those three guys, these big guys, scatter as fast as they scattered. Two of them jumped the back fence. And then she came up [to me] and said, 'There you go . . . you won't have any problems now.' She did a lot of nice things for a lot of people. She could be extremely kind-hearted when she chose to be and she could do anything for you if she chose to, but she had this volatile thing where she could go off at the drop of a hat. She didn't take shit from anybody.

Pricey and Knight often fought loudly, screaming expletives at each other before making up and having sex – also loudly. Knight told Geraldine about the video she made to get Pricey sacked and complained about him cheating when he hadn't. Knight said she would only leave him if he paid her $10,000 and if she caught him cheating she'd 'cut his dick and his balls off'. Geraldine does not believe Pricey would have cheated; if he had, news would have spread through the small town like wildfire. 'Everybody would have known about it,' she says. 'He was a really, really lovely guy. He was a real Aussie bloke. He had a big heart. Everyone loved John. His children loved him.'

Knight continually got away with actions that should have resulted in criminal charges – until she planned and executed Pricey's murder. Nor was she the only family member in trouble with the law. Patrick John Roughan, whom Knight named as the half-brother who sexually abused her, was charged in November 2006 but cleared in 2008, when he was sixty-three, of two counts of sexual intercourse by digital penetration of a nine-year-old girl (Strachan, 2008).

In 2007, Patrick John Roughan's son, James Patrick was convicted of murdering a homeless teenager after he and an accomplice attacked and decapitated their victim during a drunken argument. The Brisbane Supreme Court sentenced James Roughan, then 27, and Christopher Clark Jones, 23, to life in prison for killing Morgan Jay Shepherd, 17. They also received two years jail for interfering with the corpse. Both had pleaded guilty to being an accessory after the fact, but blamed each other for the killing. The court heard that the pair bashed their victim and stabbed him 133 times before decapitating him with a saw and an axe. The next day they allegedly buried the headless corpse after rolling the head down a hill 'like a bowling ball' ('"Bowling Ball" decapitation killer loses appeal', 2009).

Christopher Jones allegedly told friends that James Roughan stuck his hand inside the head and played with it like a puppet, and stuck the head on the stump of a paw paw tree, spinning it around and laughing at it (Meade, 2007). In late 2007, James Roughan won a new trial but was again convicted and sentenced to life in jail. In 2009, the Brisbane Court of Appeal unanimously dismissed an appeal against his conviction.

Some branches of the Roughan–Knight family were clearly dysfunctional, which affected some of the children more than others. One of Knight's half-brothers, Barry Roughan, whose wife left him to have a relationship with Knight's twin, Joy, summed it up when interviewed for Lalor's book: 'If you dig deep enough it's as grubby as all shit, our family. As grubby as shit. Mate, the family is rotten to the core' (Lalor, 2002).

Why did she do it?

We know why Katherine Knight committed her crime: to punish a partner who had tried to dump her. But why did she do it in such a brutal and shocking way? Few people kill under these circumstances and even fewer do it in the way that Knight did. Pricey's murder was the last in a line of erratic, rage-filled acts of violence that she inflicted after a number of genetic and environmental factors in her life combined to produce a pattern of behaviour consistent with her having borderline personality disorder (BPD). Three of the four psychiatrists who assessed Knight concluded that she had a BPD; hers is an extreme version and she fits all of the criteria.

Those with a BPD tend to be highly emotional and volatile, needy, irrational, manipulative, vindictive and, in cases like Knight's, violent. If they have been abused and/or abandoned they will seek care and protection but, when they find it, they don't trust the carer or protector not to withdraw it. They have a heightened sensitivity to what others say and do and to any behaviour, however small, that could possibly be interpreted as a sign of abandonment, rejection or a threat to their safety. This can result in their becoming emotionally overwhelmed and losing control, as Knight did when her partners left.

Those with a BPD also have a diminished capacity for empathy, which was probably worsened in Knight's case by working in an abattoir, which desensitised her to pain and suffering. As well as having a low IQ and limited education, she was probably genetically predisposed to high levels of irritability, emotionality and impulsivity. Some who knew her mother said she had similar traits.

There is some evidence to support Knight's claims that she was physically abused by her parents and sexually abused by a half-brother as a child. She has claimed that her father was once charged by police for physically assaulting her (Lalor, 2002), but no charges were ever laid in relation to sexual abuse. Many people with a BPD have suffered from this type of abuse in an unsafe family environment, which disrupts normal brain development in a way that leaves the child, and later the adult they become, hypersensitive to potential threats of abuse or abandonment. They focus on survival and lack the cognitive and emotional resources to self-soothe in the face of emotional distress. If, as has been suggested, Knight's mother was also a victim of child sex abuse, her parenting style may have further heightened her daughter's fears and safety concerns.

Knight's lack of education and basic literacy skills made her situation even more difficult. Leaving school in Year 8 meant she was denied the chance to learn thinking skills that could have helped her to behave more rationally when her emotions threatened to overcome her. Having an IQ probably in the lower end of the average range would also have reduced her capacity to think more rationally about how to respond to day-to-day situations and effectively manage strong feelings such as anger instead of lashing out aggressively.

From a young age, Knight had to fight to survive, becoming desensitised to the violence she saw and experienced at home and, later, at work. The longer a child lives in an environment in which they are harmed, fear being harmed or see others being harmed, the more severe their trauma will be. This can occur, for example, during war, natural disaster or when a child lives in a violent and abusive family situation without outside support. When those who are meant to protect a child also hurt them, or fail to prevent them from being hurt, the child soon develops a sense of helplessness and chronic fear. In Katherine Knight's mind, all men were potential rapists and abusers.

Abuse-related stress usually interferes significantly with the development of age-appropriate emotional maturity. A child's previous and ongoing feelings of intense fear often overwhelm them. They may react to non-threatening situations in a maladaptive way, making it more difficult for them to learn effective ways to self-soothe and identify and manage their emotions.

In many cases they haven't had a suitable adult role model to show them how to handle strong feelings or to support them in learning to manage the full range of emotions. They usually remain emotionally immature, even as adults, and their moral development is limited. In Knight's case, one of her psychiatrists concluded that she had a 'primitive conscience' and in many ways was quite childish (Lalor, 2002).

All this can make it more difficult to develop mutually supportive friendships at school and at work. Classmates and co-workers may quickly become wary of their intense emotional overreactions to minor situations. When those around her realised how extreme Knight's behaviour could be, they either left or kept out of her way.

Knight was also caught up in the process of 'violentisation', identified by Seton Hall University criminology professor Lonnie Athens (Athens and Ulmer, 2003; Rhodes, 2000). After conducting hundreds of interviews with violent convicted prisoners in jail, Athens developed a model of what he terms the violentisation process. It has four key stages:

• The brutalisation stage
• The belligerence stage
• The violent performance stage
• The virulence stage.

In the initial brutalisation stage, one or more of the following occurs:

• The individual is forced to comply with the demands of an older family member who uses violence.
• The individual witnesses a relative being forced to comply through violence.

- An older relative coaches the individual to be violent by insisting that they need to use violence to defend and take care of him/herself. This 'coaching' may be done through stories that glorify violent behaviour or by ridiculing the individual.

Next is the belligerence stage, during which the individual starts to believe that he or she must take action to protect him/herself. The message they absorb is that they need to attack anyone who seriously provokes or torments them, *but only if it is serious enough and they think they have a chance of 'winning' the interaction*. They use violence successfully in one situation.

In the violent performance stage, they begin to act aggressively towards others in some situations and become more confident that they can use violence effectively. They always consider the risk of even more violent retaliation, and exercise some caution in deciding whom to attack and to what degree. They also break from the control of the person who was using violence against them. When their 'attacks' are successful, they may attract the attention and approval of others. But they begin to develop a reputation as 'dangerous' or 'crazy'. This often develops into a warped kind of 'celebrity' or notoriety.

Finally, during the virulence stage, the individual starts to enjoy their notoriety and becomes quite pleased with him/herself, feeling almost invincible. They can see no reason not to continue this behaviour and now direct their violence towards anyone who even slightly annoys them. Others are scared of them and no-one tries to suggest that they should behave differently. They are on the path to becoming a violent criminal and have a high likelihood that they will end up in jail.

Katherine Knight clearly progressed through all four stages. Her partners ended up petrified of her violent outbursts and threats and all chose to leave the relationship when it became too much.

Like most people with a personality disorder, Knight did not learn from her mistakes, nor did she respond adaptively or resiliently to stressful situations in her life. She continued to display the same pattern of behaviour over and over, distrusting almost everyone she met and lashing out at those she thought threatened her. It was a vicious circle that led to the worst possible outcome for everyone. This certainly doesn't excuse her depraved acts of violence; it simply explains them.

Almost as difficult to explain and understand is why Knight's partners stayed with her for so long and kept forgiving her repeated acts of violence towards them. The answer partly lies in her recognition and use of the power of sexuality. Each of her partners spoke glowingly of her willingness to engage in sexual activity as a well as her 'wildness' in bed. Of Knight, her second partner David Saunders said, 'I never had a better fuck' (Lalor, 2002). She clearly used sex as a way of making up after a fight and to keep a partner who was threatening to leave.

Sadly, if Knight had been sexually abused as a child as she claimed, she could have learned the power of sex from an early age. Her emotional desperation and a fear of being alone meant she quickly moved from one man to another. But she did have some positive attributes. Many Aberdeen locals have spoken of her 'heart of gold' and her kindness to them when, for example, they were ill. Her first husband, David Kellett, claimed that for many years Knight was not only fun and devoted but also 'the most wonderful wife you could wish for. Perfect mother, perfect housewife'. But: 'Sometimes she'd just snap like a biscuit' (Charleston, 2013).

Words can't really describe the complex life and actions of Katherine Knight. But a simple children's rhyme generally attributed to US poet Henry Wadsworth Longfellow does come close. In his famous poem he writes about a little girl with a little curl right in the middle of her forehead. When she was good she was very, very good – but when she was bad she was horrid.

KATHERINE KNIGHT
DIAGNOSTIC CHART

Using DSM 5 indicators (APA, 2013), when five or more of these are present, a diagnosis of borderline personality disorder (BPD) can be made	Examples of Katherine Knight's behaviour that appear to be consistent with each indicator
Frantic efforts to avoid real or imagined abandonment. (**Note:** Do not include suicidal or self-mutilating behavior covered in Criterion 5.)	This pattern was shown in all of Knight's live-in relationships with men. She made numerous threats to kill John Price if he left her.
A pattern of unstable and intense interpersonal relationships characterized by alternating between extremes of idealization and devaluation.	This pattern was apparent in all of Knight's live-in relationships with men, e.g. she loved Pricey but, when angry with him, made him lose his mining job by filming items he had supposedly stolen from work and showing it to his employer.
Identity disturbance: markedly and persistently unstable self-image or sense of self.	This pattern was also shown in all of Knight's relationships with men. She often used the police to punish her partners by laying charges against them. Her murder of Pricey after he had rejected her was an extreme example of this behaviour pattern.

Using DSM 5 indicators (APA, 2013), when five or more of these are present, a diagnosis of borderline personality disorder (BPD) can be made	Examples of Katherine Knight's behaviour that appear to be consistent with each indicator
Impulsivity in at least two areas that are potentially self-damaging (e.g. spending, sex, substance abuse, reckless driving, binge eating). (**Note:** Do not include suicidal or self-mutilating behavior covered in Criterion 5.)	Knight's sexual behaviour was often very promiscuous. She had many live-in partnerships but also sometimes had affairs with other men at the same time. She was impulsively aggressive on a number of occasions and was known to swerve while driving to try to hit dogs and cats on the road.
Recurrent suicidal behavior, gestures, or threats, or self-mutilating behavior.	Knight made many suicidal threats and suicide attempts, usually after she felt that she had been abandoned or betrayed. Some seemed to be histrionic and others were more serious and required hospital treatment.
Affective instability due to a marked reactivity of mood (e.g. intense episodic dysphoria, irritability, or anxiety usually lasting a few hours and only rarely more than a few days).	Her emotions changed rapidly after relatively minor conflict or perceived disloyalty by her partner at the time. She often screamed at friends and neighbours, only to quickly calm down soon after.
Chronic feelings of emptiness.	Insufficient information available to comment.

Using DSM 5 indicators (APA, 2013), when five or more of these are present, a diagnosis of borderline personality disorder (BPD) can be made	Examples of Katherine Knight's behaviour that appear to be consistent with each indicator
Inappropriate, intense anger or difficulty controlling anger (e.g. frequent displays of temper, constant anger, recurrent physical fights).	Knight fought with other students while at school and had a strong history of physically assaulting or fighting with all her live-in partners when angry with them. These assaults (e.g. attacks with a hot iron or sharp knife) occurred when she believed they had behaved in small ways that offended or upset her, such as getting home from the pub a little later than expected.
Transient, stress-related paranoid ideation or severe dissociative symptoms. * Reprinted with permission from the Diagnostic and Statistical Manual of Mental Disorders, Fifth Edition, (Copyright ©2013). American Psychiatric Association. All Rights Reserved.	Knight was often convinced that her children were not safe from being sexually assaulted. Knight had one 'dissociative' episode after her first husband, David Kellett, left her and moved to another town with a new partner. She also tried to hijack a family and hold them hostage in an attempt to make them drive her to the town to which her husband had moved. Knight later placed their two-month-old daughter Melanie on a railway line shortly before the train was due. Fortunately someone saved the child and Knight was admitted to hospital.

CONCLUSION

What we can learn from the murder committed by Katherine Knight

Katherine Knight is one of a kind. Many factors combined to turn her into a sadistic killer. The key driver was the severe trauma she experienced as a child. This interacted with her low level of education and a probable genetic predisposition to some aspects of a borderline personality disorder (BPD), such as irritability, emotionality and impulsivity. Few people with a BPD become sadistic killers like Knight, but some can be extremely difficult to have in your life.

Even in milder cases, those with a BPD can be needy, manipulative, irrational and sometimes aggressive. They can twist what their friends and family do or say into rejection or a conspiracy against them, making something out of nothing. If two of their friends go out for a casual coffee without telling them, they might see it as a deliberate snub and imagine that the person who made the arrangements was trying to exclude them. Or they might become upset if they see a text message their partner has sent to another person, even if it is completely innocent.

Many people with a BPD find it hard to understand that others can disagree with them without intending to put them down. They often interpret disagreement as evidence of the other person's dislike of, or contempt for them. Insecurity can sometimes heighten their sensitivity to almost anything that might be seen as potentially negative, and this can make partnerships and friendships very difficult. If someone tells their partner they are getting tired of having chicken every Tuesday, their partner will most likely simply say 'Fine, let's have something else'. However a partner with a BPD might see it as a criticism of their planning or cooking and turn it into an angry argument.

BPD is often undiagnosed because, taken independently, its symptoms can be difficult to identify and understand, and it may be dismissed as the person simply being needy, overly emotional or immature. It is important to look at the overall pattern of behaviour in order to identify a BPD in someone you know or care about. If you think a loved one might have the disorder, consider seeking advice from a mental health professional. Their wellbeing and that of the people who care about them can be improved in small ways through support and appropriate treatment. Teachers and health professionals also need to be alert to the possibility that a child who is doing poorly in school and has difficulties focusing on their schoolwork may have suffered, or is still suffering, from some form of abuse or trauma. These children are sometimes misdiagnosed as having attention deficit hyperactivity disorder (ADHD) (Szymanski et al., 2011).

If you live with or have significant contact with someone who has a BPD, you may feel like you are on a permanent emotional roller coaster. Here are some suggestions for taking care of yourself and managing difficult situations.

Consider practising a form of mindfulness that appeals to you. A simple version of mindfulness is the 7/11 strategy. Set side five minutes to sit quietly in a peaceful place where there is something worth looking at, such as a garden plant, a favourite painting or your sleeping pet. While you continue to focus on all aspects of this, such as the detail, smell, texture and structure, breathe in slowly while mentally counting to seven and then exhale deeply while mentally counting to eleven.

Make sure that, where possible, you follow though on any promise or commitment you make to someone with a BPD. If an argument is looming, stay calm and in charge so that you don't escalate it. Stand up for yourself in a calm and non-combative way, using a quiet voice and non-aggressive body language. If you feel too angry or upset to discuss something, say that you need to take a few minutes to go away and think about things. Make sure you come back.

Disagree respectfully to validate what they are saying. This means starting with what you can agree with and then explaining what you don't agree with. For example, 'I agree with you that this last-minute change of plan is a nuisance, but I can't do anything about it.'

Remind yourself that you can't fulfil all of the other person's needs. Be mindful that they may be confusing their feelings with facts, so tell them that you are sorry they feel that way but they may not have the facts right. Don't feel guilty about their pattern of behaviour. It is likely that you can't control what they are feeling or thinking through what you do or don't do or say, even though you might sometimes be able to help them feel a little calmer (Mason and Kreger, 2010).

Don't make threats about leaving the relationship. If you decide to end a relationship or workplace position, do it discreetly, calmly and without fanfare. If an employee in your organisation whom you think might have a BPD angrily decides to leave or is 'let go', make sure they cannot access key databases and sources of information in case they decide to act vengefully.

If you have ended a relationship with someone who may have a BPD, be very careful. You might be stalked, cyberstalked or bombarded with texts and emails. Your ex-partner may use your family and friends to source information about you such as where you are going, what you are doing and any new email addresses or phone numbers. If this happens, or your ex-partner is harrassing your loved ones, consider taking out an intervention order.

Very few people with a BPD are as dangerous as Katherine Knight, but some can still make life difficult. Take reasonable precautions if needed and read some of the books about living with someone who has a BPD, which can help you to understand and deal with them (see page 382).

PART IV

ANTISOCIAL PERSONALITY DISORDER

INTRODUCTION

Antisocial personality disorder (ASPD): Life without a conscience

We find them both fascinating and repulsive. People with an antisocial personality disorder (ASPD) are predators. You probably know at least one person with an ASPD in your family, workplace or social circle – the uncle who lost his real-estate licence for misusing a client's money; the cousin who abandoned his wife and child; the friend who borrowed money from you and moved interstate without paying it back despite frequent reminders; the colleague who lied and took credit for your work.

Their underdeveloped conscience enables them to lie, cheat, steal, manipulate and mistreat other people to get what they want. Some are charming and seem normal and successful; this 'mask' can make it difficult to recognise the danger they present. Others stand out more because they regularly come into contact with the justice system from a young age. Convicted murderers Angelika Gavare, Simon Gittany and Adrian Bayley all have an APSD.

Gavare killed an elderly pensioner, Vonne McGlynn, to steal her home and other assets. Gittany threw his fiancée, Lisa Harnum, to her death from a fifteenth-floor balcony when he found out that she was trying to leave him. Adrian Bayley murdered Jill Meagher because she confronted him after he sexually assaulted her. None showed any mercy for their victims.

Recognising someone with an ASPD

Diagnosing a personality disorder is difficult and requires some professional knowledge, but you can get a general idea of it by looking at the criteria. The DSM 5 (APA, 2013) describes an anti-social personality disorder as a pervasive pattern of disregard for and violation of the rights of others, occurring since age fifteen years, as indicated by:

CRITERION A. Three (or more) of the following:
1. Failure to conform to social norms with respect to lawful behaviors, as indicated by repeatedly performing acts that are grounds for arrest.
2. Deceitfulness, as indicated by repeated lying, use of aliases, or conning others for personal profit or pleasure.
3. Impulsivity or failure to plan ahead.
4. Irritability and aggressiveness, as indicated by repeated physical fights or assaults.
5. Reckless disregard for safety of self or others.
6. Consistent irresponsibility, as indicated by repeated failure to sustain consistent work behavior or honor financial obligations.
7. Lack of remorse, as indicated by being indifferent to or rationalizing having hurt, mistreated, or stolen from another.

In addition, the individual must be at least age 18 years (Criterion B) and must have had a history of some symptoms of conduct disorder before age fifteen years (Criterion C). Conduct disorder involves a repetitive and persistent pattern of behaviour in which the basic rights of others or major age-appropriate societal norms or rules are violated. The specific behaviours characteristic of conduct disorder fall into one of four categories: aggression to people and animals, destruction of property, deceitfulness or theft, or serious violation of rules. A fourth criterion is that the behaviour must not exclusively occur during the course of schizophrenia or bipolar disorder (Criterion D).

In two of the three cases analysed in this section, this information was not readily available but it is highly likely that given the nature of their ongoing criminal activities that they had engaged in this kind of behaviour before they turned fifteen. In Simon Gittany's case there is strong evidence of his having behaved in ways that were consistent with a conduct disorder, but we are unable to publish those details.

As with other personality disorders, the severity of ASPD can range from mild to extreme. Two people with an ASPD may behave differently in some ways, depending on which criteria they meet, other personal characteristics and other factors in their lives. A distinct variant of ASPD, often termed *psychopathy* (or 'primary' psychopathy), is identified in the DSM 5 (Section iii). This psychopathic variant is characterised by low levels of anxiousness and withdrawal and high levels of attention seeking. The DSM 5 states that *'high attention seeking and low withdrawal capture the social potency (assertive/dominant) component of psychopathy, whereas low anxiousness captures the stress immunity (emotional stability/resilience) component'*. This variant corresponds with many of the features first described by Hare (1996) in his original conception of psychopathy. The specifier 'with psychopathic features' is included in the diagnosis when this is the case.

Why did they do it?

The DSM 5 notes that the ASPD pattern has also been referred to by some researchers as both psychopathy and sociopathy. The first version of the DSM in 1952 used the term 'sociopathic personality disorder', which was replaced in all newer editions by the term 'antisocial personality disorder'. The terms 'psychopath' and 'sociopath', which have been used to name individuals with many of the behaviours that are also characteristic of an ASPD, have since been used interchangeably by many writers, clinicians and researchers and within popular culture.

There has also been considerable unresolved debate over the years about whether these are identical, similar or quite different disorders. It has been argued that they are identical disorders, but that the term sociopath is more appropriate as it focuses on the fact that the suffering ('path') caused is to other people ('socio') rather than to the wellbeing ('psycho') of the person with an ASPD. Others have argued that psychopaths and sociopaths share only some of the core features of someone with an ASPD, but psychopaths are more extreme and dangerous as they are more likely to be not only callous but violent and physically cruel as well. They are also more likely to be imprisoned and to reoffend when released. Some have argued that sociopaths are more 'high functioning' than psychopaths because they are more socially effective, have a more developed conscience, have some capacity for empathy, are less likely to be cruel or violent, less likely to be imprisoned and tend to be more 'successful' than psychopaths in terms of their position in society and career. This is the assumption made by the authors of books such as *The Sociopath Next Door* (Stout, 2006), *Confessions of a Sociopath* (Thomas, 2013) and *Difficult Personalities* (McGrath and Edwards, 2009).

It has also been suggested that sociopaths are more likely than psychopaths to display additional features typical of narcissistic personality disorder, such as arrogance and grandiosity. Others have argued that sociopaths are more likely to be a product of their upbringing, while psychopaths are more likely to be a product of neurological factors (e.g. Lykken, 1995). At this stage, experts still can't agree on many of these issues, but further research is being conducted in an attempt to clarify some of them.

Prevalence
An estimated .2 to 3.3 per cent of the general population has an ASPD and it is more frequent in men (up to 5.8 per cent) than women (up to 1.2 per cent) (Lenzenweger et al., 2007; Torgersen et al., 2001). An estimated 47 per cent of male prisoners and 21 per cent of female prisoners have an ASPD (Fazel and Danesh, 2002).

Comorbidity (other disorders that often co-occur with ASPD)
In some people, an ASPD has been shown to co-occur with depression and anxiety disorders (Rotgers and Maniacci, 2006).

Typical behaviours of someone with an ASPD
A wide range of behaviours are associated with those who have an ASPD. They tend to do whatever it takes to get what they want, even if they have to deceive, cheat, steal or hurt people to do so. They have low levels of empathy and their deceitful and manipulative behaviour is callous, unemotional and indifferent to the rights, feelings or suffering of their partners, work colleagues or friends. They rarely feel guilty or remorseful and are focused on what they perceive to be 'survival'. When confronted about their deceit, they will usually try to lie their way out of it and often become aggressive. They may have an inflated and arrogant view of themselves and seem opinionated and overconfident. Many are charming in a superficial way when

they are trying to con someone and some can blend in and act like 'chameleons', merging with their social environment and disguising themselves and their intentions.

Those with an ASPD are often sexually promiscuous, unfaithful to partners and behave in other callous, manipulative and deceitful ways in their intimate relationships. They usually make poor parents as they neither notice nor respond very well to their children's feelings and needs. Some behave irresponsibly in terms of their child's physical and emotional wellbeing by neglecting nutrition, hygiene or school attendance. They usually have poor impulse control and are often sensation-seeking as they struggle to cope with boredom. They are often reckless and indifferent to their own safety and that of people around them. For example, they may drive too fast or when affected by alcohol or drugs, use drugs or alcohol in a dangerous way or waste money gambling. They tend not to learn from their mistakes.

Someone with an ASPD can become very frustrated when they don't get what they want. They are easily irritated and may respond with aggression when annoyed, often ending up in physical fights or hurting people, including their relatives. Some behave irresponsibly and experience significant periods of unemployment, often due to absenteeism. They may also ignore bills, abandon or neglect their family, default on loans or fail to pay child support. Those at the more extreme end of an ASPD, who fit into the psychopathy subtype, may use aggression and violence to get their way. They may break into homes, rape and sexually abuse others, or attack or kill those who get in their way. A few will kill simply for the excitement.

What causes an ASPD?

Like other personality disorders, an ASPD results from the interaction of genetic and environmental factors. Despite many research studies, the picture is complex and still unclear. This may reflect the different combinations of behaviours that an individual with an ASPD displays.

Some people with an ASPD have highly dysfunctional backgrounds. This may involve parental rejection, abandonment, neglect or abuse, weak parental supervision and/or inconsistent discipline, family alcohol or substance abuse, antisocial role models and associating with people living a lifestyle with antisocial elements. This picture is complicated by the fact that some parents who create dysfunctional family environments are also likely to have an ASPD themselves and may have passed the genetic predisposition to their children.

Some people who develop an ASPD come from homes where no parent modelled or stressed the importance of empathy or encouraged moral thinking. Moral decision-making and the development of a conscience require knowledge and experience of moral emotions such as compassion, respect, guilt and shame, plus knowledge of socio-cultural norms and the ability to be 'morally motivated' to care about the needs of other people.

Research into the factors that contribute to an ASPD has focused more on genetic and neurological factors than environmental factors. The disorder is more common among the first-degree biological relatives of those with the disorder – parents, children and siblings who share 50 per cent of their DNA – than in the general population. The heritability of ASPD is estimated to be .69 (Torgersen et al., 2012). This means that 69 per cent of the differences between those in research studies who had an ASPD and those who didn't were due to genetic differences between them. In particular, people with an ASPD appear to be genetically more at risk of developing lower levels of empathy and higher rates of behaviour such as irritability, impulsivity, aggression and irresponsibility (e.g. Baker et al., 2006).

Several recent studies have used neuroimaging and neuro-chemical measures to identify a range of possible neurological and biological factors that help pinpoint some of the ways in which the brains of many people with ASPD might function differently to others and what the impact of those differences might be on their behaviour. Some of the outcomes from these studies are briefly summarised below:

People with an ASPD are more likely to engage in sensation-seeking behaviour, possibly because they tend to have a lower than average resting heart rate. This can contribute to a sense of feeling calm but can also result in often feeling under-aroused and bored (Ortiz and Raine, 2004; Raine et al., 2014).

Some people who have an ASPD and are also violent tend to have a smaller volume of grey matter in the anterior rostral prefrontal cortex and temporal poles of their brain (Gregory et al., 2012). This results in difficulties with learning and experiencing 'moral' emotions, such as guilt or shame, which help to develop prosocial behaviour and encourage moral learning.

Some people who have an ASPD and are also impulsively aggressive are more likely to have lower than normal levels of the brain neurotransmitter serotonin (Moeller et al., 1996).

Many people who have an ASPD have significant abnormalities in parts of their brain, some of which have been found in sections of the orbital frontal cortex that control impulses, behavioural inhibition, attention, reasoning, decision-making, planning and consequential thinking (Blair 2007).

Some people with an ASPD, especially those who display psychopathic features, appear to be relatively 'fearless', in some ways and the following features have been identified as playing some role in this:

- Some have structural and functional impairments in the amygdala region of their brain. The amygdala is at the centre of our 'emotional brain' and is part of the 'empathy circuit' (Baron-Cohen, 2011). It alerts us to potential danger, helps us to learn to feel fear in response to certain situations and contributes to acting empathically towards those in distress. Such impairments can lead to their being less able than others to 'feel fear' and therefore less likely to respond defensively to potential threats such as punishment.

- In studies where people have been taught to antici-pate a mild electric shock when a loud buzzer goes off, those with an ASPD were less likely to act in a way that suggested they anticipated fear, such as having a higher heart rate or flinching. Their vital signs stayed the same even when there was a possibility that they would receive a mild electric shock (Hare, 1978). In other studies, compared to people who didn't have an ASPD, those who did were more likely to have a diminished or non-existent 'startle reflex', such as an automatic 'jump' or 'blink', in response to a sudden loud sound, an object suddenly coming towards them or being shown graphic, violent or unpleasant photos (e.g. Baskin-Sommers et al., 2013).

Such relative fearlessness is also found in individuals without an ASPD and who also have a normal capacity for empathy, self-control and moral behaviour. These people are often engaged in work or hobbies that most of us wouldn't be brave enough to do and which, to some extent, require not only well-developed skills but also 'nerves of steel', such as being an astronaut or deep-sea diver, aerobatic flying, parachute jumping, bomb-disposal work, military leadership or public performance. Being a daredevil does not necessarily mean you have an ASPD.

Two or more of these factors may combine to produce in someone with an ASPD the capacity to stay calm under threat, and make other people feel apprehensive in the face of such calm. With little fear of the potential consequences of their actions, they can develop 'punishment insensitivity', making it less likely that they will learn from their mistakes. Such fearlessness can make some people with an ASPD seem confident and genuine as they easily make and maintain eye contact with others. That makes it easier for them to persuade people or con them. Others will maintain eye contact in a threatening or unnerving way that warns you not to challenge or oppose them because they could be dangerous.

People with an ASPD are less accurate than other people when asked to recognise fearful or sad facial expressions in photographs (Marsh and Blair, 2008). Not recognising such emotional reactions may make it easier for them to harm or use people or to ignore their distress. However one study, in which researchers used neuroimaging techniques to monitor the brains of people with ASPD as they watched videos of people in pain or distress, obtained some interesting results. They found that the subjects initially didn't show a brain response to the distress of others in the video as measured by activation of their mirror neuron system, but if they were asked to try harder to empathise with how the people in the video were feeling, they were more likely to activate those mirror neurons (Meffert et al., 2013). This suggests that people with an ASPD *can* empathise, but choose not to do so unless it suits them. They can switch into 'non-empathy mode' while working towards a desired goal, such as conning or hurting someone, when empathy would get in the way of what they want. It appears that they share this characteristic with many people who have a narcissistic personality disorder.

Treatment

Few people with an ASPD seek treatment. Many psychologists and psychiatrists are reluctant to treat them, as their own experience and many studies suggest that insight-oriented psychological treatment is ineffective (e.g. Harris and Rice, 2006). Some are encouraged or pressured by partners or relatives to seek treatment for related issues, such as the damage they cause to those close to them. Others are ordered to have counselling after breaking the law, but their goal in joining a treatment program is usually self-serving.

One study found that prisoners with an ASPD who participated in a treatment program based on teaching anger management and interpersonal skills were more likely to reoffend after being released than those who did not participate in the program (Hare et al., 2000). It seems that, through the program, they may have learned how to more effectively exploit other people. Before killing Jill Meagher, Adrian Bayley underwent counselling following an earlier sex crime. But he later admitted to simply telling the counsellor what he thought they wanted to hear.

Like Bayley, those with an ASPD tend to have poor insight into the damage they cause and lack the capacity for the type of remorse that motivates change. They usually know the difference between right and wrong but most don't 'feel' it and often don't care about it. In many cases, people with an ASPD are among society's most dangerous citizens.

CHAPTER 8

SIMON GITTANY

The cast

Simon Gittany: The killer and fiancé of Lisa Harnum

Lamia and Sayed Gittany: Simon Gittany's parents

Simon Gittany's siblings: Barbara, Anthony, Michelle, Sue and Carol

Rachelle Louise: Gittany's girlfriend from October 2012 until after his trial

Lisa Cecila Harnum: The victim and fiancée of Simon Gittany, who called her Cecilia

Joan Harnum: Lisa Harnum's mother

Jason Harnum: Lisa Harnum's brother

Rebecca Triscaru: Lisa Harnum's friend

Paul Rokobaro: Simon Gittany's friend from his school days

Lisa Brown: Personal trainer and new friend of Lisa Harnum

Michelle Richmond: Lisa's counsellor

The crimes of Simon Gittany

19 November 1991: Soon after turning eighteen, Gittany appeared before Parramatta adult court charged with assaulting a

Merrylands cafe owner. He received a two-year good behaviour bond.

August 1993: Gittany was caught outside a Parramatta nightclub in a car allegedly loaded with stolen goods. He failed to appear in court that October, so a warrant was issued for his arrest.

23 March 1994: Gittany bit a chunk off a detective's ear and assaulted another police officer when they tried to arrest and question him.

Mid-1990s: After receiving two and a half years periodic detention for the police assaults, Gittany spent time with a Catholic order in France.

2001: Gittany was convicted of drug trafficking after police arrested him with methamphetamine tablets and more than $5000 in cash.

30 July 2011: Just before 10 am, Lisa Harnum fell to her death from her fifteenth floor balcony.

3 August 2011: Gittany was charged with Lisa Harnum's murder.

27 November 2013: Justice Lucy McCallum found Gittany guilty of murder.

11 February 2014: Gittany was sentenced to 26 years jail with a minimum of 18.

The motive

Simon Gittany became enraged, lost control and killed his fiancée, Lisa Harnum, when he discovered that she had secretly made plans to leave him and was just about to do so.

Introduction

A charming man in his late thirties delivers a short but polished speech about his undying love for his gorgeous girlfriend. They are in a restaurant with friends and family to celebrate her thirtieth birthday, but, after a nod to her milestone, the handsome romantic drops on bended knee to propose. His slender partner, who has long, black hair and almond eyes, is surprised but happy and emotional. She covers her mouth with her hand and sheds tears of joy. The room erupts in cheers as the good-looking young pair seal their engagement with a ring.

Happy scenes like this are played out by couples around Australia every day. But this one was different. A year before this grainy footage appeared on YouTube, the man, Simon Gittany, had thrown the woman, Lisa Cecilia Harnum, to her death from the balcony of their fifteenth-floor Sydney CBD apartment. At the time, Gittany told investigators that Lisa had climbed over the balcony and taken her own life or fell, possibly due to emotional problems caused by an eating disorder. But he was soon charged with murder.

While on bail awaiting trial, Gittany posted a series of personal videos online to show the world how devoted he was to Lisa and to prove that he couldn't possibly have harmed his Canadian fiancée. In the proposal video, filmed less than two months before Lisa's death on 30 July 2011, Gittany told the gathering that before meeting her he had had lost faith in women, partly because he couldn't find one to serve and love him. He described Lisa, whom he called by her middle name, Cecilia, as a beautiful person with a beautiful heart. She then embraced him (Davies, 2013).

This footage and several other videos of the pair having fun, and Lisa being baptised into the Catholic Church, showed a devoted couple who couldn't wait to start married life together. Behind the facade, however, was a turbulent relationship dominated by a man who craved the high life and control over his partner to the point where he dictated what she wore, what name she used, whom she associated with and where she could go. At one point, Gittany allegedly forced Lisa to kneel before him and submit to his authority. For several years she bowed

278

to the wishes of her partner, like many women who feel they don't deserve better. Due to his controlling ways, her self-esteem hit rock bottom and she slowly became isolated from most of her friends. Thanks to a new counsellor and personal trainer, however, in July 2011 Lisa had finally plucked up the courage to leave her partner and return to her native Canada. But she never made it: Simon Gittany, who could not stand to lose control over her, killed her rather than let her leave.

Why?

The lead-up to the crime

Toronto-born Lisa Harnum came to Australia when she was twenty-four. The former teenage dancer remained close to her Canadian friends and initially kept in contact with them. After moving to Sydney from Melbourne, she completed a hairdressing course at Australian Hair and Beauty near Bondi Junction, working part time to help fund her tuition. Lisa met Simon Gittany in early 2010. After moving into his Pitt Street apartment as a flatmate, they started dating about two months later. Lisa was a vibrant, independent young woman described by friends as 'a very bubbly, positive person'. She had been wrestling with bulimia and anorexia on and off for many years, but most of the time managed to live life to the full.

Initially the relationship was strong and loving, with Gittany fondly calling Lisa by her middle name, Cecilia. Before long, however, he started to place restrictions on her work as a hairdresser, her social activities, her gym training, what she could wear, her hairstyle and her friends. Gittany became angry if Lisa wore what he considered to be even slightly revealing clothes or talked to another man. She began to dress modestly, avoid eye contact with other men when they were out together and lost touch with most of her friends.

Why did they do it?

Lisa's mother, Joan Harnum, told Channel 7's *Sunday Night* program that she initially trusted Lisa's judgment and the couple seemed to get on well. Joan said the couple could 'talk for hours' and Lisa 'shone' after Gittany introduced her to Catholicism. But this soon changed and Lisa started to express concerns to her mother about the control her partner had over her friends, clothes and movements ('Simon Gittany's secret life', 2014).

In September 2010, the couple moved into a more expensive fifteenth-floor apartment in the prestigious Hyde building, with views over Sydney's Hyde Park. Within months, Gittany had arranged the installation of surveillance cameras that he later claimed was for security reasons. Two cameras were installed inside the apartment and one on the outside. The outside camera was a pinhole camera next to the door and faced the corridor. The secret cameras were linked to a computer in the study and also to an external hard drive hidden in the ceiling (R v Gittany, 2013).

When Lisa moved in with Gittany, she was earning $500 to $600 a week at Australian Hair and Beauty. This stopped in May 2010, after he discouraged her from working, despite the couple reportedly paying more than $1500 a week in rent. In mid-2010, Lisa told her mother that they were 'starting to have issues', after which she saw a counsellor who treated her for stress, neck and shoulder pain, anxiety and sleeping and eating complaints. A few months later, Lisa told Joan that she could not wear dresses anymore and that Gittany had told her to wear only pants and 'just basic clothes'. Lisa also said they had decided not to go to nightclubs anymore because he 'gets so uptight' and 'uncomfortable with all of the guys around'.

'This relationship sure has changed me a lot!' she texted her mother.

I'm much more calm than I was before, domesticated, conservative, and dainty. I have nails now too . . . and now I have natural French manicure! Bought a whole bunch of flat and casual shoes and no more cleavage I'm afraid. Simon is terrified of summer and the beach. He said we seedling [sic] to have to find the burka bathinsuit [sic] to wear. Hehe xoxo. (R v Gittany, 2013)

When Lisa made her last trip to Canada in December 2010, Joan noticed that her hair was pulled back, she wore no make-up and her clothes were 'blacks and greys . . . almost military, very non-revealing'. It was most unlike her daughter, who loved fashion. Lisa told her mother that she wasn't supposed to tell her Canadian friends she was home because Gittany did not want her to go out partying. He called her constantly to check up on her.

Six months before she died, Lisa texted her mother complaining about Gittany's controlling nature. 'Simon gets so uptight when we go out he makes the night turn into a nightmare,' she said. Joan then texted Gittany, asking him to let her daughter come home to Canada. He responded by installing a program on Lisa's phone that allowed him to monitor her text messages without her knowledge. Gittany later admitted this at his trial but said he did so because Lisa had revealed she had a 'secret' that she was ashamed of. He said they had several discussions about it and he became confused, upset and frustrated because Lisa was hiding something from him. He said he responded by reading her texts for two or three weeks, but didn't notice anything of note so lost interest. The judge later rejected this as fanciful.

By that stage, Lisa had not worked since leaving her hairdressing job at Bondi Junction in May 2010. In early 2011, she discussed returning to work with Gittany, who suggested she volunteer with one of his friends at a Christopher Hanna Salon, which she did for a while. In February, they argued and spent a few days apart, after which Lisa talked to her mother about possibly returning to Canada. Lisa also considered returning at the end of March but changed her mind, despite telling Joan that she and Gittany were 'having domestics' and that he had said some very hurtful things.

After Lisa spoke with her friend Rebecca Triscaru about her situation, Gittany called Rebecca and told her not to get involved or speak to Lisa again. Reflecting his increasing control over her life, on 16 April he berated Lisa by text for having her hair down: 'Since you got attitude & you made the comment about me working during the day yesterday, there are two bills worth 900 one for electricity & one for telstra. I want you to pay for them from your own money.' Lisa replied: 'If I had a job that paid me money instead of something that you are comfortable with then maybe I could pay something. You are a heartless heartless person.'

That night Gittany texted:

Who the fuck do you think you are walking around the house like you own it or coming & going without my permission?! Again I waited for you to apologize for your disgusting comment but you walk around like a peacock with your hair out & too proud to apologise. You lied to me & promised you would listen to me at all times. Obviously, you're still the proud person & nothing has changed!

Despite their ups and downs, Gittany proposed on 12 June 2011, at a surprise thirtieth birthday party he organised for Lisa. He splashed out on an expensive ring, but Lisa told friends she did not know what her partner did for a living. When Gittany proposed, she was genuinely happy and excited. But within a week they were arguing again. On 18 June he sent her a message:

Cecilia you are my fiancé [sic] & I love you but we both know you have some problems that effect [sic] the mood of our relationship at times but you refuse to admit it. Please pray to God so he can help you get rid of these habits. I love you & want a future for us. Please get rid of them! Words from my heart.

She replied in part:

I love you too Simon and I do pray every single day for God to make me a better person. Simon no one is perfect and I may have things about me that I need to work on but it breaks my heart to think that instead of helping me in a constructive way you resort to yelling and telling me to get rid of my faults or we won't work. My whole life all I wanted was to be accepted.

He replied: 'Ok so you want me to help you get through this in a constructive way? Sure no problem. Btw, I didn't like your last few lines, don't use fear of loss on me Cecilia! I'm the one asking you to fix things before we go ahead but without the fuckin games.'

The next day Lisa told her mother she was considering moving to Melbourne and contacted her friend Gisele Pratt about the possibility of living in Gisele's investment property, revealing that the engagement excitement had already fizzled. Gittany later called Gisele and demanded that she not let Lisa stay with her. In late June, the couple went skiing at Perisher with friends Rebecca Triscaru and her boyfriend Joe Filianos.

Rebecca noticed a change in Lisa, who was happy on some days but not others. 'You could just see on her that she didn't seem as vibrant and as happy as I had known her to be,' she later told Gittany's trial. Their contact after that was minimal.

In early July, Lisa started seeing personal trainer Lisa Brown, telling her that she had struggled with eating disorders and wanted to improve her health to possibly conceive. Their first session was on 13 July in the gym in Gittany and Harnum's apartment block. Brown also recommended that Lisa see her counsellor friend Michelle Richmond, who had experience with people who had eating disorders. Lisa told her trainer that she loved Gittany and wanted to have a baby with him, but asked her not to tell him she was having counselling. She later said she didn't have any friends other than her and Richmond because her fiancé 'did not like her to'.

Lisa had her first session with Richmond in the counsellor's office on 22 July. They spoke about Lisa's bulimia, which she had been unable to confide in her mother or partner about. Lisa said Gittany did not like her to leave the apartment and some-times when she did he became angry and aggressive. She was not allowed to go out alone, and when she went out with him she had to avert her eyes from other men's and keep him engaged in conversation or look down so he could never say that she was looking at someone else. Gittany went out often and Lisa did not know where he went or what he did for a living. He was appar-ently setting up some kind of home business. Her partner did not physically abuse her, but Lisa said he was very controlling and always seemed to know what she had told her mother. Richmond told Lisa about centres for abused women and they discussed putting her belongings in storage as a step towards her leaving him. Lisa told her counsellor that although she loved Gittany she was also afraid of him.

On Thursday, 28 July, Lisa saw Lisa Brown for the last time. Agitated and nervous, she gave the personal trainer two pillow-cases with clothes and shoes inside, saying she was planning to leave and wanted to return to hairdressing. After the gym session, Lisa Harnum took a bag of personal possessions and placed them in a storage unit at Metro Storage in Bondi. Gittany later confronted her with text messages about the bag and admitted to monitoring her phone. At about 7 pm, Richmond received a call from Lisa's mobile phone, but nobody spoke. When she called back, Gittany allegedly said, 'Michelle, you fucking bitch, if you ever come near Cecilia again, try to contact or meet her, have anything to do with her, I know where you live. I will fucking harm you.' Richmond also received a text message, supposedly from Lisa, saying, 'Leave me alone you have ruined my relationship. Drop all my stuff off at my concierge by no later than tomorrow 10 am. OK?'

The murder

Simon Gittany claims he broke off his relationship with Lisa on Friday, 29 July 2011, and that she was resistant. But Lisa's mother Joan says her daughter was actually desperate to leave and had told her, 'Mummy, please come and get me.' That morning, Lisa spoke to her mother for almost ninety minutes. Joan advised that if things got really bad, Lisa should grab her purse and passport and leave. Lisa went online to book plane tickets to Canada and at 1.42 pm rang migration agent Jonathan Granger about one-way tickets and visas. She was clearly planning to fly home, at least temporarily (R v Gittany, 2013).

At some point during the day, Lisa told her mother that Gittany had taken her mobile phone and knew she was trying to book a flight. She had also found files that showed he had been tracking her messages and her emails. At 2.17 pm, Michelle Richmond received a text from Lisa's phone:

I wish I never met you because you have ruined my life & I have been kicked out of the house by simon. I had everything with simon but you brain washed me Michelle & now I am out on the street with nothing! I want the money I paid you for ruining my life as I am broke & need money. You should be ashamed of yourself. Thank you for this big mess you created!

The Crown later contended in court and the judge accepted that this and several other text messages were sent by Gittany, as his texting style was different and more likely to use ampersands.

That evening, Gittany's school friend Paul Rokobaro visited. Paul arrived at 7.20 pm and noted that Simon and Lisa appeared loving. The trio ate Asian takeaway that was delivered at around 9.30 pm. After Paul left, Gittany claimed he and Lisa went to bed and watched *Romeo and Juliet* arm in arm, and he fell asleep before it finished. Soon after midnight, Lisa texted her mother asking if she was okay. At 2.15 am on Saturday, 30 July, Lisa wrote, 'good night mama. I hope you have a beautiful day today'. Gittany claims he woke between 3 and 4 am with Lisa 'still watching the cooking shows', so he went to the computer room and tried unsuccessfully to log in to the video monitoring system. Because he could not sleep, he watched some online porn and pressed the camera's record button in case Lisa walked in. When he left the study at about 5.15 am, both internal cameras were switched off.

Soon after, three international calls were made on the apartment's landline, at 5.38 am (sixty-four seconds), 5.39 am (three seconds) and 5.41 am (thirty-six minutes). During the final call, Lisa told her mother that she loved her and her brother Jason with all her heart. When Joan asked what was wrong, Lisa implored her to contact Michelle Richmond if anything happened, leaving

Richmond's details. That was the last time Joan Harnum heard from her daughter.

According to Gittany's version of events, after he heard Lisa talking and at one point laughing on the phone, he went back to sleep and woke up at around 9 or 9.30 am. He saw that Lisa had packed some bags and was ripping up a piece of paper, which she said was a note to her mother. He said he then asked Lisa whether she had changed the computer password and she said that she had changed it to 'TRUST'. He supposedly apologised for monitoring her messages, which he was not comfortable doing but felt he had to due to a 'secret' she had long kept from him.

Gittany claimed Lisa then rolled her eyes and said, 'You told me to leave, so I'm leaving.' When he asked to see her flight booking, she apparently got up, grabbed her handbag and ran for the door. He said he ran after her and reached her before she got out the door, putting his hand over her mouth to stop her screaming before bringing her back inside. The judge later discounted much of this story as being too convenient. What we know for sure is that the next-door neighbours heard the ensuing ruckus, banging on the door and a woman's voice screaming, 'Help me, help me, please God, help me', in a very distressed manner. But the screaming stopped suddenly and they did not go outside to see what was happening.

The moment when a shirtless Gittany put his hand over Lisa's mouth outside their apartment was captured on chilling CCTV footage from his own hidden pinhole camera. It was 9.54 am on 30 July and she was trying to get to the lift. Detectives calculated that only sixty-nine seconds elapsed from the time Gittany grabbed Lisa and dragged her back inside and when she dropped onto the footpath on Liverpool Street, fifteen storeys below.

Gittany later told the court that when they came inside, he removed his hand from Lisa's mouth and they both went quiet.

Lisa supposedly sat in the lounge and he went into the kitchen to make her a hot drink. Gittany claims he then said to Lisa: 'I can't believe what just happened at the door. I'm so embarrassed. The neighbours are probably outside right now and probably heard everything. Would you please just tell me what this secret is? It will all be easy if you just tell me the secret.'

Gittany said he was calm but Lisa ran outside to the balcony, so he followed. When he got outside, he claimed, she had already climbed over the balcony rail and was facing him, with just her left leg on the inside of the balcony. He said he ran towards Lisa to try to grab her, but as she got her left leg over, handbag still on her shoulder, she jumped or released herself down onto the awning above the flat below theirs.

'Cecilia looked at me,' he later told his trial.

> I reached out as far as I could to get a hand or two hands or anything to try and get hold of Cecilia's legs or any part of Cecilia. I know I screamed at least twice. After I couldn't reach her . . . she disappeared or let go, I'm not too sure, and as soon as that happened, I screamed her name out and instantly she hit the fourteenth [floor] awning from her waist and above with massive impact and that acted like a springboard and sprung her out, forward, and then Cecilia began to freefall.

Probably the only truth contained in this statement was the time. It was just before 10 am on 30 July 2011.

One witness had seen a shirtless Gittany unload an object over the balcony and another saw something fall before the man on the balcony fist-pumped the air. Both observations were in stark contrast to his protracted tale of woe. When a dishevelled Gittany appeared on the footpath, after putting on a T-shirt and taking the lift down, he was comforted by witnesses who later said he appeared relatively calm. He also tried to poke Lisa's head in a strange way, saying 'baby, baby, baby, I can't believe it'. An orthopaedic surgeon who was driving past stopped and looked for signs of life, but there were none.

On 3 August 2011, four days after Lisa Harnum's death, Gittany was charged with her murder.

The trial

Simon Gittany opted for trial by judge alone. When the four-week hearing started on 21 October 2013, he pleaded not guilty to murder. Justice Lucy McCallum had to decide whether Gittany threw his fiancée from the balcony of the apartment they shared, or whether she had climbed over herself. Crown prosecutor Mark Tedeschi QC described Gittany as a jealous, abusive partner who alienated Lisa Harnum from her friends, used CCTV cameras to monitor her inside their apartment, killed her in a fit of rage and then deliberately directed the police investigation 'towards a suicide scenario'.

Defence counsel Philip Strickland SC claimed Lisa's struggle with an eating disorder may have caused her to suicide. He said she had developed the illness as a teen ballerina, cut her wrists during adolescence, had a history of anxiety and had suicidal thoughts. Lisa was a 'conflicted, complicated and confused woman', prone to overreacting when she didn't get her way. Mr Strickland conceded that the partnership was volatile, but accused the Crown of downplaying the couple's caring, fun, affectionate and loving relationship (R v Gittany, 2013).

Gittany denied killing Lisa but admitted being a jealous partner and feeling threatened when she wore revealing clothes, sometimes without a bra. He admitted telling her to stop reveal-ing so much of her body so that she didn't give out the wrong signals or attract the wrong type of attention.

Why did they do it?

Among the few undisputed pieces of evidence was the CCTV footage that showed Gittany grabbing Lisa in the foyer outside their apartment and putting his hand over her mouth before dragging her back inside, just sixty-nine seconds before she died. A shirtless Gittany was filmed leaving the apartment fourteen seconds after Lisa's death. He put his hands on his head in the hallway and then returned inside. After thirty-three seconds, he left the apartment again, this time in a white T-shirt. He entered the lift and threw his hands in the air, clearly agitated.

ABC assistant news editor Josh Rathmell was walking to work when he saw Lisa fall to the ground. He told the court he heard what he described as a male's 'deranged' screaming and looked up to see a shirtless man carrying what appeared to be black luggage or a duffle bag horizontally across his outstretched arms. The man then 'unloaded' the object in a fluid motion and went straight back into the apartment. As the object fell, Josh watched the man run inside. He described the noise as 'guttural' and, combined with the throwing motion, it seemed aggressive.

High school student Yuto Yoshioka, fifteen, was waiting at a bus stop on the northern side of Liverpool Street, facing The Hyde, when he heard a loud noise coming from above. He saw a body fall and hit the ground. Yuto then looked up and saw a shirtless man leaning forward. The man then raised his hands, in what Yuto demonstrated in court and the judge described as a fist-pumping action, before going back inside. Justice McCallum noted in her summing up that such action spoke of triumph or anger in the accused but may also have been a gesture of despair. Gittany's defence seized on the fact the two descriptions were slightly different, but there was more damning evidence: neither Lisa's fingerprints nor palm prints could be found on the glass balustrade of the balcony, though

Gittany said she had clambered over the balustrade. While experts said this did not conclusively prove a person had not touched the surface, the judge found Lisa could not have done what Gittany said without touching the panel.

On 27 November, Justice McCallum took five hours to read her judgment and verdict, during which Gittany showed little emotion. She praised a number of defence witnesses, but repeatedly found the defendant's evidence implausible: 'At many times in his evidence, the accused struck me as a person playing a role, telling a story which fitted neatly with the objective evidence but which did no more than that. His account often appeared to rest on borrowed detail, lacking the richness and subtlety of actual experience.' Justice McCallum found defence claims that Lisa was impulsive did not establish that she was 'prone to act impulsively and perhaps dangerously when she was upset'. The suggestion Lisa had a tendency to attempt suicide was 'completely unfounded' (R v Gittany, 2013).

Instead, Justice McCallum found that a torn-up note discovered in Lisa's pocket about the surveillance cameras suggested she feared her partner and was 'quietly determined to leave'. 'Lisa Harnum was trying to leave the accused on the morning of her death,' she said.

> There is no doubt in my mind that he was in a state of rage at that point and that he had lost control of his temper. The proposition that he was able to bring himself under control so quickly after the struggle at the door is inherently implausible and I reject it. I do not accept his evidence that Lisa Harnum climbed over the balustrade. I cannot know exactly what happened in that apartment in the minute or so following the struggle at the door, but I think it is likely that Lisa Harnum was at some point

rendered unconscious. Based on my assessment of all of
the evidence, I am satisfied . . . beyond reasonable doubt
that the accused maintained his rage and, in that state,
carried her to the balcony and unloaded her over the edge.
(R v Gittany, 2013)

She concluded: 'I find the accused guilty of the murder of
Lisa Cecilia Harnum.'

As the verdict was delivered, Gittany's new girlfriend,
Rachelle Louise, screamed, 'You're wrong! You're wrong!' and
had to be restrained. After Gittany mouthed, 'I love you, baby,'
she had a cigarette outside, surrounded by dozens of reporters, before returning to the gallery, crying. Her boyfriend then
turned to face her and said: 'I'm so sorry.' Gittany's mother was
so upset an ambulance had to be called to treat her (Dale, 2013;
Bibby and Partridge, 2013).

On 11 February 2014, Justice McCallum sentenced Simon
Gittany to twenty-six years in jail with a minimum non-parole
period of eighteen years. Rachelle Louise, who led a protest outside
the sentencing proclaiming his innocence, described Gittany as
'the best boyfriend I've ever had'. His family also protested and,
when the sentence was announced, one of his sisters stood up and
declared he would not do any of that time (Dale, 'How Gittany
the bully has been crushed', 2014; Higgins, 2014).

Justice McCallum said Gittany showed no remorse and had
a low chance of rehabilitation. 'It appears to be an arid prospect,'
she said.

I am satisfied that he must have anticipated the prospect
that he would fly into a rage if ever she were to leave him.
He allowed possessiveness and insecurity to overwhelm
the most basic respect for her right to live her life as she

chose. The intention to kill . . . was facilitated by a sense of ownership and a lack of any true respect for the autonomy of the woman he claimed to love.

After Gittany's conviction, Joan Harnum told *A Current Affair*'s Tracy Grimshaw that her daughter was 'completely brainwashed' by her partner, who alienated her from life outside their apartment. Joan did not approve of the situation but wanted to let her daughter make her own life choices. While Gittany was controlling, she could only say so much and in many cases women in relationships like Lisa's were afraid to contradict their controlling partner (Tracy Grimshaw exclusive, 2013).

The torn-up note in the front pocket of Lisa Harnum's jeans, which read, 'There are cameras inside and outside the house', showed that her daughter had just realised the danger she was in. But it was too late.

Simon Gittany's background

Born in October 1973, Simon Gittany grew up in Merrylands in Sydney's west. His Lebanese migrant parents, Sayed and Lamia, had six children – two boys and four girls. Gittany told a court psychologist he had a stable, caring upbringing and the family was 'close-knit'. The Gittanys are known to be feisty and loyal. Simon Gittany completed high school and worked as a tiler while starting a TAFE training course that he did not complete. He continued working as a tiler, but did not generally stay in a job for more than about six months. Between jobs, he stayed at his parents' modest home. They did not expect him to pay rent and his mother did everything for him. He described it as 'like living in a hotel' (Dale, 'How Gittany the bully has been crushed', 2014).

Why did they do it?

Gittany had a history of trouble with the law. At eighteen, he was convicted of physically assaulting a Merrylands cafe owner, Mario Zonta, for which he was handed a $300 good behaviour bond. The assault allegedly occurred after Zonta ordered Gittany and a group of friends out of the cafe after Gittany harassed a young woman who worked there and was an ex-girlfriend of Gittany's (Owens, 2013).

On 21 August 1993, Gittany was arrested outside a Parramatta night club with a sedan loaded with electrical equipment that turned out to be stolen from a nearby house. On 13 October 1993, he failed to appear in court in relation to those matters and a bench warrant, which directs a person's arrest by police, was issued. On March 23 1994, Gittany attacked two police officers who came to his home to arrest him. After a struggle, Gittany physically assaulted Constable Peter Burgess. He also bit off a chunk of Detective Constable Keith Bristow's ear, reportedly spat it out and stood facing him, smiling. He allegedly used his younger sister as a human shield while taunting the detective and punching him in the face.

When he was tried for these offences in 1995, Gittany's defence team emphasised his devout Catholicism and his ambition to train as a priest. As a result, sentencing Judge Geoffrey Graham ordered that his original sentence, which included 12 months jail for one of the assaults, six months for the other and six months for the receiving of stolen goods, be served concurrently (i.e. all at the same time), as periodic detention rather than full-time jail. Periodic detention, which required the offender to attend a detention centre for a two day period each week for the duration of the sentence, was abolished in NSW in 2010. It usually started at 7 pm on a Friday and finished at 4.30 pm on a Sunday, but it could also be served during the week.

Judge Graham expressed scepticism about the authenticity of Gittany's supposed vocation and plans to become a priest.

However, he accepted that the probation officer, who had also been sceptical, concluded that Gittany was genuine after speaking to several Catholic priests who knew him and spoke about his involvement in and commitment to the Church. The Crown appealed against the leniency of the sentence, but that appeal was dismissed on 2 August 1995.

Father Michael Delsorte was Gittany's priest for about twenty years, beginning in the 1990s. He was teaching Roman Catholic catechism classes and Gittany was among a group of young Lebanese men seeking a more traditional form of worship. They were Maronite Catholics but came to Father Delsorte's Child Jesus and St Joseph Roman Catholic Church in Rockdale to convert to the more traditional Roman Catholicism.

At some point following his convictions, with the blessing of his Sydney church, Gittany spent time in France training to be a priest with the order of the Roman Catholic Transalpine Redemptorists, choosing it because they spoke English and were more traditional. He would have been up before sunrise and most of the day would have revolved around prayer and work. Gittany was allowed to take the habit, meaning he could wear the robes, but left and returned to Australia without completing the training to become a priest.

Eventually Gittany returned to Sydney after deciding the religious life was not for him. It is possible that he had used religion partly as a moral compass as he clearly lacked one. Gittany's pious lifestyle did not last and he soon resumed his criminal behaviour. In 2001, he was convicted of supplying a prohibited drug (fifty-five ecstasy tablets) and receiving stolen goods worth $5200. He was sentenced to three years periodic detention.

Throughout this period, Gittany worked as a waiter and for a company doing bathroom renovations. He then undertook private training for twelve months at the Australian Academy of Dramatic Art, using money his parents had banked for him.

He later claimed he could not complete that course due to the cost, but it taught him to present himself well and with confidence. Gittany also spent three years as an advertising account manager at the *Sydney Morning Herald*, and eighteen months working for a company called Reach Local.

Before his arrest for Lisa Harnum's July 2011 murder, Gittany was linked to a number of outwardly legitimate companies, including an online women's shoe business called Shoe Candy. He also claimed to be setting up a business called Health Delivered, which would offer home delivered supplements for fitness fanatics, when his fiancée died. In October 2012, Gittany started dating Rachelle Louise, who remained convinced of his innocence throughout his trial and afterwards vowed to prove it.

Others saw Simon Gittany very differently.

Why did he do it?

Justice Lucy McCallum found that Simon Gittany threw Lisa Harnum to her death from their fifteenth floor balcony, most likely in a fit of rage after he realised that Lisa was going to leave him.

Why such an extreme response to something that many couples experience?

This was no ordinary couple and Gittany was not the loving partner he claimed to be. He was a conniving, self-centred and controlling convicted drug dealer who could not stand the thought of his partner having her own life. The most significant contributing factor in this murder was the fact that Gittany's pattern of behaviour is consistent with a diagnosis of an anti-social personality disorder (ASPD), with psychopathic features and narcissistic traits. This enabled him to act without feeling any empathy or concern for Lisa Harnum. Those with an ASPD display a pattern of disregard for and violation of the rights of others and the law. Gittany showed a callous indifference to others when he bashed a shopkeeper and bit off part of a detective's ear.

Gittany's ASPD traits made it difficult for him to find true love. He wanted to settle down and have a family but could not maintain a successful long-term relationship, mostly due to his demand for a totally compliant partner. Initially charming, he became possessive and, in Lisa's case at least, emotionally abusive. The romantic restaurant video when he proposed to Lisa illustrated how he could play a part when it suited. He undoubtly honed some of those skills during his stint at an acting school.

Like others with an ASPD, Gittany was prepared to deceive, break the law or act cruelly to get what he wanted. He controlled Lisa's movements, stopped her from working and, when she finally returned to work, made her do so with no pay. He belittled her to reduce her self-esteem and kept her from friends who may have seen what he was doing to her.

For a while it appeared that Gittany had achieved his goal of finding the 'perfect' submissive partner, but when Lisa discovered he was intercepting her emails and texts, she decided she had to leave. Instead of conceding any fault, her fiancé reacted with rage. How dare she take the upper hand in a relationship he rightfully controlled? Without regard for her safety, he took control in the only way he knew how – violently. It was a pattern Gittany developed as a teenager which resulted in him responding to stresses and frustrations in his adult life by using violence with little regard for his victims. While there is no direct evidence that he physically abused Lisa before killing her, the emotional abuse was certainly crippling.

As an added complication, some reports claimed that Gittany may have used steroids (Dale, 2014). If so, this could have increased his levels of aggression. In some cases ASPD traits are exacerbated by childhood trauma or abuse, but that appears not to be the case here. By all accounts Gittany had a loving, supportive upbringing. If anything, his parents indulged him, which may have unintentionally fed his self-importance and sense of entitlement.

As well as having an ASPD, Gittany displays an authoritarian personality style. In psychological terms, authoritarianism is a state of mind or attitude characterised by blind allegiance to conventional beliefs about right and wrong and respect for submission to an acknowledged authority, such as the Church or themselves. This involves a black and white view of the world and a belief that those who disobey should be punished. The authoritarian personality was first identified by Adorno et al. in 1950. After World War II they conducted research designed to help understand the psychological factors that contributed to atrocities committed by otherwise civilised people, such as Joseph Stalin and Adolf Hitler. They found an authoritarian orientation was mainly associated with extreme right-wing conservatives and members of some fundamentalist religions (Adorno et al., 1950; Altemeyer, 1997).

Simon Gittany has a number of the characteristics various studies have identified as typical of those with strong authoritarian views. Like many others in this group, he was attracted to very traditional religious beliefs and attended a traditional branch of the Catholic church that conducted mass in Latin. His behaviour towards Lisa suggested that he believed strongly in the concept of a traditional family unit in which women were subservient to their husbands and dressed 'respectably' to avoid attracting other men. He believed that Lisa should submit to his will as the 'authority' on how she should live her life and punished her when she didn't obey his 'rules'.

Like many others with an authoritarian personality style, Gittany supported ideas that were contradictory and inconsistent. He was a devout Catholic who attended mass and church programs but also bashed and robbed people. He left the less traditional Maronite Church to join a very traditional Roman Catholic order in France, but did not last and soon after he returned he was caught up in Sydney's drug scene. In another inconsistency, while claiming to love and respect Lisa he secretly monitored her emails, controlled her movements and forced her to submit to his will. To him, none of these were contradictions because people with authoritarian personalities usually lack the capacity or motivation to think critically about themselves. To cope with potential inconsistencies, they tend to compartmental-ise different aspects of their life, have 'double standards' or come up with 'after the fact' rationales.

Authoritarian personalities also feel the need to dominate others and seek power, which Gittany sought over Lisa and possibly others through becoming a priest. Many ruthless leaders, such as Hitler, Stalin and Mussolini, had similar traits, which allowed them to kill thousands or even millions of people without feeling guilty or taking responsibility. The 'defensive avoidance' of authoritarian personalities allows them to ignore their own shortcomings and maintain an exaggerated self-image. When they have behaved in a way that even they realise is wrong, authoritarian personalities may ask God for forgiveness as a 'way out'. Some paedophile priests are a good example of this sort of thinking. In Gittany's case, he may have done this while in jail and possibly spent time in a French monastery to seek forgiveness as well as a strategy to reduce his prison sentence. He may also have believed that by entering the Church he could rise to a position of power within it, thus fulfilling a strong desire to control others.

If anyone challenges their authority, as Lisa did, those with an authoritarian personality style and an ASPD can be extremely dangerous. However, they are often skilled manipulators, so it can be difficult for their loved ones to see and accept this. Gittany's family and new partner were clearly distraught when he was found guilty – he had obviously played the caring partner, son and brother so that they would believe he was a good man. While he has been many things to many people, in reality this would-be actor, sometime salesman, thief, thug, drug dealer and one-time trainee priest was prepared to kill when the woman he supposedly loved defied him and he couldn't get his own way.

SIMON GITTANY
DIAGNOSTIC CHART

Using DSM 5 indicators (APA, 2013), when three or more of these are present, occurring since age fifteen years, a diagnosis of an anti-social personality disorder (ASPD) can be made	Examples of Simon Gittany's behaviour that appear to be consistent with each indicator
Failure to conform to social norms with respect to lawful behaviors, as indicated by repeatedly performing acts that are grounds for arrest.	Convictions for assault, drug-dealing, theft and murder.
Deceitfulness, as indicated by repeated lying, use of aliases, or conning others for personal profit or pleasure.	Lied about how he earned his money. Lied to Lisa about his lifestyle. Remade Lisa to fit his idea of what he wanted in a partner by changing her name and making her wear old-fashioned clothes to cover up her body. Claimed Lisa climbed over the balcony to suicide in order to cover up the fact that he had thrown her to her death. Regularly used several aliases, such as 'Gittoni'.
Impulsivity or failure to plan ahead.	Took the easy option in earning money from drugs and was caught.

301

Using DSM 5 indicators (APA, 2013), when three or more of these are present, occurring since age fifteen years, a diagnosis of an anti-social personality disorder (ASPD) can be made	Examples of Simon Gittany's behaviour that appear to be consistent with each indicator
	Caught several times with drugs/stolen goods. Impulsively hurt Lisa and threw her off the balcony.
Irritability and aggressiveness, as indicated by repeated physical fights or assaults.	Conviction for assault. Bit off part of a police officer's ear and assaulted another officer.
Reckless disregard for safety of self or others.	His murder of Lisa. His attack on the police officers who came to his house to arrest him.
Consistent irresponsibility, as indicated by repeated failure to sustain consistent work behavior or honor financial obligations.	
Lack of remorse, as indicated by being indifferent to or rationalizing having hurt, mistreated or stolen from another.	No remorse shown – he denied throwing Lisa from the balcony.
* Reprinted with permission from the Diagnostic and Statistical Manual of Mental Disorders, Fifth Edition, (Copyright ©2013). American Psychiatric Association. All Rights Reserved.	* In addition, the individual must be at least 18 years and must have had a history of some symptoms of conduct disorder before age 15 years. There is strong evidence of this but we are unable to publish these details.

CHAPTER 9

ANGELIKA GAVARE

The cast
Vonne McGlynn: The victim, an Adelaide aged pensioner
Donald Smallwood: Vonne's brother, who lived in Queensland
Angelika Gavare: The killer and mother of two girls; one born in Latvia, one in Australia
Inara Dombrovska: Gavare's mother who used to live in the same street as Vonne McGlynn
Agnese Dombrovska: Gavare's sister
Giuseppe Daniele: Gavare's ex-boyfriend and the father of her second daughter. After being cornered by police, Gavare tried to blame him for the murder
Ejaz Ahmed: Gavare's boyfriend at the time of the crime

The motive
Angelika Gavare was motivated by pure greed. She wanted Vonne McGlynn's home and possessions so that she could sell them and benefit from the proceeds.

Introduction

When Angelika Gavare faced an Adelaide court over the brutal murder of widowed pensioner Vonne McGlynn, seasoned court reporters did a double take. After hearing that a woman had been charged with dismembering an elderly pensioner, they'd had visions of desperate drug addicts, dishevelled down-and-outs and hard-nosed career criminals. But this alleged murderer was young, attractive, well made-up and stylishly dressed with long, light brown hair.

Sean Fewster, chief court reporter for Adelaide's *The Advertiser* and the *Sunday Mail*, was gobsmacked. How could this fetching young woman be capable of such a depraved act? Even Gavare's actions on the day of her arrest seemed incongruous. The mother of two was arrested at a Morphett Vale bus stop after dropping her daughters off at school and day care. When she later fronted court charged with murder, she appeared very much the suburban mum. 'She was absolutely not what any of us expected,' says Fewster, who observed Gavare's entire trial. But attractive or not, Angelike Gavare was a cold-blooded killer.

The evidence was strong and, despite her pleas of innocence and attempts to blame others, she was found guilty of Vonne McGlynn's murder. A video of Gavare's police interview unmasked a cold, calculating woman who only cared about her own welfare.

'When the court was played her police interview video she was glued to the screen,' Fewster recalls. 'She could not tear her eyes away. Every time Angelika on the screen cracked a joke . . . Angelika in real life would laugh at the joke. She was . . . laughing at her own jokes, months and years after they were first made.'

This woman was shameless and clearly felt no guilt. She was prepared to kill and dismember an elderly woman simply to improve her finances. Gavare had hatched a plan to kill eighty-two-year-old pensioner Vonne McGlynn so she could access Vonne's bank accounts and sell her modest outer suburban home and contents. Reasoning that old people often wandered off aimlessly, Gavare thought that others would assume Vonne had simply gone missing.

Worse still was the shocking nature of the crime. Gavare broke into Vonne's house through a manhole in the roof, killed her – probably by hitting her with a heavy statue – dismembered the body, removing the head and hands, and dumped some of the remains in a creek near her own home, putting Vonne's body parts in garbage bags and wheeling them in a child's pram. Several neighbours saw Gavare walking a pram near the creek, which flowed directly opposite her Christie Downs home, less than ten minutes drive from her victim's house. The waterline lies below a heavily treed embankment and has a walking path perfect for leisurely strolls and childhood bike-riding adventures.

Without a thought for the many people who would be walking and riding past, Gavare used this pretty bushland setting to dispose of what she saw as her meal ticket in the most callous way imaginable. But she did not count on the persistence of police and made a number of mistakes that led them to her. It soon became obvious that, like most of the murderers described in this book, she was not as clever as she thought.

Throughout, Angelika Gavare's coldness was chilling. At no stage did she show any compassion for her victim or others affected by her crime. Despite mounting evidence, she made no admissions and showed no remorse. Instead, she changed her story and tried to blame an ex-boyfriend for one of Australia's most gruesome killings. Nor would she tell police what she did with Vonne McGlynn's head and hands, which have never been recovered.

Why did she do it?

The lead-up to the crime

Widowed pensioner Vonne McGlynn lived quietly in Reynella, twenty kilometres south of Adelaide's CBD. The working-class suburb is known for its 'Junk Food Junction' on the intersection of Main South and Sherriffs roads. In late 2014, the unassuming crossroad boasted McDonald's, KFC, Hungry Jack's, Fasta Pasta and Domino's Pizza outlets. Fast food aside, Reynella is like many working-class suburbs around Australia, with quiet residential streets surrounded by schools, shopping centres, parks and sporting ovals.

Vonne lived alone in her small brick home and was fiercely independent. The spritely octogenarian was intelligent, well-travelled and in reasonably good health. Neighbours often saw her walking to and from the shops and pottering in the garden. She regularly visited the local McDonald's outlet for breakfast and was well-known to staff there.

Vonne's younger brother, Donald Smallwood, who lives in Queensland, described his sister in court as very reserved, independent and 'parsimonious' when it came to money. She had the same fridge in her kitchen that he had bought her in 1958, still in perfect working order. Donald said Vonne had few close friends, but those she did have she treasured. He spoke to her from time to time by phone and eventually persuaded her to join a Red Cross service that makes a daily phone call to check an isolated person's welfare (R v Gavare, judgment, 2011).

Vonne was friendly with neighbours Sharon and Roger Zadow. Sharon offered her lifts in the car, but the older woman rarely accepted. Sharon also occasionally cooked meals that she shared with her neighbour, who let her know if she planned to go away for more than a day. Vonne would also feed her neighbours' chickens or walk their dogs when they were away. In 2008, she broke her arm and had a plaster cast on it, forcing her to use Meals on Wheels. She also had help to shower. Later that year, Vonne told Sharon that a young woman had visited her, offering to be her carer, but Vonne declined. Vonne repeated this incident to another friendly neighbour, Therese Molloy, and to her brother Donald. She told Donald that the young woman had banged loudly on her front door and then on the back door, insisting that she could help her.

That woman was Latvian-born Angelika Gavare, who lived nearby with her two young daughters. Gavare first met Vonne in 2006, while living in the same street with her mother, Inara Dombrovska, when her second daughter was a baby. Inara, who has since moved, ran a day care centre for children from her home and knew Vonne by sight. She occasionally saw the older woman walking up and down their neat, tree-lined avenue. They had only ever spoken to say hello and Inara did not know about Vonne's disappearance until she saw it on the TV news.

On 3 December 2008, Vonne answered her Red Cross welfare check phone call at about 8.45 am. The call was the last known contact with Vonne before she died. That evening, Inara and several relatives went to Caffe Buongiorno in O'Halloran Hill to celebrate Gavare's birthday. Gavare, her boyfriend Ejaz Ahmed and her children attended. Everyone was home by about 9 pm.

Vonne McGlynn was almost certainly murdered later that night.

The murder

Sometime after leaving her birthday dinner, Angelika Gavare broke into Vonne McGlynn's home. The evidence suggests that she entered the house through a manhole in the tiled roof. Before Vonne could defend herself or alert her neighbours, Gavare probably hit the older woman with a statue from the house, killing her. At some point she took Vonne's body to her home in nearby Christie Downs, where she probably dismembered it in her garage, most likely with either an angle grinder or a chainsaw that she and Ahmed had used when they renovated Gavare's bathroom not long before. She placed Vonne's body parts in plastic bags.

Gavare then put the bags into a pram and disposed of them in Christies Creek. The creek path was directly opposite her house, so Gavare only had to wheel the pram down an embankment. It was a brazen move. The creek is only metres from houses, and the bushland path was frequented by many locals on foot and bikes. No-one knows exactly when the body parts were dumped as they were not found until almost three months later. Neighbours later said they had noticed Gavare walking around with a pram.

After killing Vonne and disposing of her remains, Gavare intended to steal her possessions and then sell the house, pocketing the proceeds. Her plan was to pretend that Vonne had entrusted her with her affairs before mysteriously disappearing. If she hid her tracks well, she reasoned, no-one would ever know. How Gavare thought she would get away with this flimsy premise, given her lack of connection with her victim, is anyone's guess. But she was supremely confident of her own cleverness.

With Vonne out of the way, Gavare stole her passport, house keys, personal photos and some furniture. She called charities and the local council, impersonating her victim as she tried to sell or dispose of unwanted items. She then searched the internet for ways to sell a house without an agent. Gavare also used a forged power of attorney document to try to withdraw money from Vonne's ANZ account and was caught in the act on CCTV. As she carried out her plan, she continued to care for her children, shop and attend a TAFE accounting course (R v Gavare, 2011).

Police first visited Vonne's home on 4 December 2008, after she failed to answer her Red Cross call. Neighbours also reported the front door was open. Police visited the house several times over the next few days but found no sign of the occupant. Meanwhile, Gavare was literally rearranging the furniture. On 4 December she tried to access Vonne's ANZ bank account online. On 5 December she called the Salvation Army store call centre using the name of Isabella McGlynn to arrange the collection of eight chairs, a sofa and dining table. On her home computer she searched for websites related to Vonne's brother, the Salvation Army, the Smith Family, Reynella and the Land Titles Office. On 8 December she phoned the Onkaparinga Council and used the name of Mrs V.I. McGlynn to request a hard rubbish collection from Vonne's house.

Police began to suspect her when she tried to withdraw $2000 from Vonne's bank account on 9 December. Her attempted use of her victim's ATM card and the forged power of attorney also led them to her. On Christmas Eve, after being challenged, Gavare effectively admitted the crime to her mother at her sister Agnese's home. Inara had seen a TV report that mentioned Gavare had been caught on camera trying to access the missing woman's bank account and gave her daughter an ultimatum: if she did not tell the truth, they could not celebrate Christmas Eve together.

Gavare admitted she had been watching Vonne for 'some time' and that she went to her house on the morning of 3 December while Vonne was out. Gavare waited until she returned and then 'made her unconscious'. She searched the house before going home and returned later that evening, wrapped the victim's body in plastic and sheets and took her somewhere south, outside the city. Gavare told her mother that she had forged a power of attorney from Vonne and ordered a fake Justice of the Peace stamp to complete the witnessing of her signature so she could sell Vonne's house and buy another one. She said she had entered the house by the roof, and was certain the police would never find the body. Shocked, Inara asked her daughter to leave.

Meanwhile, a number of witnesses reported that they had seen a woman with a pram at various locations in the Christies Creek area between December 2008 and late January 2009. When police visited Gavare's house, they noted a terrible smell like rotting flesh in her garage.

On 23 and 25 February 2009, police found a pram and some of Vonne's remains in bushes near Gavare's home. While dental records could not be used, an artificial hip joint matched the serial number of Vonne's. After seeing the pram on the television news, Gavare's sister, Agnese Dombrovska, who by now was suspicious about her sister's possible involvement, contacted police to say it looked like one she had used to take her children to the playground around the corner from her mother's home. When shown a picture of it, she noticed that it had the same fault as her mother's pram, namely a missing screw underneath that caused the lower beam to dangle down.

When she was arrested soon after, Gavare told police that she and the victim had been 'friends' and Vonne had entrusted her to deal with her affairs and renovate her home. Later, cornered by mounting evidence, she changed her story to accuse her former partner, Giuseppe Daniele, of killing the elderly woman in a hit-and-run accident.

The trial and appeal

In August 2011, Angelika Gavare pleaded not guilty to murder in the South Australian Supreme Court. Then thirty-five, Gavare was tried by judge alone – Justice Trish Kelly. South Australia's Director of Public Prosecutions, Stephen Pallaras, alleged that Gavare killed Vonne McGlynn, cut up her body and dumped it in the creek so she could sell Vonne's house and belongings. It was a simple motive for a shocking crime.

When she was arrested almost three months after committing the murder, Gavare told police she was a friend of Mrs McGlynn, who had entrusted her to deal with her affairs. She claimed that young people in her culture looked after the elderly. None of this gelled with the facts. The court heard that when she was initially questioned, Gavare had in her possession Vonne's debit card, toaster oven, table and keys. Police also found various notes written by Gavare, a folder of documents including Vonne's bank statements, expired passports and photos, and loose extracts from the accused killer's diary (R v Gavare, judgment, 2011).

Prosecutor Pallaras described Gavare as a 'chilling, amoral woman' who was unusually motivated by greed. Gavare had admitted that Vonne was dead, that she hoped to profit from selling her house and that she was a thief, liar and fraud who had falsely claimed to be Vonne's trusted friend. But she had denied killing her and claimed a former boyfriend, Giuseppe Daniele, had accidentally killed Vonne, after which she helped him move her body. Mr Pallaras told the court Gavare had ultimately demonstrated a 'moral disconnect' and changed her story when it was obvious her first version was not believed by police (Kappelle, 2011).

In Gavare's defence, Grant Algie QC argued that there was no forensic evidence linking her to Vonne's body being dismembered, Daniel's possible involvement should not be discounted and someone else could have dumped the body parts. But all the evidence pointed to Gavare – not her ex.

DNA from a blood stain on the pram was consistent with Vonne's DNA profile, as was DNA from the boot kick panel of Gavare's white Kia. Despite this, she claimed that Daniele killed Vonne in a hit-and-run and forced her to stage a robbery as a cover-up. She said he put Vonne's ATM card and personal items in her car, sparking an idea. 'It occurred to me that it was possible I could use the situation for my profit,' she said. 'I thought of benefiting from maybe transferring her [house] into my name . . . and if I was able to transfer money from her account to mine' (Fewster, 'Angelika Gavare guilty', 2011).

Not only did Gavare lie, she lied about why she lied, implying her ex-partner was dangerous. She claimed she had told police untruths to keep her family safe from Daniele, as well as to hide her greed. 'I lied because I felt once I had started lying, I could not stop lying,' she said. 'Today is not a story . . . this is my chance to say what did happen and did not happen. What I've said to police before are lies . . . today, I'm here to tell the truth.' Pallaras was unconvinced: 'You are a good liar, and lying comes easily to you.' (Fewster, 'Angelika Gavare guilty', 2011)

Giuseppe Daniele was incredulous when called to give evidence. He laughed at the 'ludicrous' suggestion that he had killed Vonne, a reaction Justice Kelly later found to be truthful. Inara Dombrovska also testified against her daughter, despite South Australian laws that allow close relatives to refuse to testify against each other. She told the court that she would not blind herself to 'what my daughter is' and recounted the Christmas Eve conversation in which Gavare had effectively confessed to the crime.

On 30 August 2011, Justice Kelly found Angelika Gavare guilty of murdering Vonne Isabelle McGlynn. 'This is one of those cases where the totality of the circumstantial evidence is as powerful as any direct evidence could ever be,' she said.

> This is not a case of an assault which went too far or a robbery interrupted which had unintended consequences. The accused wanted Ms McGlynn's house and she

wanted her money. The only way to sell or rent the house and take the property of Ms McGlynn was to ensure that she never came back to stymie the accused's plans. (R v Gavare, 2011)

When the verdict was read, Sean Fewster noted that Gavare appeared confused and stood in the dock frowning. 'Gone was any trace of the woman who had, during the three-week trial, tried to peer at documents and shaken her head at witness testimony,' he wrote at the time (Fewster, 'Greed drove Angelika Gavare', 2011).

Throughout the trial, Fewster says Gavare was calm but did react to what others said. She was curious and attentive, but sometimes struggled to comprehend what was being said, which may have been due to the recent migrant's unfamiliarity with English. 'It was a pattern that she would follow throughout the case,' he says. 'She was always calm, she was always curious, she was always very interested.'

Sean Fewster is an experienced court reporter and author of the book *City of Evil: The truth about Adelaide's strange and violent underbelly* (2011). One of the first things he noticed about Gavare was her wide, expressive eyes. 'She would listen to the evidence and react. She was clearly emotionally engaged in what was going on, but not in the sense of breaking out in a rage when someone alerted her to something.' These reactions included surprise, anger and excitement. As he observed these mannerisms and reactions, Fewster thought Gavare was either highly intelligent or wrongly thought she was. He decided it was the latter, as police were able to prove her guilt with relative ease.

In November 2011, Justice Kelly sentenced Angelika Gavare to life in prison, with a minimum non-parole period of thirty-two years. 'The circumstances in which you committed this crime – including the stalking and killing of a defenceless 82-year-old in her own home, motivated by nothing more than your own sheer greed – places your crime in the worst category,' she said. 'There is no evidence of contrition or remorse, and you've not even had the decency to reveal how you disposed of the head and hands of this most unfortunate woman. Your actions reveal a profound disregard and disrespect for human life' (R v Gavare, sentencing, 2011).

Justice Kelly said nothing could mitigate Gavare's heinous crime. 'It would be a small comfort to be able to conclude that your actions were the product of madness,' she said.

> Unfortunately, this appears to be nothing more than the actions of a greedy, narcissistic and deceitful woman with no morals or empathy. This makes you a very dangerous woman indeed. It's very sad that your two children will grow up without their mother. They are, in a very real way, also victims of your crime – but you alone are responsible for that consequence. (R v Gavare, sentencing, 2011)

Gavare barely reacted. She raised her eyebrows once when the non-parole period was announced, then walked out to the cells (Fewster, 'Pensioner killer Angelika Gavare jailed', 2011).

In December 2011, one of South Australia's top criminal barristers, Bill Boucaut, took on Gavare's case. In January 2012, she won the right to appeal her conviction and sentence. Boucaut argued the sentence and guilty verdict were based on error and Justice Kelly should have considered possibilities other than murder, such as accidental death or a burglary gone wrong (Fewster, 2012). It didn't work. In May 2012, Gavare glared as the Criminal Court of Appeal unanimously upheld the sentence and conviction.

It was an incomprehensible crime. But even more inexplicable was the fact that Gavare thought she could get away with such an ill-conceived plot. Why?

Angelika Gavare's background

Little is known about Angelika Gavare's childhood and early adult years. Born on 3 December 1975, she migrated from Latvia with her mother, sister and her Latvian-born oldest daughter in 2001 on a spousal visa after meeting her second husband. There is no available evidence about this man. A second daughter was born in Australia to Giuseppe Daniele, whom she met in 2005 and later tried to blame for Vonne's murder. Gavare and Giuseppe broke up acrimoniously in mid-2006. She moved out of their home and purchased her own home in Christie Downs. In mid-2008 she started a relationship with Ejaz Ahmed. Gavare worked in a Noarlunga newsagency and studied accounting at Noarlunga TAFE, where she completed and passed an exam around the time of Vonne's murder (R v Gavare, 2012).

Not long after arriving in Australia, Gavare began to break the law, a fact she later admitted to police. She was sacked from her newsagency job for stealing a credit card a man had given his daughter to use, along with the pin number. Gavare admitted to stealing both, as well as $34 cash that had been withdrawn. After work she went on a shopping spree, purchasing goods to the value of $1244.86. Among other things, she bought groceries, alcohol, designer clothing for one of her daughters and four bottles of perfume worth $82. The spree only ended when she tried to buy groceries at her local supermarket and the card was declined (Fewster, 'Murderer Angelika Gavare admits to stolen credit card', 2011). Gavare also stole a driver's licence from a colleague and banking records from a letterbox; she used the banking records to forge a power of attorney form in the name of the homeowner.

Why did they do it?

This pattern of behaviour was probably not new and it is highly likely that Gavare had behaved in similar ways before moving to Australia. Once here, she continued to put herself first without regard to the consequences for others. Gavare and Giuseppe Daniele were in the early stages of a custody battle when she was charged with Vonne's murder; by then she was in a relationship with with Ejaz Ahmed. She probably found it convenient to blame Daniele for Vonne's murder because their relationship ended acrimoniously and she had accused him of assault, prompting him to seek custody of their child. The allegations against Daniele were extremely serious. Not only did she accuse him of killing Vonne, Gavare said Daniele had moved Vonne into the backyard, leaving her on the pavement, and put items, including a table, into her car boot before giving her the keys to Vonne's house and telling her to leave. Gavare also said Daniele had threatened to kill her or her family if she went to the police. But the story was clearly invented – Daniele had an alibi – and designed to shift the blame. The fact that she was prepared to make such serious allegations shows a preparedness to cause distress and harm to others in order to protect her own interests.

Gavare revealed more about her complete disregard for others during four police interviews after Vonne's death. She had no qualms about lying to save her own skin, initially telling police she was a friend who helped Vonne with odd jobs around the house and that Vonne had asked her to withdraw money from her account to do some home improvements. The story about Vonne giving her power of attorney was clearly incredible given their lack of any relationship (R v Gavare, 2011).

Despite admitting to some lies, Gavare did not admit guilt nor tell police where Vonne's head and hands were. Her refusal to offer any sort of closure to her victim's loved ones was particularly cold-blooded. Gavare's sister Agnese Dombrovska told the court that her sister 'just laughed' when confronted about the crime and admitted to being the last person who saw Vonne, which was unsettling. 'She just laughed it off, and I found that a bit odd . . . it was not a laughing matter,' Agnese said.

The fact that Gavare's mother chose to testify against her was significant and suggested she may have had a past history of selfish, dishonest and ruthless behaviour. Sean Fewster found Inara to be a determined and credible witness. 'The impression of Mum I got was very stiff and cold, but of course she'd come in to give evidence against her daughter in a murder trial,' he says. 'That's a massive sign of integrity.'

While Gavare was clearly deceitful and manipulative, she could also be friendly and had no problems finding partners. Neighbours told Fewster that she was 'chatty' and 'very pretty and always well dressed'. She was often seen walking her younger daughter in a pram. To those who knew her superficially, Angelika Gavare appeared to be a typical single mother leading a quiet life in the suburbs (Fewster, 2009).

Nothing could have been further from the truth.

Why did she do it?

Angelika Gavare did not feel a twinge of guilt or remorse when she murdered an elderly woman, cut up her body and later blamed the crime on a former boyfriend. Why?

Gavare's pattern of behaviour is consistent with diagnosis of antisocial personality disorder (ASPD) with psychopathic and narcissistic features. While most people worry about taking risks or breaking the law, someone like Gavare doesn't worry about either. She feels very little empathy for other people and does not feel guilt if she hurts someone physically or emotionally, or when she steals from them. To her, other people are a means to an end. If that involves killing an elderly woman for money, so be it. She literally saw Vonne McGlynn as disposable.

After dumping Vonne's remains in garbage bags, Gavare kept her victim's new toaster, nest of tables and other belongings in her home. She then denied any wrongdoing and, when cornered by police, admitted her involvement but blamed an ex-boyfriend for the crime. That could have ruined his life. But Gavare thought she was entitled to protect herself and her own interests regardless of the harm that she caused to others. She had no regard for the welfare or rights of Giuseppe Daniele or anyone else.

People with an ASPD who also have psychopathic features tend to be relatively fearless and not learn from their mistakes. Gavare had no qualms about breaking into Vonne's house, killing her and dismembering the body. Nor did she appear nervous when she tried to access Vonne's bank account. Gavare was prepared to do whatever it took to enhance her quality of life.

An ASPD is caused by a combination of genetic and environmental factors. Little is known about Gavare's early days, but her mother pointed to a history of selfish and callous behaviour when she said that she wouldn't close her eyes to 'what her daughter was'. Gavare was probably born with a genetic predisposition to some of the traits associated with an ASPD. There are no available details about the rest of her family apart from her mother and sister, both of whom clearly have the capacity for empathy and morality. Any genetic predisposition that Gavare had may have been exacerbated by her getting away with dishonest and aggressive behaviour from when she was quite young; her classmates at school may well have been scared of her. There may have been people within her family or neighbourhood who modelled aggression and dishonest behaviour and encouraged her to do the same. All we know for sure is that by the time she arrived in Australia, she was already a cunning and ruthless manipulator who repeatedly defrauded people for her own gain. Her crimes became increasingly brazen until she came up with what she thought was the perfect way to guarantee that she could have what she wanted in life – murdering Vonne McGlynn and taking her possessions.

It was never going to end well for Gavare. She acted impulsively, overestimated her intelligence and conducted herself in a haphazard manner, keeping 'trophies' from Vonne's house and acting suspiciously. She didn't leave obvious physical evidence at Vonne's home or her own, but made many mistakes and left a number of clues, such as the security video of her trying to access Vonne's account in a bank. She also dumped part of Vonne's remains close to her home in a relatively public area. Gavare's other known crimes were sloppy as well. She was caught several times using crude methods to defraud people, such as buying goods with someone else's credit card. Yet she thought she could get away with murder.

Some criminals with an ASPD are quite intelligent and do get away with serious crimes for years. Notorious US mass murderer and sociopath Ted Bundy, for example, is known to have killed thirty young women and may have killed many more before he was executed in 1989. Like Gavare, Bundy was outwardly personable and attractive, which gave people a false sense of security when he approached them. After assaulting and killing his victims, mostly university students, he evaded police for years, coming up with cunning strategies to find more suitable victims, attack them and cover up his crimes. Bundy travelled long distances, avoided guns to prevent ballistic evidence, did not leave fingerprints, carefully researched body-disposal locations and regularly changed his appearance.

Gavare, on the other hand, left a trail of circumstantial evidence and came up with flimsy excuses that were not believable. What she did have in common with Bundy was a relative fearlessness and limited capacity for empathy. These characteristics enabled her to wheel a pram full of human body parts along a popular bushland path near her home with no signs of nervousness. Nor was Gavare nervous when she entered a bank to try to steal Vonne's money, knowing that her elderly victim was dead. Gavare's attempts to offload Vonne's possessions and house showed incredible fearlessness, but also a lack of awareness about how the world works. Suspicions were obviously going to be raised, but she appeared to be unaware of this possibility; a limited capacity for empathy can limit the development of an understanding of how 'normal' people will respond and react in certain situations.

Gavare also has narcissistic tendencies. They became obvious when she watched, enthralled, as her police video was played in the court. She smiled and laughed as she watched herself on the screen, oblivious to the disgust others would have felt.

Even in jail, Angelika Gavare appears to be using others for her own ends and amusement, without regard for their welfare or feelings. In 2012 the *Sunday Mail*'s Andrew Dowdell reported that Gavare was manipulating and taunting other prisoners and causing fights. While respectful towards prison staff, she was 'canny' and 'manipulative' of other prisoners. 'The other inmates generally want nothing to do with her, they are terrified of her because of what she has done,' one source said. Another said Gavare used her influence over other prisoners and was 'running the show in protection . . . she's pulling the strings and manipulating others' (Dowdell, 2012).

When Justice Trish Kelly imposed a thirty-two-year non-parole period for what she said was one of the state's worst

320

murders, she described Gavare as 'a greedy, narcissistic and deceitful woman completely devoid of any moral insight or empathy', adding, 'this makes you a very dangerous person indeed'. No doubt Gavare's fellow prisoners would agree with this summation (R v Gavare, 2011).

ANGELIKA GAVARE
DIAGNOSTIC CHART

Using DSM 5 indicators (APA, 2013), when three or more of these are present, occurring since age fifteen years, a diagnosis of antisocial personality disorder (ASPD) can be made	Examples of Angelika Gavare's behaviour that appear to be consistent with each indicator
Failure to conform to social norms with respect to lawful behaviors, as indicated by repeatedly performing acts that are grounds for arrest.	Convictions for theft, credit card fraud, identity theft and murder.
Deceitfulness, as indicated by repeated lying, use of aliases, or conning others for personal profit or pleasure.	Lied to the bank about having power of attorney over her victim, Vonne McGlynn. Convicted for fraudulent use of someone else's credit card. Stole banking records from a letterbox and used them to forge a power of attorney form in the name of the homeowner. Falsely blamed an ex-partner for her crime, forcing him to defend himself in court.
Impulsivity or failure to plan ahead.	Didn't consider the impact of her criminal behaviours on her children or family. Thought she could sell someone else's house and keep the proceeds without any consequences.

Using DSM 5 indicators (APA, 2013), when three or more of these are present, occurring since age fifteen years, a diagnosis of antisocial personality disorder (ASPD) can be made	Examples of Angelika Gavare's behaviour that appear to be consistent with each indicator
	Tried to use Vonne McGlynn's bank details.
Irritability and aggressiveness, as indicated by repeated physical fights or assaults.	Assaulted, murdered and dismembered Vonne McGlynn. It has been reported that she causes fights and plays people off against each other in jail.
Reckless disregard for safety of self or others.	Murdered Vonne McGlynn.
Consistent irresponsibility, as indicated by repeated failure to sustain consistent work behavior or honor financial obligations.	Sacked for stealing and using a colleague's credit card. Stole another colleague's driver's licence.
Lack of remorse, as indicated by being indifferent to or rationalizing having hurt, mistreated or stolen from another. * Reprinted with permission from the Diagnostic and Statistical Manual of Mental Disorders, Fifth Edition, (Copyright ©2013). American Psychiatric Association. All Rights Reserved.	No remorse shown – denied guilt and blamed someone else for the murder of Vonne McGlynn. *In addition, the individual must be at least 18 years and must have had a history of some symptoms of conduct disorder before age 15 years. Information is not readily available but highly likely given the nature of Gavare's ongoing criminal activities.

CHAPTER 10

ADRIAN BAYLEY

The cast

Jill Meagher: The victim
Tom Meagher: Jill's husband
George and Edith McKeon: Jill's parents, who lived in Perth
Michael McKeon: Jill's brother, who lived in Perth
Adrian Ernest Bayley: The killer. Grew up Adrian Edwards before changing his name in 2000
Debbie: Bayley's ex-wife; mother of Bayley's two older children
Second partner: Bayley had two more children with another partner
Rameeza Ali: Bayley's girlfriend at the time of the crime

The motive

Adrian Bayley raped Jill Meagher and then killed her to prevent her from reporting him to the police. He already had multiple convictions for sexual assault and knew that another conviction would almost certainly result in a maxiumum twenty-five-year jail sentence.

Introduction

After raping, strangling and burying his victim in remote bushland, Adrian Ernest Bayley returned home and had a leisurely sleep-in with his girlfriend. They watched videos and went out for a late lunch of kebabs. When reports about the disappearance of a young Irish woman filtered through the Melbourne media, Bayley warned his live-in partner, Rameeza Ali, to be careful. At that stage, just hours after the crime, Rameeza had no idea that her boyfriend had dragged ABC radio employee Jill Meagher off the street, raped and killed her.

Jill lost her life in September 2012 after a number of factors conspired to enable a clearly dangerous man to continue to harm others until he was caught. Bayley, a violent sex offender with two jail stints behind him, was on the prowl after arguing with Rameeza earlier in the night. He later told police that the argument left him feeling angry and aggressive and he transferred those feelings onto Jill because someone had to pay. Jill just happened to walk past as he stalked the streets of Brunswick, looking for a woman to abuse. He showed no mercy as he raped and then strangled the popular radio worker and left her in an alleyway, before returning to remove her body and take it to a remote spot outside Melbourne.

Adrian Bayley is among the most dangerous of criminals – those who are ruthless, repetitive and hard to pick. With close-cropped strawberry blond hair, a chiselled physique and 'boy next door' looks, he did not fit the stereotype of a social misfit. This was a man who could move freely in the community without arousing suspicion, which he did when he wasn't in jail. Bayley fathered four children with two different partners and was a regular at the gym, and no-one ever suspected he was capable of such violence. Even after doing prison time for sexual assault, he still managed to find work and girlfriends after each release.

However, Bayley's background was anything but normal. He claims to have had an emotionally and physically abusive childhood, though there doesn't appear to be any confirmation of this from other family members. As a teenager Bayley was already sexually assaulting young women. He had served two jail terms for rape and was on parole when he killed Jill. While drunk one night he had king hit a man and pleaded guilty to a physical assault charge, but appealed the three-month sentence imposed on him and was not returned to prison by Victoria's Parole Board. While free on bail until his appeal was heard, he raped and strangled Jill.

In March 2015, two years after Bayley was convicted of Jill's murder, it also emerged that he had recently been convicted of three more rapes that occurred in 2000 and 2012, before Jill's death. Those convictions could not be reported until they were all finalised and underlined the fact that Bayley is a violent sexual predator with a long history of sadistically abusing women and raping them, often in secluded alleys, whenever he felt the urge. But why would a hardened criminal who knew the justice system backwards kill an innocent young woman when, due to his previous record, it would guarantee him a life sentence?

The lead-up to the crime
The events leading up to Jill Meagher's murder could have happened anywhere. They are played out in cities around the world every weekend as colleagues celebrate the end of another working week and partners join each other for a social drink. But they rarely end like this otherwise ordinary Friday night in Melbourne, which was gearing up for the following weekend's AFL grand final. It was Friday, 21 September 2012. Twenty-nine-year-old Jill, who worked for ABC Radio, left the Southbank ABC building to join friends for a casual drink.

Meanwhile, Adrian Bayley, a man Jill had never met but who lived just one suburb away from her, was meeting up with his girlfriend at another bar across town. There, Bayley and Rameeza argued about his jealousy and possessiveness. She left the bar and, ignoring his texts and phone calls, returned alone to their small Coburg unit at the back of their landlord's home. Forty-one-year-old Bayley left the Lounge Bar in the city at around 12.25 am and took a taxi home. He couldn't find Rameeza, who was sleeping in the spare room, so he changed into a blue hooded tracksuit top and headed out. He later told police that he caught a taxi, intending to pick up his car in Newmarket, near Flemington, but the taxi driver thought he was going to vomit and ordered him to get out on Sydney Road in Brunswick, not far from where Jill Meagher was socialising with her colleagues (R v Bayley, 2013).

At about 1 am, Jill left the Brunswick Green Hotel with a colleague and walked to nearby Bar Etiquette, which was also on Sydney Road. The colleague then offered to walk her home but she declined as she lived only a few streets away and thought she would be fine. Outside a pharmacy, Jill asked a group of three people for a cigarette and had a 'short friendly, conversation'. (Anderson, 'Jill Meagher's accused killer', 2013) She then continued along Sydney Road towards Hope Street.

At 1.35 am Jill called her brother, Michael McKeon, who had recently moved to Perth, where their parents lived, to talk about their sick father. The phone connection was poor so Michael said he would call back in a minute or two. At 1.37 am, Jill's husband Tom sent her a text asking if she was okay.

She was not.

Less than ten minutes after calling her brother, Jill Meagher was attacked and killed.

The murder

After Jill spoke to Michael briefly at 1.35 am, Bayley later told police he approached her because she seemed upset. They had a brief conversation, but she 'flipped him off' and made him angry by refusing to talk to him. Bayley followed her as she turned into Hope Street from Sydney Road. At 1.38 am, as Jill neared a laneway, he approached her again, this time trying to kiss her and grab her on the bottom, after which she slapped him across the face, hit him with her mobile phone and told him she was going to call police. Bayley later told police he then 'lost it', dragged her into the laneway, raped her on the bonnet of a car and then strangled her with his hands (R v Bayley, 2013).

While this was happening, Jill's husband and brother were frantically trying to find her. Michael tried calling back several times but her phone rang out. At 1.47 am, a concerned Tom Meagher sent his wife another text: 'Answer me, I'm really worried.' He sent another at 2.07 am: 'Please pick up' (Anderson, 'Jill Meagher's accused killer', 2013).

Meanwhile, after killing Jill, Bayley returned home to Coburg to retrieve his other car and a shovel, returning to the laneway between Ovens Street and Sydney Road (where he had left Jill's body) at 4.22 am. He put her body into the boot of his Holden Astra and drove to Blackhill Road, Gisborne South, fifty kilometres north-west of Melbourne's CBD, where he buried her in a shallow grave beside the gravel road (R v Bayley, 2013).

When the Astra ran out of petrol on the way home, Bayley flagged down motorist Dayle Watkins, who drove him to a nearby service station. At 6 am Bayley filled a jerry can with petrol and Dayle drove him back to his car. In a later police statement, Rameeza said her partner arrived home at about 7 am on the Saturday. They slept until 1 pm before going to pick up his car from a Flemington hotel. 'We went in my car to Flemington [and] on the way we stopped and had kebabs,' she said. 'And then we went and picked up his car and then we got some movies' (Anderson, 'Jill Meagher's accused killer', 2013).

Rameeza said when news reports emerged about Jill Meagher's disappearance, Bayley warned her not to walk alone. 'I said, "Oh, she's pretty and . . . works for the ABC", and he goes, "Yeah . . . that's why I'm saying that this place is not safe,"' Rameeza said. 'He goes, "Don't walk alone at night."'

On 27 September, Rameeza found Jill's broken Vodafone SIM card at the bottom of her washing machine after washing Bayley's clothes. He was arrested before she could ask him about it.

That day, after investigating the crime scene and gathering evidence, including extensive CCTV footage and phone records, homicide detectives arrested Bayley on suspicion of murdering Jill Meagher. He made admissions but, on 12 March 2013, pleaded not guilty to murder and guilty to one count of rape. He later changed his murder plea to guilty, avoiding a lengthy trial.

Jill Meagher's disappearance shocked Melbourne. She was a popular ABC employee and worked with local celebrities, including ABC radio hosts Red Symons and Jon Faine, both of whom attended her funeral. Women throughout the city could relate to Jill; many had sometimes chosen to walk home alone late at night in well-lit and busy areas such as Sydney Road in Brunswick and knew that what happened to Jill could have happened to any one of them.

The story was headline news for weeks, due to the random nature of the crime, Jill's popularity and the chilling CCTV footage that captured the vibrant young woman walking past a Sydney Road bridal boutique. In the footage a man in a blue hoodie, later confirmed to be Bayley, passed the camera alone, walking north, then turned around and walked back in the direction Jill was walking on her way home. She never made it.

A week after the crime and a day after the 2012 AFL Grand Final, 30,000 people marched down Sydney Road to pay their respects to Jill Meagher and demand an end to violence against women.

Irish-born Tara Wheeler, whose husband had worked with Jill back in Ireland, told the *Herald Sun* she was one of many women who walked alone in Melbourne at night. 'We've all walked home alone after dark,' she said. 'Usually we're okay. If anything comes out of this, I hope it opens young girls' eyes up to the dangers out there.' Added Nathalie Nilsson, twenty-three, of Coburg, 'We all live in the area and we're very upset by what happened. We wanted to show our support, and we want to feel safe at night. We're all young girls. It could've been any of us' (Duck and Thompson, 2012).

Meanwhile, chilling details were emerging about Jill's killer.

Watching Adrian Bayley in court, *Herald Sun* crime reporter Andrew Rule found it hard to find outward signs of the depravity often associated with someone responsible for a violent death. 'The man escorted into Court One just after midday yesterday looks like a clean-cut Scandinavian: fair-skinned, with well-cut strawberry-blond hair,' he wrote.

He looks fit, even athletic, and has clearly done a lot of gym work. In his blue V-necked T-shirt and jeans, sporting one professionally tattooed bicep, he could pass for a soldier on leave or a ski instructor. He has none of the ugly markers that so clearly label so many of the people brought before the bench before and after him: no 'jail tatts', no scars, no bad teeth. (Rule, 2012)

Writing for the White Ribbon campaign in April 2014, Jill's husband Tom agreed, revealing that one of the most disturbing moments was watching Bayley in court during the committal and realising that he was articulate and did not look like a 'monster':

> There was a clarity of communication, sentence structure, and proper articulation. It was chilling. I had formed an image that this man was not human, that he existed as a singular force of pure evil who somehow emerged from the ether.
>
> When I heard Bayley forming sentences in court, I froze because I'd been socialised to believe that men who rape are jabbering madmen, who wear tracksuit bottoms with dress shoes and knee-high socks. The only thing more disturbing than that paradigm is the fact that most rapists are normal guys, guys we might work beside or socialise with, our neighbours or even members of our family. I wonder at what stage we will stop being shocked by how normal a rapist *seemed*. (Meagher, 2014)

All this made the crime even harder to understand. How could someone who looked so 'normal' commit such a heinous crime?

The sentencing

Adrian Bayley's 2013 sentencing heard that he killed Jill Meagher because she fought back when he attacked her. Given his criminal record, he faced a twenty-five-year maximum sentence for her rape if she lived to identify him. The court was told that Bayley didn't intend to murder Jill, but lost his temper when she 'flipped him off'. He told police she looked distraught as they walked along Sydney Road, so he offered to help her. But she fobbed him off, which he 'didn't take well' (R v Bayley, 2013).

The court heard that Bayley told a psychologist he 'lost it' after Jill slapped him because he always had trouble when someone 'put their hands on me'. After she fought back, and threatened to call police, he said he grabbed her to quieten her but she fell and hit her head, drawing blood. He then held her around the neck and maintained pressure until she stopped breathing.

In sentencing Bayley to a minimum thirty-five years jail on 19 June 2013, Supreme Court judge Geoffrey Nettle had little sympathy for him:

> You were determined to have your way with her and so you overpowered her and raped her where she stood. Then you attacked her again because she was threatening to call police and in the process you strangled her to death. You are a recidivist violent sexual offender who has had little compunction about sexual offending when the mood takes you, or about threatening and inflicting violence as part of the process.

Bayley appeared to agree. In his police interview five days after the murder, he had said people like him deserved the death penalty:

> I want to do the right thing, you know. I don't care. I'm – I'm going to jail for a long time, so it – it – right now, I just don't care, you know what I mean? I – I hope they bring back the death penalty before I get sentenced. Nah, I fuckin' do man, 'cause what – I have no life left. I'm 41 years old. I've already done eight years in prison and I know this is still going. I don't care . . . They should have the death penalty for people like me anyway. (R v Bayley, 2013)

Bayley had also told detectives he should be in jail anyway and should not have been let out. For all his bravado, this was a man who knew he could not control his urge to dominate, abuse and hurt women.

The sentencing hearing was held in April 2013, after Bayley changed his plea to guilty of one count of murder and one count of rape. In June, a plea in mitigation hearing heard that when he killed Jill, Bailey had been out of prison for two years after serving eight years of an eleven-year sentence for sixteen counts of rape against five women. In sentencing Bayley, Justice Geoffrey Nettle outlined a shocking history of sexual violence and a series of attempts by him to mitigate what he had done after being caught. Justice Nettle said when Bayley was jailed in 1991 over three sex attacks on young women, his guilty plea was 'far more dictated by an appreciation of the overwhelming nature of the case against you than by true remorse. Equally, your supposed state of depression and anxiety presented to his Honour is far more the product of fear for yourself than of any sense of contrition'.

When Bayley was charged in 2001 with sixteen counts of rape against five sex workers, he had admitted guilt only after being confronted with the evidence. For those crimes he was sentenced in 2002 to eleven years jail with an eight-year minimum non-parole period. Bayley was released on parole in March 2010, but in 2011 was charged with another offence, the serious physical assault of a man in Geelong. On 27 February 2012 he was sentenced to three months jail to be served cumulatively on the 2002 sentence, but was bailed pending an appeal.

After Jill's murder, Bayley appeared to show some remorse. Through his counsel, Saul Holt SC, he apologised in court, but did not expect forgiveness. Bayley acknowledged taking a precious life. But this was little consolation to those affected, who could only infer that, as with his previous crimes, he was saying this only as an attempt to lessen his punishment.

Justice Nettle found Bayley had intended to kill Jill when he grabbed her neck and had derived 'sadistic pleasure' from hurting women. 'It was a savage, violent rape of the gravest kind committed upon a woman whom you knew was almost certainly not consenting,' he said.

> I am also satisfied beyond reasonable doubt that you strangled the deceased with the intent to kill her. I am satisfied beyond reasonable doubt that your previous offending illuminates your moral culpability for the rape and murder of the deceased and that, taken in conjunction with them, demonstrates a dangerous propensity to subject women to rape and violence in order to satiate your perverted sexual desires. (R v Bayley, 2013)

Justice Nettle was satisfied that Bayley's guilty plea showed 'some small degree of genuine remorse', but noted: 'When you offend sexually you also invariably offend violently. I have no choice but to sentence you to prison for a very long time.'

In September 2013, Bayley tried to have his sentence reduced. The Victorian Court of Appeal took less than ten minutes to dismiss his appeal application and find that his thirty-five-year non-parole period was entirely within range given the circumstances of Jill's murder. Then in 2015, Bayley was convicted of three more rapes, one in 2000 and two in 2012 before Jill died.

Bayley's background

Adrian Ernest Matthew Edwards was born on 14 July 1971, the eldest of five children. At eighteen, he married Debbie, who was pregnant with their first child. On 8 June that year, he held a sixteen-year-old girl hostage in his home and raped her in the bed he shared with his wife. He was arrested on 10 June, charged with rape and given bail (R v Bayley, 2013).

On 30 August, Bayley attacked a seventeen-year-old girl walking home from a bus stop. He poked her in the eyes several times, ripped off her clothes and touched her on the breasts and vagina. He also tried to rape her and threatened to kill her, saying: 'You must think I'm stupid. I'm not going to do anything that will be evidence for you to go to the police with.' On 11 September, the victim identified him to police and he was arrested and charged with attempted rape but again released on bail.

Just two months after his daughter was born in late 1990, Bayley picked up a sixteen-year-old hitchhiker along the Woori Yallock–Healesville road and attacked her. She escaped before he could rape her and identified him on 17 December. Bayley had initially denied each of these three crimes, but confessed when confronted with evidence. Convicted and sentenced to five years jail with a non-parole period of three years on 7 June 1991, he was released in April 1993.

In 1995, Bayley separated from his wife, who had their second child in 1996. She retained custody of their two children. He began a new relationship in that same year and fathered two more children. His sexual assaults on women continued and, to a point, he was able to maintain relationships while leading a double life as a vicious sex offender.

In July 2000, Bayley changed his surname by deed poll from Edwards to Bayley. On 1 September that year, he raped the first of five sex workers in the St Kilda area (a sixth case emerged in 2015). Each woman was driven to a lane in Elwood and violently raped in a vehicle, with Bayley threatening violence unless they did as he wanted. In each case Bayley parked his car against a wall behind a row of shops so that his victims couldn't open the door and escape. He raped three of them anally and forced them to engage in even more painful and humiliating sex acts. In one case, after raping and brutalising his victim he told her no-one cared, adding, 'I could dump you in the fucking alley and no-one would give a shit . . . Did that fucking hurt? See, look who's got the power. See, I can do whatever I want. Well you should be loose enough now.'

While in jail for those rapes, Bayley completed a sex-offender treatment program, later admitting that he said 'whatever they wanted to hear'. He was released on parole in 2010 only to assault a man outside a Geelong cafe and then kill Jill Meagher before being jailed again. The justice system clearly failed Bayley's victims and did little to improve his attitude to women. He knew his urge to sexually abuse them was wrong, but could not or would not change. As a result, Victoria's parole laws were tightened. But it was too late for Jill and her family.

Despite this terrible dark side, Bayley was generally able to blend into the community. A *Herald Sun* investigation by Jon Kaila found that those who knew him described him as a 'smiling, easygoing average Joe' and fitness fanatic. In 1993, Bayley completed a pastry cook apprenticeship and was regularly employed. He later worked as a pipeline layer. A neighbour at the time of his name change and the breakdown of his second long-term relationship said Bayley lived in a boarding house in Wyndham Vale. 'It's a rooming house for divorced men on low incomes,' landlord Mark Stevens said. 'It's $55 a week, cheap rent, and just a room to live to start people off and get the basics. He would only have been here a year or two' (Kaila, 2012).

Bayley apparently lived in several locations before moving into a small unit with Rameeza Ali at the back of a home in a quiet Coburg street in early 2012. The home owner told the *Herald Sun* that Bayley was a respectful and cooperative tenant.

'He's been very courteous in the house,' she said. Members of his local gym remembered Bayley working out on his own. 'He was pretty easygoing. He was confident, but most of those boys are,' a woman told the paper, adding that he seemed friendly and always had a smile on his face (Kaila, 2012).

Friends said Bayley sometimes appeared nervous and edgy. 'You would consider him – if you didn't know him – to be absolutely normal,' a former friend said. '[But he had] a tendency to withdraw. He kept to himself.' Another friend said Bayley was a 'fitness freak' who was 'smart'. Bayley's Facebook page revealed that he had nine friends and listed his hobbies as the gym, movies, music and anything outdoors. He described himself as a Buddhist, with a favourite quote reading, 'Power of mind is infinite, while brawn is limited.' When it came to women, however, he clearly turned into a different person (Kaila, 2012).

In 2013 it emerged that authorities had been warned about Bayley being a continuing danger to women. The *Herald Sun* revealed that Bayley's parents had met with authorities to convey their grave concerns about their son's behaviour. The tip-off reportedly led to a confrontation between Bayley and his family, with whom he had been living after a court appearance. His family refused to comment to the press, saying they had no intention of speaking publicly about their son (Dowsley, 2013).

In July 2013, it was also revealed that Bayley owed more than $12,500 in fines for crimes including speeding and illegal parking. Melbourne Magistrates Court commuted the fines into eighty-seven days more jail time, but he didn't receive any extra time as it would be served concurrently with his murder sentence (Anderson, 'Adrian Ernest Bayley won't serve extra jail time', 2013).

For some, any release date for a serial rapist and murderer who admits he can't control his actions is too soon.

Why did he do it?

The fact that Adrian Bayley was prowling the streets late on the night that he murdered Jill Meagher clearly indicates that he could not control his impulses to rape, hurt and humiliate women. He had been fighting with his girlfriend and became angry when he couldn't find her at home. His response was to hit the streets looking for someone to take his anger out on. Despite having a partner and, presumably, regular sex, he still craved the thrill of forcing himself onto strangers.

This violent urge to abuse women has been a constant theme of Bayley's adult life. Consultant psychologist Professor James Ogloff concluded that he had a borderline personality disorder (BPD). Ogloff's report, which was presented in court, noted that he had relied on claims by Bayley that his Melbourne childhood was traumatic and that he was physically abused by his father from the time he was nine years old, and sexually abused by a female relative between the ages of nine and fifteen. The sexual abuse had supposedly begun with inappropriate touching and led to sexual intercourse (R v Bayley, 2013). Ogloff concluded that as a result of what he had supposedly experienced, Bayley had ongoing feelings of guilt, remorse and self-loathing. However there is no other evidence to support this claim (Russell and Bucci, 2013).

This seems an improbable diagnosis given the available evidence and Bayley's overall behavioural history, which was not consistent with a BPD. It is more likely that Bayley's behaviour pattern is consistent with an antisocial personality disorder (ASPD) with psychopathic features. An ASPD is characterised by a pattern of disregard for and violation of the rights of others. Those with ASPD are indifferent to the rights, feelings or suffering of others and have little regard for the law or general expectations of society. Professor Ogloff did agree that Bayley was a cunning predator who enjoyed dominating his female victims and typically blamed them for his violent actions rather than taking responsibility for his own behaviour.

People with an ASPD tend to be preoccupied with doing whatever it takes to satisfy their desires. This may include violence, deceit, law-breaking, calculated cruelty or domination. Some, like Bayley, are physically violent and their behaviour is consistent with the psychopath variation of an ASPD as described in the DSM 5. They may break into homes, rape and sexually abuse, or attack or kill those who get in their way. Some kill simply for the excitement. In Bayley's case, he killed because he didn't like the fact that Jill fought back when he assaulted her. He also wanted to protect himself as she had threatened to report him to the police. Bayley, like most people with an ASPD, isn't very resilient and has always dealt with angry feelings or with people challenging him by responding in the same maladaptive ways through violence.

Like others with an ASPD, Bayley didn't learn from his mistakes and kept repeating the same behaviour patterns. Only when he was caught did he admit that what he did was wrong, but this was probably a ploy to secure a more lenient sentence. It is unlikely that his demonstrated remorse was genuine, although according to some he did show a small glimmer of insight into his behaviour when he acknowledged that he couldn't or wouldn't change and suggested that people like himself should be executed.

When Bayley attended a sex-offenders program in jail, he later admitted 'saying what it took' to impress those running it. The program didn't change his attitude or behaviour, which fits with the results from one research study that evaluated the effects of a treatment program for teaching anger management and social skills to prisoners with a psychopathic variation of an ASPD (Hare et al., 2000). The study found that program participants reoffended more upon release than other prisoners with the same diagnosis who hadn't taken part. It seems the program may have actually helped them to better understand the behaviour and motivation of potential victims and they then used this knowledge for their own ends. However, recent reviews of the effectiveness of treatment programs for such individuals are more optimistic about the potential positive outcomes for at least some of the participants (e.g. Harris and Rice, 2006).

Bayley also fits into a specific sub-category of serial rapists described by Hazelwood (Hazelwood, 2009) called the angry, revenge rapist. This type of rapist is physically brutal and wants to degrade and humiliate the person they rape. The act is impulsive rather than planned. The most common trigger is a recent argument with a female in his life and the act of raping another woman is a way of expressing his fury. He sees it as an act of punishment which leaves him feeling justified. This appears to have been the case with many of his rapes, including Jill's.

Whether or not he felt any genuine remorse, Adrian Bayley is a dangerous sexual predator who cannot or won't control his aggressive urges. Violence is a way of life for him. In October 2012, while in a protection unit of the Melbourne Assessment Prison awaiting his court appearance, Bayley cut himself when Rameeza Ali said she no longer wanted to see him. Staff found him unconscious in his cell during morning muster with cuts to his wrist, elbow and ankle. The wounds required surgery and a hospital stay (Dowsley, 2012). Once again, violence had been the answer for this deeply flawed and dangerous man. Given his ASPD and criminal history, this is unlikely to change. The only consolation for society and the families of his victims is that Adrian Ernest Bayley is unlikely to be released until he is a very old man – if at all. On 28 May 2015, Bayley was set a new non-parole period of 43 years following his conviction for three other sexual assaults, so he will not be eligible for parole until 2058, when he will be 86.

Adrian Bayley

Those long years in jail will seem even longer after Bayley's crime led to Victoria's parole conditions being tightened, putting the onus on criminals to prove they are no longer a danger to the public, former victims or witnesses. In 2014, Bayley was still being held in protection at the Melbourne Assessment Prison after long-term prisoners blamed him for the changes, prompted by public outrage after Jill Meagher died. *The Age*'s John Silvester revealed that notorious criminals with long maximum terms, particularly murderers, would be affected most. 'They are now looking at much longer jail time and they blame Bayley,' a source told him (Silvester, 2014).

For the first time in his life it looks like Adrian Ernest Bayley, who spent many years terrorising others, will find out what that feels like.

ADRIAN BAYLEY
DIAGNOSTIC CHART

Using DSM 5 indicators (APA, 2013), when three or more of these are present, occurring since age fifteen years, a diagnosis of an anti-social personality disorder (ASPD) can be made	Examples of Adrian Bayley's behaviour that appear to be consistent with each indicator
Failure to conform to social norms with respect to lawful behaviors, as indicated by repeatedly performing acts that are grounds for arrest.	History of multiple sexual assault convictions.
Deceitfulness, as indicated by repeated lying, use of aliases or conning others for personal profit or pleasure.	Told counsellors 'what they wanted to hear' when doing a sexual offenders' course in jail. Initially denied killing Jill. Lured women into his car by pretending he was a nice guy prepared to give them a lift, and then attacking.
Impulsivity or failure to plan ahead.	Didn't consider the effects of his crimes on his four children. Raped and killed Jill Meagher in a public laneway. Said he decided to kill Jill to avoid a twenty-five-year rape sentence, yet a murder sentence is often longer.

Using DSM 5 indicators (APA, 2013), when three or more of these are present, occurring since age fifteen years, a diagnosis of an anti-social personality disorder (ASPD) can be made	Examples of Adrian Bayley's behaviour that appear to be consistent with each indicator
Irritability and aggressiveness, as indicated by repeated physical fights or assaults.	Convicted for physical assault of a man in Geelong.
Reckless disregard for safety of self or others.	Conviction for murder. Multiple sexual assault convictions.
Consistent irresponsibility, as indicated by repeated failure to sustain consistent work behavior or honor financial obligations.	Failed to pay more than $12,500 in fines for speeding and illegal parking.
Lack of remorse, as indicated by being indifferent to or rationalizing having hurt, mistreated or stolen from another. * Reprinted with permission from the Diagnostic and Statistical Manual of Mental Disorders, Fifth Edition, (Copyright ©2013). American Psychiatric Association. All Rights Reserved.	No genuine remorse for Jill's murder. He blamed her because she 'flipped him off' when he tried to talk to her and because she kicked out at him and threatened him after he had raped her. He spoke insultingly and condescendingly to many of his rape victims, particularly the sex workers. *In addition, the individual must be at least 18 years and must have had a history of some symptoms of conduct disorder before age 15 years. Information is not readily available but highly likely given the nature of Bayley's ongoing criminal activities.

CONCLUSION

What we can learn from the murders committed by Simon Gittany, Angelika Gavare and Adrian Bayley

No-one is completely safe in a relationship with someone who has an antisocial personality disorder (ASPD). These people are deceptive, manipulative and potentially dangerous, especially if they don't get their way. They have no qualms about using others to fulfil their needs, even if it means hurting people in the process, such as getting a colleague fired so that they can have her job, stealing a stranger's money, crushing their partner's self-esteem or physically assaulting them.

Vonne McGlynn, Lisa Harnum and Jill Meagher were all victims of callous killers who acted entirely in their own interests and did so without guilt or remorse. In hindsight, the previous behaviour of these murderers sent out strong signals that they were dangerous people. They all had previous 'form' and contact with the justice system. Simon Gittany was already a violent convicted criminal when he killed Lisa Harnum and Angelika

344

Conclusion

Gavare was a classic example of someone who had already demonstrated that she was prepared to do whatever it took to satisfy her selfish needs.

Before he killed Jill Meagher, Adrian Bayley was a convicted rapist. When it comes to rape, research has found that the perpetrator is more likely to succeed if the attempt happens at night, the perpetrator has been using alcohol or drugs and if they use a weapon in an isolated location. However, studies have concluded that those who are targeted for rape who don't fight back physically and who use non-forceful resistance such as crying, pleading, reasoning, trying to talk the perpetrator out of it or 'physically freezing' and 'going limp' are more likely to be raped as the perpetrator intended (Ullman, 2012).

Conversely, the rape is less likely to be completed if the potential victim immediately and forcibly resists by screaming, swearing and yelling, guarding their body with their arms, struggling, biting, scratching or hitting and trying to flee. This doesn't *guarantee* a better outcome, but makes completion less likely (Ullman, 2012). In some cases, though, fighting back may see the violence escalate. Jill Meagher was extremely unlucky. She did try to forcibly resist Bayley, but he was an experienced rapist with a history of successful completion. He also had a lot to lose – with several convictions and imprisonments for rape he faced the maximum twenty-five-year sentence if she reported him. The murder also occurred at night in an isolated area and he had consumed alcohol.

Others will encounter someone with an ASPD in less dangerous everyday situations. If you meet someone who seems 'too good to be true', they possibly are. If possible, check them out with others who already know them and their history. If you suspect that someone already in your life has an ASPD, consider minimising or terminating contact with them. Anyone can mistreat you or lie to you once, but people with an ASPD will keep doing it. Be careful about giving them too many 'chances' once you become aware of the possibility that they may have an ASPD. Be very cautious about engaging with them in any activity where you could get burned, such as investing or lending money.

Anyone who is involved with someone they suspect might have an ASPD should seek advice from a psychologist or health professional. At the very least they should discuss their fears with a trusted friend or relative who may also have an insight into the person's behaviour. Those around someone who is being mistreated or controlled may have picked up signals or noticed antisocial behaviour; often it is someone outside a relationship who notices something is not right before the person being abused realises it themselves. In Lisa Harnum's case, her friends noticed that she did not contact them as much, and not long before she died she did not seem to be her usually bubbly self.

The appendix of this book lists a number of resources for those whose lives may be affected by someone with a personality disorder, including ASPD. While it may turn out they do not have the disorder, if you feel concerned, it is better to consider the possibility than wait until it's too late. While some can lead relatively normal lives if they make a conscious effort, many with ASPD are among society's cruellest and most dangerous people. If you think a person you have significant contact with has this personality disorder, consider talking to a psychologist to discuss whether they might actually have it and what to do about it.

APPENDIX

WHERE TO GO FOR HELP

Note: if your life is in immediate danger, call police on 000.

Australian federal government crisis support page
Website: www.humanservices.gov.au/customer/subjects/
crisis-and-special-help

Lifeline
Crisis support and suicide prevention 24/7.
Telephone: 13 11 14
Website: www.lifeline.org.au

Kids Helpline
Free, confidential 24/7 telephone and online counselling service.
for those aged 5–25.
Telephone: 1800 551 800
Website: www.kidshelp.com.au

1800 RESPECT
Free, confidential 24/7 national family violence and sexual assault counselling service.
Telephone: 1800 737 732 to speak to a professional counsellor
Website: www.1800respect.org.au

Family Relationship Advice
Information and advice on family relationship issues and parenting arrangements after separation.
Telephone: 1800 050 321
Website: www.familyrelationships.gov.au

Mensline Australia
Telephone and online support, information and referrals regarding domestic violence and relationship and family problems.
Telephone: 1300 789 978
Website: www.mensline.org.au

Victorian Centres Against Sexual Assault
Help and counselling for those who have been sexually assaulted.
Sexual Assault Crisis Line telephone: 1800 806 292.
Website: www.casa.org.au

White Ribbon
Provides domestic violence information and lists national and state-based support organisations.
Website: www.whiteribbon.org.au

Translating and Interpreting Service
Access to an interpreter in your own language for the cost of a local call.
Telephone: 13 14 50
Website: www.tisnational.gov.au

Australian Childhood Foundation
Help for children and young people affected by abuse.
Telephone: 1800 176 453
Website: www.childhood.org.au

Relationships Australia
Support groups and counselling on relationships, and for abusive and abused partners.
Telephone: 1300 364 277
Website: www.relationships.com.au

ASCA (Adults Surviving Child Abuse)
Helps adult survivors, their friends and family and the health-care professionals who support them.
Telephone: 1300 657 380
Website: www.asca.org.au

GLOSSARY

Adrenalin
Adrenalin is a hormone produced in the body's adrenal cortex and medulla. Adrenalin is the natural hormone of speed and energy. It speeds up the heart rate, increases blood sugar levels and reduces appetite so you can do everything more quickly. It also prepares you to leave a situation that you perceive to be challenging or dangerous (flight) or confront it (fight). By directing energy away from other areas of functioning (e.g. eating and sleeping), adrenalin enables you to concentrate on several things at once and produce a higher level of performance and concentration.

Amygdala
This area of the brain is like a security camera that is responsible for monitoring what you see, touch, smell and hear so that you can decide what's 'safe' and what's 'dangerous'. If it perceives 'danger', it quickly sends a message to the **hippocampus**, where stored personal memories provide further information to allow

you to decide whether the danger is 'real'. The hippocampus then connects to the prefrontal cortex to help you decide what action, if any, needs to be taken.

Antisocial personality disorder

A personality disorder characterised by pervasive pattern of disregard for and violation of the rights of other people, occurring since the person was fifteen years old. Some of the typical features of this pattern include deceit, manipulation, impulsivity, irresponsibility, lack of remorse and, in some cases, aggression.

Authoritarian personality

This type of personality (pattern of behaviour) has been identified by Professor Robert Altemeyer (1997), building on the earlier work of psychologists Adorno, Frenkel-Brunswik and their colleagues (1950). People with this pattern of behaviour have a preference for order, power, status and structured lines of authority. They believe that there should be unquestioning obedience to those in authority and that disobedience should be punished. They tend to endorse conventional values and traditions including, in most cases, traditional family structures in which women are subservient to their husband. Most people with this personality trait tend to be hostile towards non-traditional groups such as homosexuals.

Avoidant personality disorder

A personality disorder characterised by a pervasive pattern of social inhibition, feelings of inadequacy and hypersensitivity to negative evaluation, beginning by early adulthood and present in a variety of contexts.

Behavioural inhibition
The tendency of a child to react, more than most children, with fear, restraint, withdrawal or all three to unfamiliar persons, situations or experiences.

Borderline personality disorder
A pervasive pattern of unstable interpersonal relationships, self-image and emotions combined with impulsive behaviours that begins by early adulthood and presents in a variety of contexts. Its severity is strongly connected to negative experiences in childhood.

Cognitive behaviour therapy
A form of (usually) short-term psychotherapy, developed by Dr Albert Ellis, which focuses on supporting a patient to identify and change irrational thinking and expectations and unhelpful thinking habits.

Comorbidity
The presence of one or more additional disorders co-occurring with a primary disorder, either at the same time or, in some cases, with one contributing to the development of the other.

Cortisol
The body makes only limited amounts of adrenalin per day and if it is used up due to daily stressors or a major challenging event, the brain produces another hormone called *cortisol* as an emergency replacement. Cortisol is the 'stress' chemical which provides speed and energy but can also make one irritable and exhausted and, sometimes, angry and argumentative.

Dialectical behavioural therapy
A specific type of cognitive-behavioural psychotherapy developed by psychologist Marsha M. Linehan as a treatment for people with a borderline personality disorder. It focuses on assisting the patient to identify errors in their thinking about other

people's behaviour and their responses to it, and to replace these thoughts with more realistic and helpful thinking.

Dopamine

Dopamine is a neurotransmitter (i.e. a chemical in the brain which sends messages to other parts of the brain). Dopamine affects brain processes that control movement, emotional responses and the ability to experience stimulation, pleasure and pain.

DSM 5

Published by the American Psychiatric Association, *The Diagnostic and Statistical Manual of Mental Disorders*, Fifth Edition (2013) is a classification and diagnostic reference manual outlining a range of mental disorders and the diagnostic criteria for each of them. It enables mental health professionals to diagnose mental disorders in a relatively consistent and reliable way. The DSM 5 is the most widely-used classification system in the world for this purpose and provides a common language for research and analysis. The descriptions, symptoms and indicators of the mental disorders in the DSM 5 are based on a combination of extensive research from scientific journals and conferences, plus input from 160 world-renowned clinicians and researchers from a range of mental health disciplines including psychiatry, psychology, paediatrics, nursing and social work. The DSM 5, published in 2013, is the most recent edition.

Empathy

Empathy is the ability to understand and share the feelings of another person and is the most important building block of respect, compassion and moral behaviour. There are three main components of empathy:

The first is *cognitive* empathy, which is the capacity to read and understand the emotions, behaviours and intentions of another.

The second is *emotional* empathy, which is the capacity to emotionally 'feel' some of the same emotion that another person is experiencing.

The third is *empathic concern*, which is the willingness to respond to another person's feelings of distress with words or actions of kindness or support.

Epigenetics

DNA provides a genetic plan for each person, but various factors affect how that plan will be 'expressed'. Epigenetics is the study of factors that can influence whether a gene is switched 'on' or 'off'. Some of the factors that have been identified as potentially influencing whether or not a gene is expressed include diet, exercise, smoking, obesity, exposure to chemicals, periods of starvation, stress, trauma, viral infections and the use of illicit drugs.

Familicide

The killing of one's whole family, i.e. partner and biological children.

Filicide

The killing by a parent of one or more of their biological children under the age of eighteen.

Genetic predisposition

A genetic predisposition is an inherited risk of, or an increased susceptibility to, developing a particular condition, disease or specific behavioural tendency. Some people with a genetic predisposition will develop a specific disease, condition or behavioural tendency while others who also have the same genetic predisposition will not.

Grandiosity
An exaggerated belief in one's importance and level of success.

Heritability
The degree to which genetics plays a role in developing a disorder. Heritability is an estimate of how much of the observed differences between people within a specific population (e.g. people in a research study) is due to genetic differences between them. The closer a heritability estimate is to 100 per cent, the more strongly that characteristic or behaviour is influenced by genetic factors. Heritability can range from 0 (no genetic influence) to 1 (100 per cent genetic influence). If a study of 'singing ability' in 600 adults found that the heritability of 'singing ability' was .45, that would mean that 45 per cent of the differences between them in terms of their singing ability was due to specific genetic differences between them. Heritability estimates are usually obtained through studies comparing identical twins with non-identical twins.

Hippocampus
The part of your brain that stores memories (sights, sounds, smells, actions, words) and long-term records of your knowledge and experiences. It sends information to the prefrontal cortex to help it interpret information received and decide how to respond. When the brain's 'fear circuitry' is working properly there is a strong connection between the hippocampus and the prefrontal cortex.

Infanticide
The act of killing an infant under the age of twelve months.

Interpersonal psychotherapy
This type of psychotherapy focuses on helping the patient to build social support through enhancing problem-solving and

social skills and addressing relationship issues in the patient's family, workplace and social contexts.

Maladaptive
Unhelpful and unproductive behaviours that interfere with a person's ability to effectively adjust to and manage difficult or challenging situations and, as a result, prolong their distress.

Mental illness
A clinically significant medical condition that significantly impairs (temporarily or permanently) a person's mental functioning, perceptions and judgment and strongly indicates that they need care, medical treatment and/or control. It is characterised by the presence of one of more of the following:

- Disturbance in thought, emotions, orientation, mood, perceptions, memory and/or decision-making.
- The presence of one or more of the following symptoms: delusions, hallucinations, serious disorder of thought, a severe disorder of mood, and/or sustained or repeated irrational behaviour that indicates the presence of one of the symptoms above.

Mindfulness
Mindfulness is an approach to managing stress and self-calming that can be learned. Mindfulness can be used in many different contexts, not just in a therapy session. It has some similarities with meditation and relaxation training. When a person is being mindful, they are intentionally focusing and concentrating on one selected aspect of the present moment (e.g. watching a flower moving in the breeze) and not thinking about current worries or what has happened in the past.

Narcissistic personality disorder

A personality disorder characterised by a need for admiration, exploiting others and arrogance. Those with a narcissistic personality disorder see themselves in a class of their own when it comes to looks and ability and therefore entitled to the best of everything.

Melatonin

Melatonin is the sleep chemical which also 'sets' your body clock. It works alongside serotonin. When your pineal gland detects light in the morning, your body 'wakes up'. When it detects a loss of light in the early evening, it starts to produce melatonin. Over the next few hours it will produce enough to make you feel sleepy at roughly the same time each night. When melatonin takes over, production of serotonin is temporarily turned off. Decreasing levels of melatonin trigger the production of serotonin and you wake up.

Neurotransmitters

Neurotransmitters are chemicals in the brain that help neurons (brain cells) to send messages to each other. The three most significant neurotransmitters that affect behaviour are **serotonin**, **melatonin** and **dopamine**.

Each neurotransmitter has a chemical relationship with one or more sites in the brain (called 'receptors'). Some specific neurotransmitters and receptor sites have almost a 'lock and key' arrangement where only one specific neurotransmitting chemical can be received by a specific neuroreceptor site. But it's not *quite* that simple. Distortions in the function of neurotransmitting chemicals can occur as a result of gene or protein abnormalities, injury, illness or the effects of both illicit and (some) prescription drugs.

Passive-aggressive behaviour
An intentional but indirect expression of hostility that can be difficult to detect, such as not performing a task that a partner has requested and then claiming that the partner never made the request.

Personality disorder
The **DSM 5** (APA, 2013) describes a personality disorder as: 'an enduring pattern of inner experience and behavior that deviates markedly from the expectations of the individual's culture, is pervasive and inflexible, has an onset in adolescence or early adulthood, is stable over time, and leads to distress or impairment'.

These are the more specific criteria provided by the DSM 5 for a General Personality Disorder:

A. An enduring pattern of inner experience and behavior that deviates markedly from the expectations of the individual's culture. This pattern is manifested in two (or more) of the following areas:
   - Cognition (i.e., ways of perceiving and interpreting self, other people, and events).
   - Affectivity (i.e., the range, intensity, lability, and appropriateness of emotional response).
   - Interpersonal functioning.
   - Impulse control.
B. The enduring pattern is inflexible and pervasive across a broad range of personal and social situations.
C. The enduring pattern leads to clinically significant distress or impairment in social, occupational, or other important areas of functioning.
D. The pattern is stable and of long duration, and its onset can be traced back at least to adolescence or early adulthood.

E. The enduring pattern is not better explained as a manifestation or consequence of another mental disorder.

F. The enduring pattern is not attributable to the physiological effects of a substance (e.g., a drug of abuse, a medication) or another medical condition (e.g., head trauma).

Prefrontal cortex

This more rational area of your brain interprets and coordinates emotional signals from your **amygdala** and memories from your **hippocampus** and integrates them to help you reason, problem-solve, plan, make decisions and manage your feelings. It also helps you to empathise with the feelings of others.

Psychopath/sociopath

Terms that are sometimes used interchangeably with the term 'antisocial personality disorder', although some have argued that there are differences between the three.

Pyschotic

When a person is 'psychotic' they are under the influence of a 'psychosis'. A psychosis is a symptom of **mental illness** and the term indicates that there has been a loss of contact with reality.

Resilience

The capacity to adapt flexibly to the ever-changing challenges of life, cope with inevitable setbacks, losses and disappointments and 'bounce back' to a state of emotional wellbeing (McGrath and Noble, 2011).

Serotonin

Serotonin has been described as the chemical of good mood and motivation. You need sound and regular levels of this neurotransmitter to feel motivated and relaxed during the day, to sleep well at night, to have a good and predictable appetite, and to cope with change and challenge. Low levels of serotonin can make you feel sad, tired and demotivated, and, eventually, anxious and depressed. Low serotonin levels have also been linked to aggression.

Social anxiety disorder

Also known as social phobia, social anxiety disorder is an anxiety disorder in which a person has an excessive and unreasonable fear of making a fool of themselves in specific types of social situations such as public speaking, eating in public etc. Although there are some similarities with avoidant personality disorder, they are different conditions.

Sociopath (see psychopath)

SSRI medication (selective serotonin reuptake inhibitor)

Medications that are predominately used to treat depression and/ or anxiety. **Neurotransmitters** regulating our moods are inactivated if they are reabsorbed in the brain. SSRI medications can block this reabsorption or 'reuptake' and ensure that **serotonin** is available to enable necessary brain functions related to mood. Drugs in this category of prescription medication (e.g. Aurorix, Zoloft, Lexapro and Luvox) operate on a long-term preventive basis rather than providing short-term symptom relief.

REFERENCES AND FURTHER READING

Introduction

American Psychiatric Association, *Diagnostic and Statistical Manual of Mental Disorders*, Fifth Edition, American Psychiatric Publishing, Arlington VA, 2013

Coid J, Roberts A, Yang M et al., 'Prevalence and correlates of personality disorder in Great Britain', *British Journal of Psychiatry*, vol. 188, (5) 423–431, 2006

Millon, T., Millon, C.M., Meagher, S. and Grossman, S, *Personality Disorders in Modern Life*, Wiley, Hoboken, NJ, 2004

Vassallo, S., Sanson, A. and Olsson, C.A. '30 years on: Some key insights from the Australian Temperament Project'. *Family Matters* 94, 2014: 29–34

Vassallo, S. and Sansone, A., *The Australian Temperament Project: The First 30 Years*, 2013, Australian Institute of Family Studies, http://www.aifs.gov.au/atp/pubs/reports/first30years/atp30.pdf also more detail at: http://www.aifs.gov.au/atp/

World Health Organization, *The ICD-10 classification of mental and behavioural disorders: clinical descriptions and diagnostic guidelines*, World Health Organization, Geneva, 2010

PART I Avoidant personality disorder
Introduction
American Psychiatric Association, *Diagnostic and statistical manual of mental disorders*, Fifth Edition, American Psychiatric Publishing, Arlington VA 2013

Brown, T., Tyson, D. and Fernandez Arias, P., 'Filicide and parental separation and divorce'. *Child Abuse Review*, 23 (2), 2014: 79–88

Cox, B.J., Pagura J., Stein M.B. and Sareen, J., 'The relationship between generalized social phobia and avoidant personality disorder in a national mental health survey', *Depression and Anxiety* 26 (4), 354–62, 2009

Francia, C.A., Coolidge, F.L., White, L.A., Segal, D.L., Cahill, B.S. and Estey, A.J., 'Personality disorder profiles in incarcerated male rapists and child molesters', *American Journal of Forensic Psychology*, 28, 55–68, 2010

Gjerde, L.C., Czajkowski, N., Røysamb, E., Orstavik, R.E., Knudsen, G.P, Ostby, K., Torgersen, S., Myers, J., Kendler, K.S. and Reichborn-Kjennerud, T., 'The heritability of avoidant and dependent personality disorder assessed by personal interview and questionnaire', *Acta Psychiatrica Scandinavica* 126 (6), 448–57, 2012

Grant, B.F., Hasin, D.S., Stinson, F.S. et al., 'Prevalence, correlates, and disability of personality disorders in the United States: Results from the national epidemiologic survey on alcohol and related conditions', *Journal of Clinical Psychiatry* 65 (7), 948–58, 2004

Johnson, J.G., Cohen, P., Chen, H., Kasen, S. and Brook, J.S., 'Parenting behaviors associated with risk for offspring personality disorder during adulthood', *Archives of General Psychiatry*, 63, 5, 579–587, 2006

Kauppi, A., Kumpulainen, K., Karkola, K. et al., 'Maternal and paternal filicides: A retrospective review of filicides in Finland'. *Journal of the American Academy of Psychiatry and Law* 38, 2010: 229–38

Laajasalo T., Ylipekka, M. and Häkkänen-Nyholm, H., 'Homicidal behaviour among people with avoidant, dependent and obsessive-compulsive (cluster C) personality disorder'. *Criminal Behaviour and Mental Health*, 1, 18–29, 2013

Meyer, B. and Carver, C.S., 'Negative childhood accounts, sensitivity, and pessimism: A study of avoidant personality disorder features in college students, *Journal of Personality Disorders*, 14, 233–248, 2000

Millon, T., Millon, C.M., Meagher, S. and Grossman, S., *Personality Disorders in Modern Life*, Wiley, Hoboken NJ, 2004

Pineiro, B., Fernandez Del Rio, E., Lopez-Duran, A., Martinez, U. and Becona, E., 'The association between probable personality disorders and smoking cessation and maintenance', *Addictive Behavior*, 38, 2369–73, 2013

Rettew, D.C., Zanarini, M.C., Yen, S., Grilo, C.M., Skodol, A.E., Shea, M.T., McGlashan, T.H., Morey, L.C., Culhane, M.A. and Gunderson, J.G., 'Childhood antecedents of avoidant personality disorder: A retrospective study', *Journal of the American Academy of Child and Adolescent Psychiatry* 42 (9), 1122–30, 2003

Rigonatti, S.P., de Padua Serafim, A., de Freitas Caires, M.A., Guerra Vieira Filho, A.H. et al., 'Personality disorders in rapists and murderers from a maximum security prison in Brazil', *International Journal of Law and Psychiatry*, 29 (5), 361–9, 2006

Stravynski, A., Elie, R. and Franche, R.L., 'Perceptions of early parenting by patients diagnosed with avoidant personality disorder: A test of the overprotection hypothesis', *Acta Psychiatrica Scandinavica*, 80, 415–420, 1989

Torgersen S.I., Myers, J., Reichborn-Kjennerud, T., Røysamb, E., Kubarych, T.S. and Kendler, K.S., 'The heritability of Cluster B personality disorders assessed both by personal interview and questionnaire'. *Journal of Personality Disorders* 26 (6), 2012: 848–66

West, S., Friedman, S.H. and Resnick, P.J., 'Fathers who kill their children: An analysis of the literature', *Journal of Forensic Sciences*, 4 (54), 2009: 463–8, 6: 137–41

Yardley, E., Wilson, D. and Lynes, A., 'A taxonomy of male British family annihilators, 1980–2013', *The Howard Journal of Criminal Justice*, 53 (2), 117–40, 2014

Chapter 1 Robert Farquharson

'Across the Night Sky', *Australian Story*, ABC TV, 28 March 2011 http://www.abc.net.au/austory/specials/acrossnightsky/

Anderson, P. and van den Berg, L., 'Child killer Robert Farquharson to appeal sentence', *Herald Sun*, 14 October 2010

Australia Bureau of Statistics, *Divorces, Australia, 2007*, 3307.0.55.001, 2007 http://www.abs.gov.au/ausstats/abs@.nsf/mf/3307.0.55.001

Bice, K., 'Dam boys murdered, says QC', *Herald Sun*, 27 September 2014

Cleary, P., Source: Robert Farquharson: Murder in the Dam, October 2007 www.philcleary.com.au

DPP v Farquharson, Supreme Court of Victoria, sentencing, 16 November 2007, Cummins J

Fallon, J., Interview. South Melbourne, 18 April 2013

Garner, H., *This House of Grief: The story of a murder trial*. Text Publishing, Melbourne, 2014

Hunt, E., 'Witness Dawn Waite speaks of relief at Robert Farquharson's conviction', *Herald Sun*, 23 July 2010

Kissane, K., 'In the name of the father, how could he?', *Sydney Morning Herald*, 6 October 2007

Liem, M., Levin, J., Holland, C. and Fox, J.A., 'Nature and incidence of familicide in the United States, 2000–2009', *Journal of Family Violence*, 28, 351–358, 2013

Millon, T., Millon, C.M., Meagher, S. and Grossman, S., *Personality Disorders in Modern Life*, Wiley, Hoboken NJ, 2004

Norris, M., *On Father's Day: Cindy Gambino's shattering account of her children's revenge murders*, The Five Mile Press, Melbourne, 2013

Portelli, E., 'Killer dad Robert Farquharson has been denied a final chance to appeal against his conviction', *Herald Sun*, 16 August 2013

R v Farquharson, Supreme Court of Victoria Court of Appeal, 17 December 2009, Warren CJ, Nettle and Redlich JJA

Rintoul, S., 'Robert Farquharson's "unspeakable" revenge', *The Australian*, 23 July 2010

Rule, A., 'Police officer who made a difference by accident', *Herald Sun*, 25 July 2013

'Sins of the Father', *60 Minutes*, Nine Network, 28 October 2007

Chapter 2 John Myles Sharpe

Berry, J., 'Family murder "too awful to contemplate"', *The Age*, 27 April 2005

Currie, I., Interview, Phone interview, 10 June 2014

Francia, C.A., Coolidge, F.L., White, L.A., Segal, D.L., Cahill,

B.S. and Estey, A.J., 'Personality disorder profiles in incarcerated male rapists and child molesters', *American Journal of Forensic Psychology*, 28, 55–68, 2010

Goldsmith, B., Interview, Phone interview, 10 June 2014; in-person interview, Mornington, 11 July 2014

Hadfield, S., 'Speargun killer John Sharpe's elaborate deceit and murder of his pregnant wife and toddler Gracie shocked Melbourne', *Herald Sun*, 7 March 2014

Healey, K., 'Sharpe's secret family letters reveal a history of sexual abuse', *Sunday Herald Sun*, 13 November 2005

Millon, T., Millon, C.M., Meagher, S. and Grossman, S., *Personality Disorders in Modern Life*, Wiley, Hoboken NJ, 2004

R v Sharpe, Supreme Court of Victoria, 5 August 2005, Bongiorno J

Suter Linton, J, *Blood Ties*, ABC Books, Sydney, 2012

Part II Narcissistic personality disorder
Introduction

American Psychiatric Association, *Diagnostic and statistical manual of mental disorders*, Fifth Edition, American Psychiatric Publishing, Arlington VA, 2013

Buffardi, L.E. and Campbell, W.K., 'Narcissism and social networking web sites', *Personality and Social Psychology Bulletin*, 34, 1303–14, 2008

Baskin-Sommers, A., Krusemark, E. and Ronningstam, E., 'Empathy in narcissistic personality disorder: From clinical and empirical perspectives', *Personality Disorders: Theory, research, and treatment*, 5(3), 323–33, 2014

Blackburn R., Logan, C., Donnelly, J. and Renwick, S., 'Personality disorder, psychopathy, and other mental disorders: Co-morbidity among patients at English and Scottish high security hospitals', *Journal of Forensic Psychiatry and Psychology*, 14, 111–37, 2003

Dhawan, N., Kunik, M.E., Oldham, J. and Coverdale, J., 'Prevalence and treatment of narcissistic personality disorder in the community: A systematic review', *Comprehensive Psychiatry*, 51 (4), 333–39, 2010

Kohut, H., *The search for the Self*, Vol. 2, International Universities Press, New York, 1972

Millon, T., Millon, C.M., Meagher, S. and Grossman, S., *Personality Disorders in Modern Life*, Wiley, Hoboken NJ, 2004

Ritter, K., Dziobek, I., Preissler, S., Rüter, A., Vater, A., Fydrich, T., Lammers, C.-H., Heekeren, H.R. and Roepke, S., 'Lack of empathy in patients with narcissistic personality disorder'. *Psychiatry Research* 187, 2011: 241–47

Stinson, F.S., Dawson, D.A., Goldstein, R.B., Chou, S.P., Huang, B., Smith, S.M., Ruan, W.J., Pulay, A.J., Saha, T.D., Pickering, R.P. and Grant, B.F., 'Prevalence, correlates, disability, and comorbidity of DSM-IV narcissistic personality disorder: Results from the Wave 2 National Epidemiologic Survey on Alcohol and Related Conditions', *Journal of Clinical Psychiatry*, 69 (7), 1033–45, 2008

Torgersen, S.I., Myers, J., Reichborn-Kjennerud, T., Røysamb, E., Kubarych, T.S. and Kendler, K.S., 'The heritability of Cluster B personality disorders assessed both by personal interview and questionnaire', *Journal of Personality Disorders*, 26 (6), 848–66, 2012

Twenge, J. and Campbell, K., *The Narcissism Epidemic: Living in the age of entitlement*, Simon & Schuster, New York, 2010

Chapter 3 Peter Caruso

Buttler, M., 'Greg Brazel's killer swindle', *Herald Sun*, 6 June 2012

Caruso, S., Interview. Numerous in-person and phone interviews, December, 2011 to early 2015

Caruso, [name withheld (son of Rosa)]. Interview. Several phone interviews across 2013 and 2014.

Crawford, M. and Gartner, R., *Woman Killing: Intimate Femicide in Ontario 1974–1990*, Ontario Woman's Directorate: Ministry of Community and Social Services, 1992

Dutton, D. and Kerry, G., 'Modus operandi and personality disorder in incarcerated spousal killers', *International Journal of Law and Psychiatry*, 22, 287–99, 1999

Millon, T., Millon, C.M., Meagher, S. and Grossman, S., *Personality Disorders in Modern Life*, Wiley, Hoboken NJ, 2004

Paganella, P. and Paganella, T., Interview. Melbourne, 23 December, 2011

Pallante, J., Interview. Several phone interviews, 2013 and 2014

R v Caruso, Supreme Court of Victoria, 6 September 2010, King J

Ross, N., 'Murder trial a test of wills', *Herald Sun*, 8 August 2008

Chapter 4 Gerard Baden-Clay

Baden-Clay, G., Blog. http://expertrealestate.blogspot.com.au/

Baden-Clay, N., Blog. http://web.archive.org/web/20080718224602/ http://century21.com.au/westside/agenthome.htm)

Baskin, B., 'Day 5: Gerard Baden-Clay on trial accused of murdering wife Allison', *Courier-Mail*, 17 June 2014

Baskin, B., 'Gerard Baden-Clay trial forces shattered families together in court', *Courier-Mail*, 21 June 2014

Baskin, B., 'Day 12: Gerard Baden-Clay on trial accused of murdering wife Allison in 2012', *Courier-Mail*, 1 July, 2014

Baskin, B., 'Day 17: Gerard Baden-Clay on trial accused of murdering wife Allison in 2012', *Courier-Mail*, 9 July 2014

Bath, C., 'Allison Baden-Clay's secret letter discovered', *Sunday Night*, Channel 7, 20 July 2014

Calligeros, M., 'Gerard Baden-Clay Trial Live Coverage: Day 4, Week 2', *Brisbane Times*, 16 June 2014

Calligeros, M., 'Gerard Baden-Clay guilty: What jury didn't hear', *Brisbane Times*, 15 July 2014

Calligeros, M., 'Gerard Baden-Clay, consummate salesman, narcissist and killer', *Brisbane Times*, 20 July 2014

Chamberlin, T., 'Gerard Baden-Clay, husband of Allison, once touted as LNP MP', *Courier-Mail*, 6 May 2014

Jeal, T., *Baden-Powell*, Yale University Press, London, 2007

Kyriacou, K., 'Gerard Baden-Clay's life and career built on honesty', *Courier-Mail*, 27 April 2012

References And Further Reading

Kyriacou, K. and Murray, D., 'Prosecution launches tirade of accusations against Gerard Baden-Clay, on trial accused of murdering wife Allison', *Courier-Mail*, 3 July 2014

Kyriacou, K. and Murray, D., 'The lady vanishes: The angry red welts on his face that made Gerard suspect number one', *Courier-Mail*, undated

Laskaris, T., Queensland Police witness statement. Brisbane, 3 May 2012

Malmquist, C.P., *Homicide: A Psychiatric Perspective.* American Psychiatric Press, Inc., Washington DC, 1966

Millon, T., Millon, C.M., Meagher, S. and Grossman, S., *Personality Disorders in Modern Life*, Wiley, Hoboken NJ, 2004

Murray, D., *The Murder of Allison Baden-Clay: All marriages have their secrets*, Random House Australia, Sydney, 2014

Murray, D., 'Day 13: Gerard Baden-Clay on trial accused of murdering wife Allison in 2012', *Courier-Mail*, 1 July 2014.

Murray, D., 'Allison Dickie had to choose between two men – her first love and Gerard Baden-Clay', *Courier-Mail*, 29 November, 2014

Murray, D., 'Accused wife killer Gerard Baden-Clay created web of lies to continue affairs, court told', *Courier-Mail*, 5 July 2014

Murray, D. and Kyriacou, K., 'Gerard Baden-Clay stood to gain $600,000 from media deal if he was acquitted of murdering wife Allison', *Courier-Mail*, 18 July 2014

Queensland Heath, Forensic and Scientific Services, Autopsy report on Allison Baden-Clay, 5 September, 2012

R v Baden-Clay, Supreme Court of Queensland, summing up 9 July 2014; and sentencing 15 July 2014, Byrne J

Remeikis, A., '"Taking the fifth": The case against alleged wife-killer Gerard Baden-Clay', *Brisbane Times*, 27 June 2014

Rosenthal, M., *The Character Factory: Baden-Powell and the origins of the boy scout movement*, Pantheon Books, New York, 1986

Sandy, A., 'Family Can't stop Allison Baden-Clay's secret property sale deal from going through', *Courier-Mail*, 7 September, 2012

Sutton, C., '"Married but don't want to be – looking for some sex on the side!": Inside Gerard Baden-Clay's depraved secret life', *Daily Mail*, 15 July 2014

Sutton, C. and Crane, E., 'Teddy bears, family portraits and children's drawings: Chilling crime scene photographs inside the Baden-Clay family home four days after Allison disappeared', *Daily Mail*, 13 June 2014

'The Baden-Clay story, Chapter 1: Til death do us part', [no byline], *Courier-Mail*, 16 July 2014

Wilson, R., 'Court hears Allison Baden-Clay reacted to anti-malarial drug', *The Queensland Times*, 26 June 2014

Wilson, R., 'Gerard Baden-Clay's phone log shows early morning charge', *The Queensland Times*, 25 June 2014

Chapter 5 Roger Dean

Arnold, P., Interview. Various phone interviews from July to December 2014

Bibby, P., '"I feel I'm under attack, under spiritual attack": Killer nurse explains why he did it', *Sydney Morning Herald*, 29 May 2013

Bibby, P., 'Nursing home did not check Roger Dean's CV before Quakers Hill fire: inquest', *Sydney Morning Herald*, 8 September 2014

Bibby, P., 'Nurse Roger Dean might have lit three fires at Quakers Hill nursing home, not two', *Sydney Morning Herald*, 29 September 2014

Cooper, H., 'Interview gives glimpse inside mind of a killer', *7.30*, ABC TV, 29 May 2013 http://www.abc.net.au/7.30/content/2013/s3770435.htm

Crawford, S., 'Supervisor knew Roger Dean had stolen painkillers but felt "helpless" and "tired" when handing him keys to drug cabinet', *Daily Telegraph*, 10 September 2014

Crawford, S., 'Nursing home killer Roger Dean's boss Tracey Sheehan was warned off reporting him for stalking her', *Daily Telegraph*, 30 September 2014

Gardiner, S., 'Dean "stressed and anxious" in months before nursing home fire', *Sydney Morning Herald*, 5 June 2013

Hall, L., 'Nursing home killer had history of incidents at work', *Sydney Morning Herald*, 30 September 2014

Hoerr, K., 'Police release interview with Roger Dean, convicted of murder from Quakers Hill nursing home fire', 29 May 2013, www.abc.net.au/news

Marcus, C., 'Quakers Hill Nursing Home manager called police before Roger Dean's fatal fire', *Sunday Telegraph*, 2 June 2013

Millon, T., Millon, C.M., Meagher, S. and Grossman, S., *Personality Disorders in Modern Life*, Wiley, Hoboken NJ, 2004

R v Dean, Supreme Court of New South Wales, sentencing, 1 August 2013, Latham J

Slattery, L., 'Night of infamy', *Sydney Morning Herald*, 22 February 2014

Wells, J., 'Prosecutor says Quakers Hill nursing home fire killer Roger Dean should be jailed for life', 17 June 2013, www.abc.net.au/news

Chapter 6 Keli Lane

Arlington, K., 'Lane driven to overcome pregnancy trauma: doctor', *Sydney Morning Herald*, 12 March 2011

Cadzow, J., 'Secrets and lies', *Good Weekend* magazine, 30 July 2005

Chin, R.J., *Nice Girl: The story of Keli Lane and her missing baby, Tegan*, Simon & Schuster, Sydney, 2011

Davies, L., 'Keli Lane climbed down fire escape with baby', *Daily Telegraph*, 10 August 2010

Davies, L., 'What happened to Tegan Lane?', *Daily Telegraph*, 14 August 2010

Davies, L., 'Hospital cleared Keli Lane to leave with Tegan', *Daily Telegraph*, 18 August 2010

Duff, E., 'You don't know my dad: Keli Lane's secret fear', *Sydney Morning Herald*, 19 December 2010

Exclusive report on Keli Lane, *Sunday Night*, Channel 7, 3 April 2011

Hatters Friedman, S. and Resnick, P.J., 'Child murder by mothers: Patterns and prevention'. *World Psychiatry* 6, 2007: 137–41

'How Keli Lane's secret life was exposed. Part one: Public Keli, Private Keli' [no byline], *The Age*, 14 December 2010

Lane v R, Supreme Court of New South Wales Court of Appeal, 13 December 2013, Bathurst CJ, Simpson J, Adamson J

Millon, T., Millon, C.M., Meagher, S. and Grossman, S., *Personality Disorders in Modern Life*, Wiley, Hoboken NJ, 2004

Putkonen, H., Weizmann-Henelius, G., Collander, J., Santtila, P. and Eronen, M., 'Neonaticides may be more preventable and heterogeneous than previously thought: Neonaticides in Finland, 1980–2000', *Archives of Women's Mental Health*, 10, 15–23, 2007

Resnick, P., 'Murder of the newborn: A psychiatric review', *American Journal of Psychiatry*, 126, 1414–2, 1970

Saunders, K., *Deadly Australian Women*, ABC Books, Sydney, 2013

Shelton, J., Corey, T., Donaldson, W. and Dennison, E., 'Neonaticide: A comprehensive review of investigative and pathologic aspects of 55 cases', *Journal of Family Violence*, 26 (4), 263–76, 2011

Warren, A., 'My dear teacher killed her baby', *Daily Telegraph*, 17 April 2011

Welch, D., 'Cold case squad renew dig for baby Tegan', *Sydney Morning Herald*, 4 August 2008

Williams, S., 'Man on a mission', *Sydney Morning Herald*, 20 July 2013

Elder, J., 'Sins of the mother: The tragedy of neonaticide', *The Age*, 19 December 2010

Part III Borderline personality disorder
Introduction

American Psychiatric Association, *Diagnostic and statistical manual of mental disorders*, Fifth Edition, American Psychiatric Publishing, Arlington VA, 2013

Birn, R.M., Patriat, R., Phillips, M.L., Germain, A. and Herringa, R.J., 'Childhood maltreatment and combat posttraumatic stress differentially predict fear-related fronto-subcortical connectivity'. *Depression and Anxiety* 31 (10), 2014: 880–92

Black, D.W., N. Blum, B. Pfohl, and N. Hale., 2004. "Suicidal Behavior in Borderline Personality Disorder: Prevalence, Risk Factors, Prediction, and Prevention." *Journal of Personality Disorders*: Vol. 18, Suicide and Borderline Personality Disorder, pp. 226–239

References And Further Reading

Black D.W., Gunter T, Allen J, et al., 'Borderline personality disorder in male and female offenders newly committed to prison', *Comparative Psychiatry*, 48, 400–405, 2007

Bremner, J.D., Randall, P., Vermetten, E., Staib, L., Bronen, R.A., Mazure, C., Capelli, S., McCarthy, G., Innis, R.B., Charney, D.S., 'Magnetic resonance imaging-based measurement of hippocampal volume in posttraumatic stress disorder related to childhood physical and sexual abuse: A preliminary report'. *Biological Psychiatry* 41, 1997: 23–32

Dinsdale, N. and Crespi, B.J., 'The borderline empathy paradox: Evidence and conceptual models for empathic enhancements in borderline personality disorder', *Journal of Personality Disorders*, 27, 172–95, 2013

Edmiston, E.E., Fei Wang, B.A., Mazure, C.M., Guiney, J., Sinha, R., Mayes, L.C. and Blumberg, H.P., 'Corticostriatal-limbic gray matter morphology in adolescents with self-reported exposure to childhood maltreatment'. *Archives of Pediatrics and Adolescent Medicine* 65 (12), 2011: 1069–77

Grant B.F., Chou S.P., Goldstein R.B., et al., 'Prevalence, correlates, disability, and comorbidity of DSM-IV borderline personality disorder: Results from the Wave 2 National Epidemiologic Survey on Alcohol and Related Conditions', *Journal of Clinical Psychiatry*, 69 (4), 533–545, 2008

Herringa, R.J., Birn, R.M., Ruttle, P.L., Burghy, C.A., Stodola, D.E., Davidson, R.J. and Essex, M.J., 'Childhood maltreatment is associated with altered fear circuitry and increased internalizing symptoms by late adolescence', *Proceedings of the National Academy of Science USA*, 110, 19119–24, 2013

Koch, W., Schaaff, N., Popperl, G., Muller, T.C., Juckel, G., Reicherzer, M., Hegerl, U., Tatsch, K. and Pogarell, O., 'ADAM and SPECT in patients with borderline personality disorder and healthy control subjects', *Journal of Psychiatry and Neuroscience*, 32, 234–40, 2007

Leaming, B., *Marilyn Monroe*, Three Rivers Press, California, 2006

Lieb, K., Vollm, B., Rucker, G., Timmer, A. and Stoffers, J.M., 'Pharmacotherapy for borderline personality disorder: Cochrane systematic review of randomised trials', *The British Journal of Psychiatry*, 196, 4–12, 2010

Lim, L., Radua, J. and Rubia, K., 'Gray matter abnormalities in childhood maltreatment: A Voxel-Wise meta-analysis', *American Journal of Psychiatry*, 171 (8), 854–63, 2014

McGowan, P.O., Sasaki, A., D'Alessio, A.C., Dymov, S., Labonté, B., Szyf, M., Turecki, G. and Meaney, M.J., 'Epigenetic regulation of the glucocorticoid receptor in human brain associates with childhood abuse', *Nature and Neuroscience*, 12, 342–8, 2009

Miller, J.M., Kinnally, E.L., Ogden, R.T., Oquendo, M.A., Mann, J.J. and Parsey, R.V., 'Reported childhood abuse is associated with low serotonin transporter binding *in vivo* in major depressive disorder'. *Synapse* 63, 2009: 565–73

Monroe, M., Hecht, B., and Green, J., *My Story*, Taylor Trade Publishing, Maryland, 2007

Soloff, P.H. Kevin, G.L. Thomas, M.K., Kevin, M.M., Mann, J.J., (2000). "Characteristics of Suicide Attempts of Patients With Major Depressive Episode and Borderline Personality Disorder: A Comparative Study". *American Journal of Psychiatry* 157 (4): 601–608

Soloff, P.H., Lynch, K.G. and Kelly, T.M., 'Childhood abuse as a risk factor for suicidal behavior in borderline personality disorder, *Journal of Personality Disorders*, 16 (3), 201–14, 2002

Sansone, R.A. and Sansone, L.A., 'Borderline personality and criminality', *Psychiatry*, 6 (10), 16–20, 2009

Sansone, R.A. and Sansone, L.A., 'Fatal attraction syndrome: Stalking behavior and borderline personality'. *Psychiatry* 7, 2010: 42–46

Scannapieco, M. and Connell-Carrick, K., *Ecological and Developmental Perspective on Child Maltreatment*, Oxford University Press, New York, 2005

Soloman, E.P. and Heide, K.M., 'The biology of trauma: Implications for treatment', *Journal of Interpersonal Violence*, 20, 51–60, 2005

Stoffers, J.M., Völlm, B.A., Rücker, G., Timmer, A., Huband, N. and Lieb, K., 'Psychological therapies for people with borderline personality disorder', *Cochrane Database of Systematic Reviews* 8, 2012

Taraborrelli, R., *The Secret Life of Marilyn Monroe*, Grand Central Publishing, New York, 2009

Teicher, M.H., Andersen, S.L., Polcari, A., Anderson, C.M., Navalta, C.P. and Kim, D.M., 'The neurobiological consequences of early stress and childhood maltreatment', *Neuroscience and Biobehavioral Reviews,* 27 (1–2), 33–44, 2003

Torgersen, S., 'The nature (and nurture) of personality disorders', *Scandinavian Journal of Psychology*, 50 (6), 624–32, 2009

Torgersen, S.I., Myers, J., Reichborn-Kjennerud, T., Røysamb, E., Kubarych, T.S. and Kendler, K.S., 2012. 'The heritability of Cluster B personality disorders assessed both by personal interview and questionnaire'. *Journal of Personality Disorders* 26 (6), 2012: 848–66

Yen, S., Shea, T., Battle, C.L., Johnson, D.M., Zlotnick, C., Dolan-Sewell, R. and Skodol, A.E. et al., 'Traumatic exposure and posttraumatic stress disorder in borderline, schizotypal, avoidant, and obsessive-compulsive disorders: Findings from the Collaborative Longitudinal Personality Disorders Study', *Journal of Nervous and Mental Disease*, 190, 510–18, 2002

Chapter 7 Katherine Knight

AAP, '"Bowling ball" decapitation killer loses appeal', *Sydney Morning Herald*, 20 February 2009

AAP, 'Ex-Minister pleads innocent to sex crime', *Sydney Morning Herald*, 13 September 2007

Athens, L. and Ulmer, J.T., (eds), *Violent Acts and Violentization: Assessing, applying, and developing Lonnie Athens' theories*. Emerald Group Publishing, London, 2003

Charleston, L-J., *Fatal Females: 13 cases that gripped a nation*. Sydney: Random House, 2013

Edwards, G., Interview. Phone interview 4 July, 2014, plus several other phone interviews in late 2014

Lalor, P., *Blood Stain*, Allen and Unwin, Sydney, 2002

Lee, S., *Beyond Bad: The Life and Crimes of Katherine Knight, Australia's Hannibal*, Random House, Sydney, 2002

Mason, P.T. and Kreger, R., *Stop Walking on Eggshells: Taking your life back when someone you care about has borderline personality disorder*, New Harbinger Publications, Oakland CA, 2010

Meade, K., 'Family ties of grisly teen killer', *The Australian*, 5 April 2007

R v Knight, Supreme Court of New South Wales, sentencing, 8 November 2001, O'Keefe J

Rhodes, R., *Why They Kill: The discoveries of a maverick criminologist*, Vintage Books, New York, 2000

Strachan, J., 'Man cleared of two sex charges', *Newcastle Herald*, 9 February 2008

Szymanski, K., Sapanski, L. and Conway, F., 'Trauma and ADHD: Association or diagnostic confusion? A clinical perspective', *Journal of Infant, Child and Adolescent Psychotherapy*, 10 (1), 51–59, 2011

Part IV Antisocial Personality Disorder
Introduction

American Psychiatric Association, *Diagnostic and statistical manual of mental disorders*, Fifth Edition, American Psychiatric Publishing, Arlington VA, 2013

Baker, L.A., Bezdjian, S. and Raine, A., 'Behavioral genetics: The science of antisocial behavior', *Journal of Law and Contemporary Problems*, 69 (1–2), 7–46, 2006

Baron-Cohen, S., *The Science of Evil: On Empathy and the Origins of Cruelty*, Basic Books, New York, 2011

Baskin-Sommers, A.R., Curtin, J.J. and Newman, J.P., 'Emotion-modulated startle in psychopathy: Clarifying familiar effects', *Journal of Abnormal Psychology*, 122, 458–68, 2013

Blair, R.J., 'The amygdala and ventromedial prefrontal cortex in morality and psychopathy'. *Trends in Cognitive Science* 11, 2007: 387–92

Blair, R.J., 'Psychopathy, frustration, and the role of reactive aggression: The role of the ventromedial prefrontal cortex'. *British Journal of Psychology* 101, 2010: 383–99

Fazel, S. and Danesh, J., 'Serious mental disorder in 23000 prisoners: A systematic review of 62 surveys', *Lancet*, 359 (9306), 545–50, 2002

References And Further Reading

Glenn, A.L. and Raine, A., 'Antisocial personality disorders'. In J. Decety and J. Cacioppo (eds), *The Oxford Handbook of Social Neuroscience*. New York: Oxford University Press, 2011

Gregory, S., Ffytche, D., Simmons A., Kumari V., Howard M., Hodgins S. and Blackwood N., 'The antisocial brain: Psychopathy matters', *Archives of General Psychiatry*, 69, 962–72, 2012

Hare, R. D., Psychopathy: A clinical construct whose time has come', *Criminal Justice And Behavior,* 23(1), 25–54, 1996

Hare R.D., Clark, D., Grann, M. and Thornton D., 'Psychopathy and the predictive validity of the P.C.L-R: An international perspective', *Behavioral Sciences and the Law*, 18, 623–45, 2000

Hare R.D., 'Electrodermal and cardiovascular correlates of psychopathy', in Hare, R.D. and Schalling, D. (eds), *Psychopathic Behavior: Approaches to research*, Wiley, Chichester, England, 1978

Harris, G.T. and Rice, M.E., 'Treatment of psychopathy: A review of empirical findings', in C.J. Patrick (ed.), *Handbook of Psychopathy*, Guilford, New York, 2006

McGrath, H.L. and Edwards, H., *Difficult Personalities: A practical guide to managing the hurtful behaviour of others* (2nd edition), Penguin, Melbourne, 2009

Lenzenweger, M.F., Lane, M.C., Loranger, A.W. and Kessler, R.C., 'DSM-IV personality disorders in the National Comorbidity Survey Replication', *Biological Psychiatry*, 62 (6), 553–64, 2007

Lykken, D.T., *The Antisocial Personalities*, Erlbaum, Hillsdale NJ, 1995

Marsh, A.A. and Blair R.J.R., 'Deficits in facial affect recognition among antisocial populations: A meta-analysis', *Neuroscience and Biobehavioral Reviews*, 32, 454–65, 2008

Meffert, H., Gazzola, V., den Boer, J.A., Bartels, A.A. and Keysers, C., 'Reduced spontaneous but relatively normal deliberate vicarious representations in psychopathy', *Brain* 136, 2250–562, 2013

Moeller, F.G., Dougherty, D.M., Swann, A.C., Collins, D., Davis, C.M. and Cherek, D.R., 'Tryptophan depletion and aggressive responding in healthy males', *Psychopharmacology*, 126 (2), 97–103, 1996

Ortiz, J. and Raine, A., 'Heart rate level and antisocial behavior in children and adolescents: A meta-analysis', *Journal of American Academy of Child and Adolescent Psychiatry*, 43 (2), 154–62, 2004

Raine, A., Fung, A.L.C., Portnoy, J., Choy, O. and Spring, V.L., 'Low heart rate as a risk factor for child and adolescent proactive aggressive and impulsive psychopathic behavior', *Aggressive Behavior*, 40 (4), 290–9, 2014

Rotgers, F. and Maniacci, M., *Antisocial Personality Disorder: A practitioner's guide to comparative treatments*, Springer Publications, New York, 2006

Stout, M., *The Sociopath Next Door: The ruthless vs the rest of us*, Broadway Books, New York, 2006

Thomas, M.E., *Confessions of a Sociopath: A life spent hiding in plain sight*, Crown Publishers, London, 2013

Torgersen, S., Kringlen, E. and Cramer V., 'The prevalence of personality disorders in a community sample', *Arch General Psychiatry*, 58 (6), 590–6, 2001

Torgersen, S.I., Myers, J., Reichborn-Kjennerud, T., Røysamb, E., Kubarych, T.S. and Kendler, K.S., 'The heritability of Cluster B personality disorders assessed both by personal interview and questionnaire'. *Journal of Personality Disorders*, 26 (6), 848–66, 2012

Ullman, S., 'A 10-year update of "Review and critique of empirical studies of rape avoidance"'. In C.R. Bartol and A.M. Bartol (eds), *Current Perspectives in Forensic Psychology and Criminal Behavior* (3rd edition). Thousand Oaks: Sage Publications 2012

Chapter 8 Simon Gittany

Adorno, T.W., Frenkel-Brunswik, E., Levinson, D.J. and Sanford, R.N., *The Authoritarian Personality*, Norton, New York, 1950

Altemeyer, B., *The Authoritarian Specter*, Harvard University Press, Cambridge, 1997

Bibby, P. and Partridge, E., 'Simon Gittany guilty of murdering fiancee Lisa Harnum', *Sydney Morning Herald*, 27 November 2013

Dale, A., 'Simon Gittany's moment of truth: The cold-blooded killer of Lisa Harnum expected to get away with murder', *Daily Telegraph*, 30 November 2013

Dale, A., 'Four things you didn't know about the Simon Gittany Case', Random House Books blog, 16 September 2014, http://www.randomhouse.com.au/blog/four-things-you-didnt-know-about-the-simon-gittany-case-2170.aspx

Dale, A., 'How Gittany the bully has been crushed by losing his power'. *Daily Telegraph*, 15 February 2014.

Davies, L., 'Accused fiancee killer posts online video of surprise marriage proposal', *Sydney Morning Herald*, 13 January 2013

Delsorte, M., Interview. Tyong, 1 May, 2014

Higgins, E., 'Simon Gittany sentenced to 18-year minimum for murder of Lisa Harnum', *The Australian*, 11 February 2014

Owens, J., 'From petty crim to killer', *The Australian*, 28 November 2013

'Simon Gittany's secret life', *Sunday Night*, Seven Network, 9 February 2014

R v Gittany, New South Wales Court of Criminal Appeal, judgment, 2 August, 1995, Cole JA, Allen J, Hulme J

R v Gittany, Supreme Court of New South Wales, judgment, 27 November 2013, McCallum J

Tracy Grimshaw exclusive interview with Joan Harnum, *A Current Affair*, Nine Network, 28 November 2013

Chapter 9 Angelika Gavare

Dowdell, A., 'Pensioner killer becomes queen bee in prison', *Sunday Mail*, 23 June 2012

Fewster, S., 'Police search Vonne McGlynn's alleged killer's house', *Adelaide Now*, 27 February 2009

Fewster, S., *City of Evil: The truth about Adelaide's strange and violent underbelly*, Hachette, Sydney, 2011

Fewster, S., 'Angelika Gavare guilty of Vonne McGlynn's murder', *Adelaide Now*, 30 August 2011

Fewster, S., 'Greed drove Angelika Gavare to Vonne McGlynn's murder', *Adelaide Now*, 31 August 2011

Fewster, S., 'Pensioner killer Angelika Gavare jailed for 32 years', *Adelaide Now*, 4 November 2011

Fewster, S., 'Murderer Angelika Gavare admits to stolen credit card shopping spree', *Adelaide Now*, 21 December 2011

Fewster, S., 'Angelika Gavare wins right to appeal murder conviction in Vonne McGlynn case', *Adelaide Advertiser*, 23 January 2012

Fewster, S., Interview. Phone interview, 28 August, 2014

Kappelle, L., '"Chilling" Angelika Gavare murdered pensioner', *Courier-Mail*, 23 August 2011

R v Gavare, Supreme Court of South Australia, judgment, 30 August 2011, Kelly J

R v Gavare, Supreme Court of South Australia, judgment of the Court of Criminal Appeal, 4 May 2012, Vanstone J, Anderson J, White J

R v Gavare, Supreme Court of South Australia, sentencing, 4 November 2011, Kelly J

Chapter 10 Adrian Bayley

Anderson, P., 'Jill Meagher's accused killer Adrian Ernest Bayley watched movies after attack, court documents show', *Herald Sun*, 13 March 2013

Anderson, P., 'Adrian Ernest Bayley won't serve extra jail time over unpaid fines', *Herald Sun*, 23 July 2013

Dowsley, A., 'Authorities warned about Jill Meagher's killer Adrian Ernest Bayley by his own family', *Herald Sun*, 11 June 2013

Dowsley, A., 'Jill Meagher's accused killer returns to prison after receiving treatment for self-harm in St Vincent's Hospital', *Herald Sun*, 30 October 2012

Duck, S. and Thompson, A., 'Police dismantle shrines to Jill Meagher on Sydney Road in Brunswick', *Herald Sun*, 1 October 2012

Hare R. D., Clark D., Grann M. and Thornton D., 'Psychopathy and the predictive validity of the P. C. L-R: An international perspective', *Behavioral Sciences and the Law*, 18, 623–645, 2000

Hazelwood, R.R., Analysing the rape and profiling the offender. In Hazelwood, R.R., and Burgess. A.W. (ed.). *Practical Aspects of Rape*

Investigation: A Multidisciplinary Approach (4th ed.). Boca Raton: CRC Press, 2009

Kaila, J., 'Locals reveal background of man charged with rape and murder of Jill Meagher', *Herald Sun*, 29 September 2012

Meagher. T., 'The danger of the monster myth', blog, http://whiteribbon blog.com/2014/04/17/the-danger-of-the-monster-myth/

R v Bayley, Supreme Court of Victoria, sentencing, 19 June 2013, Nettle JA

Rule, A., 'We all hoped for the best, but the story of Jill Meagher ended in grief and tears', *Herald Sun*, 29 September 2012

Russell, M. and Bucci, N., 'Bayley on parole when he killed', *The Age*, 12 June 2013

Silvester, J., 'Long-term prisoners blame Adrian Bayley for changes to Victorian parole system', *The Age*, 19 February 2014

Conclusion
Ullman, S., 'A 10-year update of "Review and critique of empirical studies of rape avoidance"'. In C.R. Bartol and A.M. Bartol (eds), *Current Perspectives in Forensic Psychology and Criminal Behavior* (3rd edition). Thousand Oaks: Sage Publications 2012

Glossary
Altemeyer, B., *The Authoritarian Specter*, Harvard University Press, Cambridge, 1997

Adorno, T.W., Frenkel-Brunswik, E., Levinson, D.J. and Sanford, R.N., *The Authoritarian Personality*, Norton, New York, 1950

McGrath, H. and Noble, T., *Bounce Back: A Classroom Resiliency and Wellbeing Program*, Pearson, Sydney, 2011

Recommended books for further details on the crimes
Anderson, P., *Dirty Dozen: Bodies, bullets and betrayal*, Hardie Grant Books, Melbourne, 2007

Cameron, L. and Ross, F., *Killer in the Family. Shocking Accounts of Domestic Tragedy*, The Five Mile Press, Melbourne, 2008

Charleston, L-J., *Fatal Females: 13 cases that gripped a nation*. Random House, Sydney, 2013

Chin, R.J., *Nice Girl: The story of Keli Lane and her missing baby, Tegan*, Simon & Schuster, Sydney, 2011

Dale, A., *The Fall: How Simon Gittany killed Lisa Harnum*, Random House, Sydney, 2014

Fewster, S., *City of Evil: The truth about Adelaide's strange and violent underbelly*, Hachette Australia, Sydney, 2010

Lalor, P., *Blood Stain*, Allen and Unwin, Sydney, 2002

Lee, S., *Beyond Bad: The Life and Crimes of Katherine Knight, Australia's Hannibal*, Random House, Sydney, 2002

Murray, D., *The Murder of Allison Baden-Clay: All marriages have their secrets*, Random House Australia, Sydney, 2014

Norris, M., *On Father's Day: Cindy Gambino's shattering account of her children's revenge murders*, The Five Mile Press, Melbourne, 2013

Suter Linton, J., *Blood Ties*, ABC Books, Sydney, 2012

Further reading
Books to read about narcissistic personality disorder

Ronningstam, E.F., *Identifying and Understanding the Narcissistic Personality*, Oxford University Press, New York, 2005

Lechan, C. and Goodman, B.L., *The Everything Guide to Narcissistic Personality Disorder. Professional, Reassuring Advice for Coping With the Disorder – at Work, at Home, and in Your Family*, Adams Media, Avon MA, 2012

Books to read about antisocial personality disorder

Thomas, M.E., *Confessions of a Sociopath: A life spent hiding in plain sight*, Crown Publishers, London, 2013

Stout, M., *The Sociopath Next Door: The ruthless vs the rest of us*, Broadway Books, New York, 2006

McGrath, H.L. and Edwards, H., *Difficult Personalities: A practical guide to managing the hurtful behaviour of others* (2nd Edition), Penguin, Melbourne, 2009 (and also published internationally in 2010)

Babiak, P. and Hare, R.D., *Snakes in Suits: When psychopaths go to work*, Harper Collins, New York, 2006

Dutton, K., *The Wisdom of Psychopaths*, Scientific American / Farrar, Straus and Giroux, New York, 2013

Books to read about borderline personality disorder

Mason, P.T. and Kreger, R., *Stop Walking on Eggshells* (10th edition), New Harbinger Publications, Oakland CA, 2010

Manning, S.Y. and Lienhan, M., *Loving Someone with Borderline Personality Disorder: How to keep out-of-control emotions from destroying your relationship*, Guilford Press, New York, 2011

Books to read about domestic violence

Bancroft, L., *Why Does he Do That? Inside the Minds of Angry and Controlling Men*, Berkley Books, New York, 2003

Court material that appears in this book is reproduced with the following permission:

Supreme Court of NSW

Material from R v Roger Dean [2013] NSWSC 1027; Lane v R [2013] NSWCCA 317; R v Simon Gittany [2013] NSWSC 49; R v Katherine Knight [2001] NSWSC 1011 is reproduced with the permission of the Supreme Court of NSW: © State of New South Wales through the Department of Justice and reproduced with the approval of the Supreme Court of NSW.

Supreme Court of Queensland

Material from R v Baden-Clay [2014] QSC 154 and QSC 155 is reproduced with the permission of the Queensland Department of Justice and Attorney General, which has copyright of the original material.

Supreme Court of South Australia

Material from R v Gavare [2011] SASC 142 and subsequent sentencing remarks is reproduced with permission from the Attorney-General for the State of South Australia and the South Australian Courts Administration Authority.

Supreme Court of Victoria

Material from Supreme Court of Victoria and Supreme Court of Victoria Court of Appeal cases R v Farquharson [2009] VSCA 307; R v Sharpe [2005] VSC 276 (Bongiorno J); R v Caruso [2010] VSC 354 (King J); and R v Adrian Bayley [2013] VSC 313 (Nettle JA) is reproduced with permission from the Council of Law Reporting.

Note

The views in this book are not necessarily those of *Nice Girl* author Rachael Jane Chin.

Names
The names of children have only been used in this book where they are deceased or their names have been widely reported in the media and referred to publicly by their next of kin. Several sources requested that they remain anonymous, and we have respected this.

Accuracy
The authors have made every effort to ensure that the material used in this book is accurate and up to date. Any errors or omissions are unintentional and we invite readers to contact Pan Macmillan if anything needs correcting for future editions.

ACKNOWLEDGEMENTS

Many people helped to make this book possible, and we thank them all. In many cases the subject matter was distressing, but a number of people either directly or indirectly involved with the cases covered helped us with our research and with insightful comments about the perpetrators.

Special thanks to our publisher, Pan Macmillan, particularly our talented copy editor, Ali Lavau, who did a brilliant job, our supportive editor Libby Turner, who expertly guided and supported us through the process, our excellent photo editor Alex Lloyd and non-fiction publisher Ingrid Ohlsson, who showed faith in this project from the start. Thanks also to The Honourable Alastair Nicholson AO, RFD, QC, who took the time to write the insightful foreword.

We would also like to thank the authors' families and friends for their support and special thanks to, in no particular order, Judi Fallon, Barry Goldsmith, Ian Currie, Santo Caruso, Rosa Caruso's other son, Tina and Pat Paganella, Mac and Julie Pallante, Peter Arnold, Father Michael Delsorte, Father Eric Hodgens,

Phil Cleary, Sean Fewster, Bob Gambino, Geraldine Edwards, David Murray, Andrew Rule, Libby-Jane Charleston, Kim Arlington, John Silvester, John Elder, Sue Williams, Jane Cadzow, Kate Kiriacou, Brooke Baskin, Shelley Hadfield, Anthony Dowsley, Paul Anderson, Norrie Ross, Mark Buttler, Jon Kaila, Andrew Dowdell, Amy Remeikis, Katie Bice, Elissa Hunt, Tom Chamberlin, Siobhan Duck, Angus Thompson, Amy Dale, Rae Wilson, Stuart Rintoul, Marissa Calligeros, Tom Salom, Tracey Linguey, Peter Lindeman, Tom Meagher, Rachael Jane Chin, Hardie Grant Books, Julia Taylor, Megan Norris, Cindy Gambino, The Five Mile Press, Sandra Lee, Random House Books Australia, Australian Broadcasting Commission, Channel 7, Channel 10, Channel 9, World Health Organization and the Supreme Courts of Victoria, New South Wales, Queensland and South Australia. A number of writers, courts and media outlets allowed us to use their material and we are grateful for their help.

Thanks also to those who gave us information anonymously, whom we cannot thank by name. You know who you are.